JOHN DE WITT

JOHN DE WITT

Statesman of the " True Freedom"

HERBERT H. ROWEN

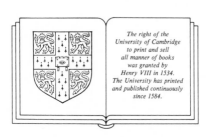

The right of the
University of Cambridge
to print and sell
all manner of books
was granted by
Henry VIII in 1534.
The University has printed
and published continuously
since 1584.

CAMBRIDGE UNIVERSITY PRESS

Cambridge

London   New York   New Rochelle
Melbourne   Sydney

Published by the Press Syndicate of the University of Cambridge
The Pitt Building, Trumpington Street, Cambridge CB2 IRP
32 East 57th Street, New York, NY 10022, USA
10 Stamford Road, Oakleigh, Melbourne 3166, Australia

First published 1986

Printed in Great Britain by the University Press, Cambridge

Library of Congress catalogue card number: 84-29387

British Library cataloguing in publication data

Rowen, Herbert H.
John de Witt: statesman of the 'True Freedom'.
1. Witt, John de   2. Statesmen–Netherlands
–Biography
I. Title
949.2′04′0924   DJ173.W7
ISBN 0 521 30391 5

UP

Contents

Preface

This book is based upon a much larger one by the same author, *John de Witt, Grand Pensionary of Holland, 1625–1672*, published in 1978 by Princeton University Press. It is, unabashedly and even proudly, a work of self-plagiarization, but it is not an abridgment. It is a new book from first page to last, in which I have sought to make my picture and my understanding of the great Dutch statesman of the seventeenth century more easily available to general readers.

The initiative for this book came from the publisher of the Dutch translation, the famed publishing house of Martinus Nijhoff. Originally a full-scale translation of the book of 1978 was undertaken by the Zutphen publishers De Walburg Pers, but it proved too costly a project for an audience most of whom read English easily. They therefore ceded to Martinus Nijhoff at my request the right to publish the smaller book on the same subject, and I wish here to thank them again for their gracious deed. I owe a special debt of gratitude to two readers, Professor Ragnhild Hatton and Dr. Simon Groenveld, for their percipient criticism.

Rocky Hill, N.J.　　　　　　　　　　　HERBERT H. ROWEN
May 13, 1983

Prologue

Political greatness, it is plain, arises from the conjunction of difficult circumstances with personal force of character and mind. A nation's need creates a man's opportunity.

Thus it was in the Netherlands in 1650 when a young man of twenty-five years stepped forward upon the political scene for the first time. He would soon become the leader of the Dutch Republic and remain its directing mind and will during two decades of hard struggle and impressive achievement. But before John de Witt could take his place of leadership, another, still younger man, Prince William II of Orange, had to depart.

When the mid-century year began, it was William who held the forefront of the stage. In 1647 he had succeeded his father, Prince Frederick Henry, as stadholder and captain general, the political and military leader of the Dutch nation. His administration started with a bitter failure. He had opposed the conclusion of the Treaty of Münster of January 1648 that ended the Eighty Years War of independence against Spain, but he lacked the skill and the strength to prevent its ratification.

Peace had been the work of the leaders of Holland, the leading Dutch province. They wanted peace so that they could enjoy the fruits of the country's long struggle, and they insisted upon a reduction of the army so that taxes could be cut and repayment of the huge wartime debt be begun.

William, contrariwise, wished to maintain intact the instrument of war. He shared the wide popular hatred of Spain and was committed to restoring the alliance with France forged by his father in 1634 and shattered by the separate peace with Spain. After the beheading of his father-in-law, King Charles I of England, in 1649, William was no less intent upon using the political, economic and military resources of the Republic on behalf of the Stuart cause.

I

For almost two years the Prince and Holland – the two foci of power in the Republic – argued, and gradually the difference between the numbers each would accept for the size of the army was narrowed. But an irreducible difference remained. Each insisted that the other make the final concession, for doing so meant accepting the rival's ultimate predominance. In June 1650 William decided to break the deadlock by means of the majority he controlled in the States General, where each province had one vote, no matter its size or how much or little it contributed to the national treasury. With a vague but broad grant of authority from the States General, he journeyed through the voting towns of Holland, seeking to break the majority against him in the States of Holland. When neither argument nor intimidation availed, William turned to the ultimate argument – force.

On the last day of July, he arrested six deputies to the States of Holland whose towns had stood most firmly against him and sent them to the prison castle of Loevestein to await their fate. The next day, at his command, army forces appeared before the gates of Amsterdam, but, word of their approach having forewarned the great city, it refused entry to the troops. Total triumph escaped William, and he came to terms with his opponents. The differences over the size of the army were bridged at last, and the Bicker brothers, who had led the opposition to him in the government of Amsterdam, were barred from office.

Over the next few weeks, the towns whose deputies were held at Loevestein abandoned their opposition, and the six prisoners were released. Although the Prince seemed to hold the upper hand, he had won only a half-victory. Resentment of his bold deed ran deep among the ruling class of Holland. But it was not they but the Prince who held the initiative.

Yet he held back from using it at once to consolidate his political domination. Instead he went off to Gelderland, in the eastern Netherlands, to hunt. In October he came down with a fever and was carried back to The Hague by boat. On November 6 he died of smallpox.

The political situation changed, suddenly and totally.

The Prince's party was left leaderless. Ever since the foundation of the Republic seven decades earlier, there had always been a Prince of Orange to take the helm of state. William himself, while yet a boy, had been elected to succeed his father on his death. But

2

now, although William's widow, Mary Stuart, was huge with a still unborn child, there was as yet no living successor to William. A week passed before she gave birth to a son, William III.

By that time the leaders of Holland had already acted with swift decisiveness to regain their predominance in the nation. And they were intent to share it no longer with the stadholders, as they had always done before, but to keep it wholly for themselves. The Orangist party, in dismay and disarray, was in no position to thwart them.

The six prisoners at Loevestein, who had been released in August at the price of abandoning all political office, were restored to their seats in the municipal governments. Dordrecht, whose deputy to the States of Holland, Jacob de Witt, had been the most forceful and outspoken of the six, went further. Not only did it return him to his posts, but it elected his son, John, who had been practicing law in The Hague for the previous two years, as one of the city's two pensionaries, as its legal and political secretaries were called.

A political career was launched that would bring John de Witt to the pinnacle of power and then hurl him to the depths.

I

To the threshold
1625–1650

If difficult times are the anvil on which the hammer of personal merit forges historical greatness, the circumstances in which John de Witt took his first office were not favorable.

Things were going extraordinarily well, in fact, for the Republic of the seven United Provinces of the Netherlands. One of the smallest states in Europe, it had built itself into a great power. Spain's century-old predominance had been smashed, and the Dutch even more than the French had been the artisans of its defeat. France itself was in the grip of civil war, which for all that men knew in 1650 might augur for it the same fate that had befallen Spain. England too had come through a decade of civil war, although the firm hand of General Cromwell had already taken control. Germany had ceased to exist as an effective political entity; the settlement at Westphalia consecrated its conversion into a congeries of middling, small and miniature states over which the Habsburg emperor reigned but did not rule.

The Dutch Republic, however, had soared while contemporaries had floundered and fallen. Its navy and army were among the most powerful in Europe, and its strength rested upon the solid foundation of unexampled riches, drawn from Dutch domination over the trade and shipping of Europe from the Baltic to the Levant. The Dutch population numbered only about one and a half million, but what it lacked in numbers it made up in economic prowess. Holland was the entrepôt of Europe where international trade converged and spread out again, where the grain and timber of the North were exchanged for the wines and luxury goods of the South. Behind the prosperity of fishermen, shippers and traders, there lay a substantial and varied industry and a sturdy agriculture.

The Dutch economic ascendancy was more fragile than one would have assumed from the sight of its massive wealth. The

4

entrepôt function was new, inherited from Antwerp in the previous century; and it could pass into the hands of another country in turn, or disappear as multilateral trade developed, with countries trading directly with each other rather than through Dutch intermediaries. England and France in particular had often displayed a desire to shake off their maritime and commercial dependence upon the Dutch, and once they recovered from civil war they possessed the means to challenge them.

Politically, too, the strength of the Dutch derived not only from their own resources, considerable as they were, but even more from the coincidence that the great powers were all facing grave problems at one and the same time. It was a conjunction of circumstances that was not likely to last, and again it was England and France who presented the most dangerous eventual threat. Each had a vastly larger territory than the United Provinces, and each had a much more numerous population, the English three times as many, the French ten. Furthermore, each was self-sufficient in foodstuffs, whereas the Dutch had to import great quantities of grain or starve, and they had to trade in order to find the wherewithal to buy their supplies.

Finally, if it came to a showdown between the Dutch and either of these erstwhile and uncertain friends and potential competitors, the fundamental strategic advantages lay with the English and the French. Britain lay safe from invasion behind the wide moat of the Channel and the North Sea; France was difficult to assault even though it lay on the continent. The powerful Dutch navy might deflect English power at sea, reviving under Cromwell's guidance, but it could not do more against the island state. It could do equally little against the French, the greatest land power in Europe, for whom the navy was always secondary. Indeed, only the intervening buffer of the Spanish Netherlands – modern Belgium – protected the Dutch against the immensity of French military power.

Furthermore, the Dutch rise to political power had been a victory, in a way, over the Dutch political system itself. The revolt of the Netherlands in the sixteenth century had been intended to protect provincial and local power against the destructive intrusions of central authority directed from Brussels and ultimately from Madrid. The creation of a new, independent state in the northern Netherlands had been an unintended result of the rebellion. It was not created from above by a monarch imposing his authority upon

5

restless barons and rebellious towns, but by the provinces and their constituent elements – towns and nobilities – joining together in a loose-knit federation. To the outside world the United Provinces were a single state in the shape of the States General, but within there was an assemblage of seven provinces, each with its own provincial States that were effectively sovereign over its internal affairs. The structure of national decision-making was complicated, slow-moving and uncertain, and the rule of majority was seldom recognized or practiced.

That the system worked, and worked as well as it did, was the joint accomplishment of the Princes of Orange, who were stadholders in five of the seven provinces (cousins held the same office in the other two), and of the province of Holland, where the wealth and hence the tax-paying capacities of the Republic were concentrated. When the Princes and the province of Holland worked hand in hand, all went smoothly; but when they came into conflict, the fragile unity of the Dutch state was in peril.

This had happened twice. The first time had been the struggle between Oldenbarnevelt and Prince Maurice after the conclusion of the truce with Spain in 1609. The bitter rivalry of the political architect of the Republic and its military defender, who had worked so closely with each other for decades, ended with Oldenbarnevelt's trial and beheading in 1619, but Maurice won not only by using the voice of the other provinces against Holland but also by rallying strong forces within Holland to his side. He did not employ his opportunity to reorganize the Dutch state upon either a monarchical or a unitary basis; the dream of the Prince of Orange reigning as duke and count had lit up the eyes of many of Maurice's courtiers, but he had been satisfied with the reality of political domination. The notion of unifying the Republic into a state on the pattern of Spain or France or England did not occur to anyone as either dream or practical goal.

The second time had been the crisis through which the country had just come. William II's coup d'état had broken the traditional if often troubled alliance of Orange and Holland. The ruling party in Holland was determined now to prevent any recurrence of such events as the seizure of the six deputies and the near assault upon Amsterdam. But if they were not to waste the chance that had come their way so unexpectedly, they needed leadership of their own that would create a single will and a coherent policy out of the multiple

6

needs and aspirations first of Holland itself, and then of the whole republic. They needed a new Oldenbarnevelt, not as a builder but as a rebuilder; and they wanted no new Maurice to stand alongside him, either as collaborator or competitor. It was the task that would come to John de Witt, not at once but over the course of three years.

While dynastic monarchs – or quasi-dynasts like the Princes of Orange – were born to leadership of states, John de Witt entered the world of politics with a lesser opportunity. He was not born to power but only to the chance that it would be given to him. He was a member of the class from which the "regents," as the Dutch called members of the governing bodies in the Republic, were all recruited.

The De Witt family had provided aldermen, burgomasters and magistrates to Dordrecht for three centuries, almost as far back as the recorded history of Holland's first city goes in any detail. During the seventeenth century, John's father and uncle had both served in the government of the province, always as allies of the Prince of Orange until the recent dispute between William II and Holland. Yet the De Witts were not the first family of Dordrecht, a rank disputed between the Muys van Holy and Van Beveren clans; but the De Witts were linked to both of them by marriage. The family wealth had been earned in a timber business, but like so many of the prospering bourgeois of Holland, Jacob de Witt had sold out his direct stake in commerce in order to devote himself fully to work in government, while drawing his income from real estate and government bonds. He was well known in intellectual circles in Holland, more as a friend of the truly creative minds than as himself a significant poet or thinker.

He had married outside the confines of his city, choosing as a bride Anna van den Corput, from one of the leading Calvinist families in the Brabant city of Breda. It was politically an alliance of mixed value. States Brabant, as the northern part of the province conquered by the Dutch was called, remained stubbornly Catholic and was not admitted to participate with a vote in the States General; on the contrary, it was administered by officials named by the States General, always Reformed and reserving to their brethren in the Calvinist faith, however few in number, the benefits of government patronage and office. The Van den Corputs and their friends were in the front ranks of these beneficiaries of

"Generality" rule. Anna therefore brought to her husband not political allies, although her family had once been quite eminent, but political clients. On the other hand, it had established numerous links with regent families in many of the cities of Holland. Over the years John would address as "cousin" – a tie of more than sentimental value in the world of Dutch politics – many whose connections with him were through his mother.

John was born on September 25, 1625. The year is given as 1623 in several contemporary records, but the figure is an obvious error, even though the hard proof of a baptismal entry for him in the family church, the Grote Kerk near the De Witt home, is missing. But since there is a proper entry in 1623 for his brother Cornelius, who was two years older, the issue is beyond serious dispute. Perhaps John was born in Dordrecht and baptized in a village nearby. In any event, his rights as a natural-born citizen of Dordrecht were never challenged, as they would certainly have been had he been born, say, in The Hague, as one writer has suggested.

He was the youngest of four surviving children. The family life was a blending of the stern demeanor of parents committed to the strict tenets of Dutch Calvinism as laid down at the Synod of Dort, and the warm intimacy characteristic of the Dutch in their private life. Strong ties of affection – what we would call filial and fraternal love if we did not live in an unsentimental age – bound the children to their parents and to each other. The two eldest, both daughters, at first treated their little brother with the superior wisdom of their years. When he grew older and displayed an intelligence quite beyond the ordinary, they learned to mingle admiration with their admonitions. In later life, when he held high office and his abilities and powers were public knowledge, they gave him due deference and respect, and even sought reassurance of his love. Cornelius and John were so close in age that they became virtual equals, going to school and then to university at the same time and at the same level. We cannot say how early Cornelius learned to look to his brother as his superior in intelligence and judgment, but he too came to defer to him with an easy acceptance that infuriated his own wife, Maria. If the psychologists are right in holding that a childhood marked by strength of affection and steadiness of relations prepares the adult for meeting challenges with controlled emotions and self-assurance, then John de Witt the Grand Pensionary was shaped for his great task as a man by the character of his life at home as a boy and a youth.

The brothers began their education at the local Latin school, which had an excellent reputation. John in particular showed high aptitude in his studies. Like other lads of his generation, he learned to write in the Gothic hand that would remain in use in the Netherlands for another half-century, but he wrote it with a characteristic clarity and strength that few of his contemporaries possessed. It probably was a hint of the qualities of mind and personality that he would show in later life. But then we should remind ourselves that its very regularity, which nothing, neither endless hours of toil nor perplexities without number, could seem to shake – nothing, indeed, but the death of a beloved wife – may have been the sign of a soul too perfectly controlled. Be that as it may, he became fluent in Latin and French, the indispensable linguistic tools, and acquired a bit of English and German.

In 1641, when he was sixteen, he and Cornelius went to Leiden to begin university study of law. He soon discovered an intellectual love other than law, mathematics. So far as we know, he did not meet the French mathematician–philosopher René Descartes, who was living near Leiden in these years, but he studied informally with Descartes's friend, the professor of mathematics Frans van Schooten, who was one of the very first to teach mathematics in the Cartesian mode.

John mastered law in both the forms necessary for a Dutch jurist, the Roman law common to most of western and central Europe and the customary law of the Netherlands. By the time he ended his formal studies three years later, he had the formal body of law (which included the generally accepted political theory of the age) at his fingertips. A friend of his father's who was a noted juridical scholar was astounded by his command during an informal examination. For the rest of his life De Witt (as we shall now call him, except when necessary to distinguish him from his brother) was to use his legal knowledge with skill and accuracy, although it required the usual apprenticeship in a lawyer's office to learn the actual operating principles of Dutch courts, which were not touched upon in the highly theoretical law taught in the university. Yet there is no sign that the law ever captured his imagination or enthusiasm for itself, as had mathematics. It never occurred to him, however, to seek to make a living as a mathematician: that was a

9

career limited to a few university professors and a handful of military engineers. Most mathematicians, like Descartes himself, were brilliant amateurs of independent means. De Witt's choice of career was simple: either he would become a practicing lawyer or he would enter political life. But for the moment he did not need to make the choice.

In 1645 Jacob de Witt traveled to Denmark and Sweden as leader of a Dutch diplomatic mission. He took with him his two sons and their cousin, John de Wit (actually a namesake of our John, but one who wrote his name with a single "t"). They served as "noblemen" (*edellieden*), as unpaid junior aides to the accredited envoys were called; thus they were initiated into the forms and content of diplomacy. In Stockholm the young queen, the brilliant and erratic Christina, gave her hand to the young "noblemen" to be kissed during the embassy's public audience. When Jacob had to stay on alone for continued negotiations, he kept with him his nephew, who had been serving as secretary to the embassy. His sons left for home by way of Germany. Although the major fighting of the Thirty Years War was past, the country was still dangerous for travelers and they hired an armed guard. They got through without difficulty, but it was the young men's first direct experience with what war can do to a country. Their homeland had been at war for almost eighty years, of course, but no major campaigns had been fought on its own territory for decades. Yet, so far as we can tell, the travelers' concern was for themselves, not for a war-scarred and war-wearied nation. To ask them to have had such compassion is to read modern sensibilities into seventeenth-century man. What did strike to their hearts was the news when they reached The Hague early in 1645 that their mother had died in Dordrecht only three days before.

The brothers had to handle their grief without their father, who did not return from his mission until September. Within a month he had arranged for them to go on a grand tour of France and England to complete their education, formal and informal, as was becoming common among young Dutchmen of good birth and education.

Their journey lasted twenty-one months. They saw France as it slid toward the civil war of the Fronde that broke out in 1648, and England as Cromwell's New Model Army was on the verge of final victory, but they spent much more time acquiring the social graces and playing the tourist than imbibing the nectar of political knowledge at the source. In Paris they saw not only such notables as Cardinal Mazarin and the Prince of Condé but also gazed at the boy-king Louis XIV as he dined at the palace of the Tuileries, surely without premonition of how great a part he would play in their lives. They stayed three months at Angers, where they took their doctorates in law, which entitled them to practice at home and to be known as "Master," a form of address reserved for lawyers in the Netherlands to this day.

Afterwards they returned to their journeying. Considering that they were Calvinists to the core, they viewed an astonishing number of Catholic churches and shrines; their curiosity was marked by mild mockery, however, not by temptation. Natural wonders, fortified places and the remains of Roman antiquity also drew their interest. At some of their stops, they met members of local Protestant communities whom they found "very good company." Whether they were equally delighted with the famed Calvinist theologian Jean Deodati, a friend of their father's whom they visited at Geneva, John does not tell us in his record of the journey, but we may well imagine that this was more the work of duty than of desire.

Their stay in France ended in June 1647 when they crossed the Channel from Calais to Dover. In England they resumed their sightseeing. In London they took in the Houses of Parliament, Westminster Abbey and the Tower. Then, with two Dutch merchants as their guides, they crossed southern England all the way to Bristol. They saw Stonehenge, bathed at Bath and visited a number of English gentlemen at their estates. They enjoyed hunting at Marlborough, quite unaware of what that name would mean for the Dutch as well as the English in another half-century.

The climax of their stay in England was a visit almost at its very end to King Charles I at Reading, where he was under arrest. They were in the company of the aged but well-informed Dutch ambassador, Albert Joachimi, yet there is no indication in John's account of the journey that they discussed with him the larger significance of the political events occurring about them. What we can read back from what was later characteristic of John's career as a statesman is that he gained then no insight into the inner workings of violent politics. If anything, the sight of a captive king may have confirmed his dislike of public disorder, just as the picture of royal panoply in Paris may have stiffened his preference for republican simplicity.

The brothers' tour of England was over in little more than two months, as compared to the nineteen that they had spent in France. What English they learned was small and halting, from the evidence of their later experience. We may take for granted that their French acquired a fluency and an accuracy of accent that otherwise would probably have escaped them. This would help John in future negotiations with foreign diplomats in The Hague, most of whom spoke French but few Dutch.

It may well be that the most significant aspect of the brothers' grand tour is the cast of mind it reveals in John himself. While he was away, he kept a logbook in which he recorded what they saw and did, and little notebooks in which he set down with meticulous precision a list of letters received from home, moneys spent and miles traveled. On his return he transferred this information into a journal, but instead of using the occasion to comment upon what he had heard and learned, or to reminisce and reflect, he merely made it a neater, drier account. He was already, it is obvious, a man whose thoughts turned out to the world around him, not inward to himself and to his place in the world. For all his intellectual gifts, he was matter-of-fact to the extreme. Should we say that he was intelligent but not an intellectual? That, although he had the powers of mind we associate with a philosopher, he would never become a philosopher–statesman such as Plato dreamed of? The judgment may be a bit harsh, but it is certainly at bottom true.

Had he anticipated such a comment from his biographer, he would no doubt have protested that he had no ambition to be a philosopher, and he would not have understood what we mean nowadays by an "intellectual." He would probably have explained that he had not undertaken a career in politics because that had been chosen for his brother, and Dordrecht had rules against multiplying offices in the same immediate family.

Their paths did not diverge, however, until both had taken their oaths as lawyers before the Court of Holland a few months after their return, Cornelius in October and John on November 11. But Cornelius went back to Dordrecht to follow in his father's footsteps and was named to his first post as sheriff less than a year later, as soon as he came of age. John stayed on at The Hague, entering the office of a prominent lawyer and friend of Jacob de Witt's, John van Andel, to begin his practical apprenticeship.

The choice of Van Andel to be John's guide and host was significant in one respect. He was not a member of the official Reformed church but a Remonstrant, one of the sect formed by the Arminians purged after 1619 by the triumphant Gomarians. Yet Jacob de Witt had been one of the Gomarians, in fact the treasurer of the Synod of Dort. What happened to his religious convictions during the intervening three decades? We know almost nothing about how the change occurred, but a complex man had grown out of the simple young one. He remained an orthodox Calvinist in his religious principles. It is also evident, however, that he had sloughed off the persecuting propensities of the Gomarians in favor of a religious tolerance that few of the orthodox clergy as yet professed. The choice also displayed Jacob's courage, for the hostility of the dominies could have untoward political consequences: but what, looked at one way, may be courage of conviction, may be, looked at another way, stiff-necked determination to go one's own way.

Life for John de Witt, now all of twenty-two years of age, became a mixture of work, enjoyment and study. He put to use the social graces he had acquired or polished while in France. He flirted with the maidens and was accused of jilting one who also lived in the Van Andel home as a guest. He played the violin. He may even have written poetry; at least some attributed to him was read by a nineteenth-century Dutch scholar who thought it poor stuff, but it has since been lost and we cannot make up our own mind. Yet our best guess is that the critic was right: De Witt's was not a soul from which poetry was made. He went to the theater and the fair, dressed well and ate well. No self-denying puritan, he continued to be a precise disciplinarian for himself. He kept a methodical record of his expenditures down to the last stiver. He found relaxation, however, in mathematics. He took up the study of conic sections and drafted a major treatise which worked out solutions in a modern manner, but allowed it to slumber in manuscript.

The one topic that does not seem to have interested him was politics. It goes utterly unmentioned in all his letters written during the years 1648 and 1649, the very years so agitated by the conflict over army reduction. It was as if, having left a political career to his brother, he had also decided to leave to him interest in affairs of state. But we are speculating without any hard facts. All we can say is that he was not drawn to politics like a moth to the flame: it was no compulsive activity without which he wilted, the only work he felt worthy of him.

Events caught him up in the mid-summer crisis of 1650. The arrest and imprisonment of his father wrenched him from his lackadaisical attitude toward politics, and he sped down to Dordrecht to work for his father's release. After a brief discussion with the Old Council, the town's governing body, he continued on to Loevestein a few miles upriver to be on the spot. There was no question of offering resistance to Prince William's blow, only of softening its impact. John sought his father's release without loss of honor, and Jacob inside the castle took the same approach. Even before the Prince gave permission first for letters and then for personal visits, John managed to smuggle in a note to his father.

The settlement at Amsterdam set the pattern for one at Loevestein. William told a deputation from the prisoners' towns that he would let them go if they gave up their offices, as the Bickers had done. One elderly deputy accepted the Prince's terms at once, but Jacob's sons rejected them as implying that their father had been guilty of a crime or misdeed. Only after the States of Holland officially abandoned their insistence upon army reduction on August 13 did the impossibility of further resistance become evident.

Jacob thereupon asked the Old Council to relieve him of his seat in its ranks and of his other offices "in view of the present state of times and circumstances," and his request was granted. Even then John was insistent that there must be no indication that they had negotiated with the Prince with the city as intermediary: it had to be clear, even if unstated, that they were giving way only to force. William, having won the essentials, released the prisoners. On August 19, Jacob de Witt was again a free man.

That was all that could be hoped for. Political aspirations for Jacob and his sons could be written off. Of itself this was no loss to John, whose prospects as a lawyer remained excellent, and he returned to The Hague to pick up his tasks in Van Andel's law office.

The acceptance of defeat seems to have been total. The only thing to fear was that William would be vengeful, and during the months of life that remained to him there was no sign that he was.

Many years later a French visitor to the Netherlands, the Count of Guiche, reported in his memoirs that Jacob de Witt was irredeemably embittered, each day instructing his son at their first meeting in the morning, "John, remember Loevestein!" But Guiche was not in Holland at the time and, although he claims to know that this happened "from first hand," there is no contemporary source to confirm it. Besides, Guiche was a notoriously inventive memoir writer. In any case, John's own correspondence would indicate the contrary, if anything. He seldom mentioned politics at all until late October. Then, in a letter to a cousin, he discussed two new pamphlets that stirred public interest. One was favorable to the Prince, the other hostile, and John judged the former to show knowledge and good sense. The latter he did not characterize at all. This was the attitude we would expect from someone observing politics with curiosity and not commitment, the placid acceptance of a decree of fate.

William's death on November 7 shattered that placidity. Fate, ironic, unpredictable fate, had reversed her decree, and the door to politics was once again open to John de Witt. This time he was ready to enter.

2

Apprenticeship of power
1651–1653

It had taken the chance of two deaths, in fact, to open the way for John de Witt's political career. The first had been, of course, the demise of William II on November 7. The second was that of Cornelius Musch, the *griffier* or secretary of the States General, on December 15. Musch, apart from his fabulous venality, had been a pliant instrument in the hands of the Princes of Orange. The *griffier*, although he had no power in his own name, was crucially situated to influence policy, especially in foreign affairs. Holland moved at once to get its own man into the office. Only two days later, it put forward the candidacy of Nicholas Ruysch, one of Dordrecht's two pensionaries. He was duly elected and took the oath on December 23.

His pensionary's post was therefore empty, and Dordrecht, as if to seal the restoration of Jacob de Witt to honor and power, had already named his son John on December 21 to replace Ruysch. John went at once to The Hague to take up his duties as the town's permanent deputy to the States of Holland. Dordrecht's "residence" on the Vijverberg, across the moat from the Binnenhof, became his home.

Of itself his office was one of limited powers. Like all other deputies to the States of Holland, he did not act in his own name but in that of the town he represented. He was bound to follow the instructions of the burgomaster, and because he was not a member of the town council (called the "Old Council" in Dordrecht), unlike the other deputies from Dordrecht, he did not even have a share in the making of policy, as they did. But he stayed in The Hague even when the States of Holland was not in session, while they returned home, and he gave the business of the States his full attention, while it was only one of the questions with which they were concerned. He therefore acquired an expertness of knowledge that made his judgment valuable, and although he was an agent, he was one whose first task was to give advice. Furthermore, in the constant interplay of politics in the province, the deputies of the other towns looked to him as Dordrecht's spokesman.

There was another, special role that the permanent deputy of Dordrecht could play in the States of Holland. Dordrecht had long since been surpassed in economic and political importance as well as in population by several other towns in the province, notably Amsterdam, but still it was the oldest and hence the first in precedence. Thus, when opinions were polled in the States of Holland – there was no formal casting of votes in the modern sense – Dordrecht was the first to give its view after the Nobility. And it was normally the resident deputy, who was now John de Witt, who spoke for the city. He was therefore able to set the tone of debate because he defined its subject and because other towns' deputies found themselves stating their views in his terms, whether for or against.

There was one more duty that could come to the pensionary of Dordrecht because of his town's precedence. If the councilor pensionary, who was the highest official of the province (after the stadholder, if there was one), and the chief manager of the States of Holland, was absent, it was the Dordrecht deputy in residence who filled in for him. At the moment this was not a major responsibility or opportunity because the councilor pensionary, Jacob Cats, was present and active. Cats has maintained lasting fame as a poet for Everyman, but in his own time he was generally respected as a competent legist. He was not, however, a strong individual force in Dutch politics; he was essentially the servant of whoever dominated Holland, the stadholders Frederick Henry and William II in the past and now the newly prevalent anti-Orangist forces. But he was quite old and suddenly confronted with the task of leadership he had neither contemplated nor wanted. It was one that he had to assume, however, no matter how modest or tired he was.

On January 18 an extraordinary meeting of the States General opened in the Knights Hall of the Binnenhof with the purpose of deciding the shape and course of Dutch national government in the wake of William's death. Holland was already determined that no new stadholder would be named as its governor, and it desired that the other provinces where the late Prince of Orange had been stadholder do the same. It had taken the initiative for the Great Assembly, as the special session of the States General was called because it included not only the regular deputies from the provinces who resided in The Hague, but also a substantial fraction of the membership of each of the provincial States. Holland had wanted more, the attendance of the full membership of every province, so that decisions could be taken at once without the necessity to await approval of the provincial bodies, but that had been refused. Only the States of Holland participated as a body, but the other States sent their most influential members* to The Hague.

In practice the partial Great Assembly proved enough. The Hollanders were able to discuss the problems of the country personally with the most important leaders of all the provinces, both formally and away from the Knights Hall, in discussions at inns and residences that were even more important. The guidance of Holland's negotiations fell by right and necessity to Cats, but more and more during the seven months for which the Great Assembly sat, the councilor pensionary depended upon the energies and intelligence of several of the younger members. Not least among them were Conrad van Beuningen, an up-and-coming deputy for Amsterdam, and John de Witt of Dordrecht, Cats's designated substitute.

The other provinces were only too aware that in the absence of the counterweight of the Prince of Orange as stadholder, it would be almost impossible to thwart the will of the leading province. They were worried lest the Hollanders, confident in their own strength, should decide to go it alone and reduce the Union of Utrecht, the constitutional bond of the United Provinces, to a thin and meaningless shell. They were also concerned that Holland might take revenge upon William II's political henchmen who had played a leading part in the coup of the previous summer. Their fears turned out to be exaggerated, although it was soon clear that Holland intended to abandon the institutions of the stadholdership and the captaincy general. But most of the provinces gladly imitated the decision of the States of Holland to abolish the stadholder's right to name the members of the town councils,

---

* In contemporary usage, it was the towns and the order of Nobility in each province who were the "members," and the deputies were only their representatives.

instead authorizing the councils themselves to fill seats which became vacant.

De Witt, who alone of the Dordrecht deputies was always on hand, reported the proceedings in detail to his masters at home. Yet he avoided detailed discussion of the first major decision, adopted little more than a week after the Great Assembly convened. This was a resolution proposed by Holland on the always ticklish matter of religion. It was not an outright rejection of the demand of the Calvinist synods for action by the States General – not the States of the provinces – against religious groups outside the pale, like Catholics, Socinians (Unitarians) and Jews, as well as against violators of public morality. Instead it was a formal reaffirmation of the government's acceptance of the decrees of the Synod of Dort, reenactment of the decisions against religious outsiders, and silence about matters of public morality...and no provision for enforcement. This was a continuation of the old policy of seeming to give in to the Calvinist dominies that had been followed by Frederick Henry and the dominant political groups in Holland since 1625. It was a clever solution to a difficult problem, to be sure, but it infuriated the preachers, who knew that they had been paid with words and not with deeds. Their distrust of the political leaders of Holland was intensified, and their commitment to the cause of the House of Orange was made only the firmer. No wonder that De Witt preferred not to spell out the significance of the resolution.

Holland did not have its way so easily with regard to the central question before the Great Assembly – the future of the stadholderate and the captaincy general. The stadholderate continued intact in Friesland under Count William Frederick of Nassau, a cousin of the infant Prince of Orange, and the deputies of his province argued vehemently that the stadholderate was assumed by the Union of Utrecht in all provinces, and that it was therefore an integral part of the constitution of the country. No such fundamental claim was made with regard to the captaincy general, but the Orangists asserted that election of a commander of the forces of the United Provinces required only a majority in the States General, not unanimity.

Holland rejected both assertions, but as yet its rebuttal reflected only revulsion at William II's conduct – misconduct, as they saw it. They had as yet no specifically republican theory aimed at the stadholderate with which to sustain their argument. Dutch republicanism had been a matter of rejection of the tyranny of the kings of Spain rather than of monarchical rule as such, and it had not been directed against the Princes of Orange, even though some of the courtiers serving them had dreamed of converting the stadholderate into a monarchy, or at least a quasi-monarchy. But though republican theory would take shape in the course of the debate, it remained unstated during these first months of 1651.

Holland had little to fear from Friesland's arguments and assertions so long as it could hold the other provinces in line. But that was more easily said than done, since Orangism in them rested not only upon loyalty to the house that had led the nation for eight decades but also upon resentment of the predominance of Holland, to which there was now no barrier. The key resistance came from Zeeland, and De Witt became deeply involved in dissuading the neighbor province from continuing its advocacy of election of William III as stadholder of both provinces, with an adult – obviously, Count William Frederick as his nearest male relative – acting as his lieutenant until he came of age.

When it became evident that Holland would not yield, Zeeland recalled its deputies from the Great Assembly. Holland thereupon sent a delegation to Middelburg to seek an agreement based upon concessions in the matter of the army. De Witt, who acted as spokesman for the delegation, presented the arguments of Holland against election of a lifetime captain general in a lengthy address, but the Zeelanders were willing only to send their deputies back to The Hague. As a result Friesland, as well as its neighbor province Groningen which had named William Frederick as its stadholder after the death of William II, knuckled under to Holland's refusal to permit election of a captain general. Thus De Witt's first venture into the art of persuading the other provinces to do as Holland wished was a success.

He repaid the Frieslanders by accepting their proposal that a general amnesty be declared for the events of 1650. He headed a committee investigating the responsibility for the orders that brought the troops to the gates of Amsterdam. Despite bitter attacks upon William's close collaborators, De Witt saw the necessity for reconciliation, and he won over the States of Holland to his position. He earned little appreciation for it from staunch Orangists, however, although some provincial leaders, like the pensionary of Zierikzee in Zeeland, considered the decision of Holland to be an act of "great wisdom, foresight, moderation and temperateness."

When the Great Assembly held its final session on August 21, it had accomplished what the leaders of Holland had sought. Leadership of the republic had passed from the hands of the Princes of Orange to their own province. De Witt had not been the dominant figure in the work of the assembly, but he had made his mark as an intelligent, flexible and resolute member.

Difficult as these matters of domestic policy had been, they were almost as nothing compared to the relations with the newly established Commonwealth of England. It might have been imagined that parallel republican ideologies would bring the two countries together, all the more since the new régime in England was founded on the overthrow and execution of a king, while Holland's revulsion with the stadholderate was the result of the wilfulness and violence of a Prince of Orange who was the son-in-law of the late Charles I.

The similarity was more apparent than real, however. For one thing, as we have seen, Dutch republicanism as an explicit movement built upon the rejection of the stadholderate was utterly new. For another, although the triumphant Puritan party in England was quite close to the Dutch Calvinists in dogma, they were separated both by different views of church government (the Dutch Reformed church was presbyterian in structure, while in Britain the Presbyterians were losing out to the congregationalist Independents) and by the horror of the Dutch dominies at the killing of the English king. The commercial rivalry between the Dutch merchants and shippers, at the peak of their domination of European trade, and the envious English added the fuel of a powerful material interest to an already smoldering flame of mistrust and dislike. The political situation in the Netherlands, inordinately complex as it was, was made even more complicated as the Stuart cause became entangled with the Orangists' hopes and plans.

At first it seemed, indeed, that the two governments would come to an accord. The States General accepted without demur Holland's proposal to recognize the Commonwealth "as a free and sovereign republic." It was a good start, for it showed that William II's policy of implacable hostility to the republican government in England was being set aside. But it was not at all a good sign that an extraordinary embassy that came over from England in March was insulted and threatened at The Hague, and that its safety had to be assured by placing a military guard before its residence.

More serious was disagreement over the proposal brought by Cromwell's envoys for an alliance between the two countries "for the maintenance of the freedom of the people." Pressed as to what so broad a phrase meant in practice, they admitted it was directed against supporters of the Stuarts. The Dutch balked at this involvement in what they saw as the domestic concerns of the English. The negotiations bogged down at this point, and by the time the Great Assembly came to an end, no progress had been made beyond a decision to send an extraordinary embassy to England.

It had been intended to have Cats head the embassy, but he declined, arguing that the seventy-four years of age he had attained entitled him to terminate his duties rather than take on a new task that was certain to be lengthy and arduous. In May he asked permission to resign, but it was not granted until July, and the resignation would not take effect until a new councilor pensionary was chosen. There proved to be a dearth of candidates of obvious ability who still had most of their adult years before them. After two months, the States of Holland acknowledged this situation by asking Adrian Pauw van Heemstede, who had been Cats's predecessor, to become councilor pensionary for the second time. He was only a few years younger than Cats and accepted with extreme reluctance. He was not expected to remain very long in office, but at least there would be time to find someone capable of assuming what everyone knew was the most onerous task in the Dutch state.

Once Pauw went to England in June 1652 to join the extraordinary embassy, De Witt, as Dordrecht's permanent deputy, was called upon to do much of the councilor pensionary's work. It was a supreme opportunity to make his abilities known, but it came to him by virtue of Dordrecht's position in the order of precedence, not because anyone had as yet marked him out for this high office.

De Witt's principal duty not only while Pauw was in England but even after the councilor pensionary returned was to help him in the conduct of foreign policy. There was no foreign minister as such in the Dutch Republic, but ever since the days of Oldenbar-nevelt the councilor pensionary of Holland had acted as such.

And Dutch foreign policy at that moment consisted primarily in relations with England, all bursting with the pride and self-confidence of a successful revolution. Nothing spoke more elo-quently of the difficulties that the extraordinary embassy faced than the passage two months before it sailed of the Navigation Act by the English Parliament. This "notorious ordinance...to the disadvantage of trade," as De Witt called it, was designed to break the Dutch stranglehold on the European carrying trade by permitting Dutch shippers to bring into England only goods made or grown in the Netherlands, a minor part of Dutch exports. The English rivalry extended to the far-off East Indies, where the English wished to gain a larger share of the spices trade and the nascent empire controlled by the Dutch. They revived the decades-old controversy over the so-called "Amboina massacre," the trial and execution of English merchants in 1632, to inflame popular hatred of the Dutch.

But the Dutch themselves were divided about what policy to follow toward the English. The ruling party especially in Holland knew that the Dutch had little to gain even from a victory in the event of war with the Commonwealth, and much to lose from defeat. They were not committed by political sympathy to either side in the English civil war, neither to the triumphant republicans nor to the vanquished royalists. This was not at all true of the Orangists, however. They wanted such a war, thinking only of the Stuart restoration which they took for granted would be the first result of a Dutch victory.

Although the conduct of foreign affairs was in the hands of the States General, the power of decision lay ultimately with the States of the seven provinces. As the most important of these, the States of Holland saw, in the complicated and dangerous business of relations with England, the necessity to determine their policy on a systematic basis even before it was discussed in the States General. A new committee on English affairs was formed by Their Noble Great Mightinesses of Holland in February 1652, and De Witt was named to it as a matter of course, in view of his status as Dordrecht's pensionary-deputy. He soon became its leading member and put his personal touch on the way it handled its business. He saw to it that it reported regularly to the States of

Holland, not just now and then, and that its records were kept methodically.

He was at the center of its most important work. He arranged for money to be sent to the envoys in England to enable them to find out what was being discussed in the Council of State; the ugly word "bribe" was not used. When Holland decided to send its own unofficial representatives to England to smooth along the negotiations if possible, it was he who went around the towns to try to talk likely candidates into accepting the difficult and probably thankless task, and it was his friend William Nieupoort of Leiden who was appointed in May. He continued to favor making every effort to preserve the peace, but recognizing that England seemed determined to make the appeal to arms, he supported measures to give Admiral Martin Tromp a fleet strong enough to daunt the English or defeat them if it came to battle.

Battle was what it did come to on May 29, when Tromp was met by the English admiral Blake off Dover and the Dutchman refused to dip his flag first in salute to the Englishman. It was no more than an indecisive clash of fleets, not a fight to the death, but it could furnish the English with an easy pretext for the war they seemed to be seeking.

The news of the encounter reached The Hague on June 4. The hopes and fears it set off were to be characteristic of the political conflict that would tear at the United Provinces for the next two decades.

For the supporters of the Prince of Orange's cause, war with England would provide a double opportunity. Constantine Huygens, the great poet who served as secretary to all the Princes of Orange from Frederick Henry to William III, wrote to an English Royalist friend that a crisis might soon break out in which the populace in the Netherlands could be stirred up against the new government before it had time to tighten its grip upon the state. It was probably much the same fear – not hope as with Huygens – that Quentin de Veer, the bailiff of The Hague, had in mind when he wrote De Witt, his nephew, that when he returned from Dordrecht there were things he had to tell him that he did not dare to put down in writing. De Veer had just dispersed a demonstration of youths before the stadholder's quarters in the Binnenhof, waving orange banners and shouting to see the infant William. To restore the Prince of Orange and the Stuart king in exile, Charles II, in one great combined effort was a glorious dream that to the Orangists seemed also utterly realistic politics.

For the dominant party in Holland, the threat of war with England presented on the contrary a double burden. The first was to rescue peace if at all possible, although without conceding English demands that would be disastrous to Dutch trade, the second to prepare to wage war if it came anyway. It was decided that a final effort should be made to persuade the English that the clash had only been an unfortunate accident and that another extraordinary ambassador, this time an official envoy, unlike Nieupoort, should be sent to London. The choice for arguing the Dutch case fell upon the elderly Pauw, whose reluctance was softened by permission to return at his own discretion if he saw no hope of success. Pauw left for London on June 15, and his duties as councilor pensionary of Holland were assumed, in accordance with the usual practice, by De Witt as pensionary-deputy from Dordrecht.

Pauw was not at all encouraged by what he saw on his arrival in England. The English would make another trial of arms, he foresaw, and their demands would go up if they won, and their thirst for revenge would do the same if they lost. He asked De Witt to cool Dutch tempers while he was negotiating. But De Witt thought that the time had come to beat the English at their own game. At his proposal, the States General sent orders to Tromp to fight whenever he would find the advantage lay with him. The ambassadors in England were told to come home unless the English settled down to serious negotiations. They departed on July 10, and Parliament declared war on the Dutch on July 31. Pauw thereupon returned to The Hague.

The Orangists were delighted. The war was a "sure bridge" over which Charles II would return to his throne and the young William III would regain his father's offices. The common people in the Netherlands gleefully anticipated an easy victory. The regents of Holland saw more realistically that England held the strategic advantage. The Dutch had to win in battle or pay a heavy price.

De Witt, all afire for victory, was confident that Tromp could win because he had more ships than Blake. He soon learned that numbers were not enough. Blake twice beat off Tromp's attacks and then brought his own fleet across the North Sea to the Dutch coast. Tromp, reporting to the States General, told Their High

Mightinesses that the fleet was in no condition to undertake an attack. In October his vice admiral, Witte de With, was defeated, and in December Tromp himself met Blake off the Downs and came off somewhat better, although Blake escaped up the Thames, having lost only two ships.

For a little while in February 1653 De Witt thought that the English were sufficiently impressed by the new war fleet that the Dutch were making ready to be willing to talk peace. He became wary, however, when an unofficial English representative came over with the message that the government in London would resume negotiations if the Dutch took the formal initiative. The Englishman was sent back with assurances of Dutch interest, but De Witt suspected that the real purpose of the visit was to slow Dutch naval preparations while Blake was getting his fleet out to sea.

At the end of the month the hostile navies met again off Portland Bill. A three days' battle ended with Tromp managing to save part of the merchant fleet he was convoying from France, but otherwise it was Blake's victory. Once back home, Tromp told Their High Mightinesses that he could not win with numbers alone: Blake's ships were larger and specially built for combat, not converted merchantmen like the majority of his own craft. De Witt learned this lesson well, but for the moment there was little that could be done about building a new kind of Dutch navy. It was necessary rather to follow up the chance of peace negotiations.

New secret talks were undertaken by Holland, without the participation of the other provinces, through an English officer in the Dutch army who went to England in December for a visit (travel between belligerents was not as tightly barred in the seventeenth century as in the twentieth). De Witt continued to play a central role, drafting a letter that Their Noble Great Mightinesses the States of Holland sent in March to Parliament and the Council of State that played up the religious comradeship of the two countries. But the English wanted to treat of peace not with a single province but with the whole States General, and the Hollanders had to inform Their High Mightinesses of what they had been doing.

The willingness of the English to talk peace did not calm the wrath of the deputies from the other provinces against the Hollanders for their initiative. The furious debate in the States General set the fundamental arguments against each other. The

Groningers accused the Hollanders of having violated the Union of Utrecht. It was Cromwell who really started the business, it was said, and the Hollanders, with De Witt the worst of them, were doing his work. Deputies whose Orangist sympathies were notorious demanded that the war be carried on with greater vigor and that restoration of Charles II be made one of the official war aims. Nicholas Stellingwerff of little Medemblik, who had been one of the six deputies imprisoned by William II at Loevestein, gave a blunt retort. You should know why we cannot go on with the war, he told them, it is your provinces which refuse to pay their share of its costs.

The States of Holland, although unwilling to go so far as to propose an immediate truce, as De Witt urged, pressed the States General for continuation of the negotiation, perhaps in a neutral Protestant country. The Hollanders won by a bare majority, and a letter drafted by De Witt was sent to London by two couriers, each going by a different route. The one who went directly by sea returned in a few days with news that Cromwell had sent Parliament packing and was ruling by his own authority, more sovereign, he thought, than any king of England had ever been. But the new ruler wanted peace with the Dutch, not continued war. The reply that came officially from the Council of State late in May was that the English were ready for peace talks, but they would have to be held in London.

It took a month of acrimonious debate before the English proposal was accepted by the States General and an extraordinary mission of four ambassadors, including Nieupoort and another Hollander, Jerome (Hieronymus) van Beverningk of Gouda, was named and left for London. Van Beverningk, like De Witt, was one of the bright young men in Dutch politics.

The ambassadors could not harbor much longer their hope that the Dutch fleet would provide them with persuasive arguments. Another battle at sea on June 12 brought Tromp another defeat, and Witte de With put the situation in the simplest words: the English "are now our Masters." Commodore Michael de Ruyter, who was equally plain spoken and was not tainted with Orangist sympathies, declared that he would not put to sea again unless he had more and better ships.

De Witt, as the most influential member of the naval committee of the States of Holland, had been trying his best for more than a year to provide a stronger fleet, but he failed to gain the new taxes and the improved administrative measures in the admiralties that would have made it possible. And, himself without experience at sea, he did not easily grasp the admirals' insistence upon having bigger ships constructed specifically for combat.

A worse problem for the negotiators was the outbreak of Orangist riots at home. English naval predominance might well make their price for peace higher, but, as De Witt foresaw, it might also increase their readiness to conclude a peace that would certainly be to their advantage. On the other hand, if the Orangists regained power in the Dutch Republic, they would put its forces at the service of Charles II. This made them common enemies of the ruling powers in both Holland and England. The ambassadors were therefore told that the terms for peace might well include combined action by both governments against the two Houses of Orange and Stuart. The internal politics of the Dutch Republic thus became an integral part of its foreign policy.

The Orangist movement had held De Witt's attention ever since the outbreak of war with England had provided it with its great opportunity. It rested upon many elements of strength. The army and navy were loyal by force of tradition and habit to the family that had given them their commanders since the birth of the Republic. The populace was moved by simple affection for the national leaders consecrated by more than eight decades of struggle for independence, and they also saw the Princes of Orange as protectors against the regents, the ruling authorities in the towns. These feelings were shared by wide circles of those the Dutch called "burghers," not a capitalist bourgeoisie but craftsmen and small merchants who were clearly distinguished from and superior to the populace of wage-workers, but who were excluded from participation in political power by the increasingly oligarchic regents. De Witt thought that "hardly one out of a thousand" of the common people did not support the House of Orange. The six outer provinces all resented Holland's single-minded determination to pursue its own interests; for them to back the Orangist cause was to put all the passion of the movement behind their own self-interest. All the disparate groups received the encouragement and the blessing of the bulk of the Calvinist clergy, who had annexed Orangism to their own religious loyalties despite the Erasmian tolerance that had characterized both William the Silent and

Frederick Henry. They were not principled republicans, no more than Calvin himself had been, and when they scoured the text of Scripture, they updated the kings of the Old Testament to fit the stadholders in their own republic.

The power of the movement lay in its ability to work both sides of the street. The outer provinces, led by Zeeland and Friesland, provided a legal form of action for the Orangist drive to regain power. They might not be able to prevent Holland from going its own way, but they could delay and hamper the adoption of its policies. The populace, and to a lesser extent the burghers, were ready to act outside the framework of legality, using the weapon of riot and threatening that of outright rebellion. In this assault upon the established authorities, they were encouraged and even incited by the preachers, who lent it moral legitimacy.

All the same, the Hollanders held the upper hand. Ever since the death of William II, they alone occupied the strategic heights of Dutch politics. Money was the sinews not only of war but also of all government, and the single province of Holland earned more from all branches of economic life and paid more revenue to meet the needs of state, both within purely provincial agencies and through the States General, than all the other provinces combined.

The regents of Holland had the habit of governance. Even during the years when the Princes of Orange had been most powerful, the regents had ruled in the towns and held the final authority in the provincial States. The regular police force in the cities was tiny, consisting only of the sheriff and his assistants; but the burgher guard was normally quite able to put down any civil disturbances. True, its members in the ranks were not participants in government and they usually resented their exclusion; but their officers were named by the regents and came from their class. Furthermore, if rioting proved more than the burgher guard could handle, a detachment of the army could be dispatched to put an end to the disorder, and, in the absence of a Prince of Orange as commander-in-chief, there was no question of the army's disobeying its provincial paymasters.

The regents, lastly, had no doubt about their right to rule or any compunctions about the use of force against the "rabble." Unless popular rioting became so widespread that it overwhelmed the armed forces, or unless the self-confidence of the regent régime was undermined, the Orangist hope of restoration on purely internal forces was idle.

The most serious challenge came from Zeeland within weeks of the English declaration of war. On August 22, Middelburg, the capital, put before the provincial States a proposal to call upon the States General to name William III captain and admiral general. The States of Holland responded quickly. A delegation of four, including De Witt, was sent to Middelburg to urge the Zeelanders to stand by the policy of collaboration with Holland which they had accepted during the Great Assembly.

The delegates were confronted by repeated threats of violence in Zeeland. In Middelburg a mob broke into the meeting hall of the States intent upon killing the Hollanders, who luckily had left for an inspection of the harbor of Flushing. There too, a crowd with obviously hostile intentions gathered before the inn where they had stayed, but found that their expected victims had already departed.

De Witt, who stood out as the strong man of the delegation, sniffed disdainfully at the threats. The populace, he wrote sardonically to a cousin, are so concerned for our welfare that they wish to spare us both the long torture of Zeeland fever and the expense of a return journey. But disdain did not mean reckless unconcern for their own safety. The Hollanders protested to the Zeeland authorities, who gave them a heavy guard when they came to the provincial States to ask that a delegation be sent to The Hague for continued discussion. But they did not put sole reliance upon the Zeelanders. On their own they arranged for troops on Holland's payroll that were stationed in nearby garrisons to stand watch over them in the streets and at the assembly hall. Thus, they emerged safely and returned home unharmed.

Two months passed before a delegation from Zeeland arrived at The Hague. It reaffirmed the province's proposal to name the Prince of Orange as captain general, with a lieutenant general commanding for him until he came of age. The States of Holland replied with an "Advice" drawn up by De Witt. It did not argue in general terms against the House of Orange but only specifically that there was no need at the moment to elect a commander of the armed forces and certainly none to elect a child.

In the ensuing discussions, De Witt took the place of the absent Pauw. The Zeelanders' essential argument was that the election was needed in order to calm the public, and they refused to desist from presenting their proposal to the States General. De Witt was pleased that the discussions went smoothly, without personal animosity, and that the Hollanders had maintained their unanimity. It was a pattern to which he would remain faithful for the rest of his life – to keep his own province united, and with its strength behind him to persuade the other provinces to accept Holland's policy.

When the Advice was presented formally to the Zeelanders on December 5, a final paragraph written by De Witt had been added. It spelled out arguments of principle ostensibly against the appointment of a captain general but in fact against the institution of the stadholdership itself. The stadholder's position was like that of a monarch; it was dangerous to the community because there was no counterweight to the tendency inherent in human weakness. Popular government – which in the language of the times meant a broad aristocracy, not a universal democracy – with its power widely distributed among many assemblies, was better.

It is doubtful that the Zeelanders were persuaded by these arguments, for over the next two decades they would be in the forefront of the movement for Orange restoration. Yet at this time they refrained from presenting their proposal to the States General, as they had intended to do. Skeptics suggested that the whole business had been a charade on their part, soothing their populace with a show of firmness while actually they were glad to be rid of the domination of their province by the Prince of Orange as its "First Noble."

The succession of disasters at sea did, however, lead to a surge of Orangist demonstrations, some of which spilled over into rioting. The first demonstration occurred in The Hague in May 1653 after a ceremony in which the Prince of Orange, now two and a half years of age, was inducted into the English Order of the Garter by a herald-at arms of Charles II. The burgher guard marched along the Vijverberg the next day in little William's honor, while bands of youths celebrated by breaking windows. There were Orangist demonstrations in Dordrecht a month later, and the town government preferred the prudence of inaction to the boldness of repression. In Delft, demonstrators compelled naval recruiters to carry the Prince's flag, not that of the States General as the law required.

In Enkhuizen, a port town on the Zuider Zee, the burgomaster and council refused to permit this to be done. Demonstrations followed, and the order was withdrawn, but not quickly enough to forestall fierce rioting. The town government, unable to put it down with the meager forces available to it, asked the States of Holland to send in soldiers. This was done, but Their Noble Great Mightinesses also named a committee to investigate the disorders and bring the ringleaders to The Hague for trial – a plain intrusion upon the autonomy of the town. The arrival of troops outside Enkhuizen was sufficient to restore order, but the committee was not allowed to enter. For De Witt the whole affair was disturbing. He did not believe it was spontaneous, and it was an example that might be followed elsewhere. His anxiety was justified, for rioting spread to many towns in the province, with the populace demanding that the Prince of Orange's flag be displayed by recruiters. De Witt did not approve of Medemblik's capitulation to the rioters. He considered that Alkmaar's action in bringing in two companies of cavalry and arresting rioters was the right way to handle such troubles; the other towns should follow its example.

During June the De Witt family itself became the butt of threats. A drunken and armed German hanger-on of the Orange court confronted Jacob de Witt in the streets of The Hague, promising to teach him a lesson for speaking out against the Prince. Jacob walked on as if nothing had happened, but his son John did not treat the matter so lightly. He had the man arrested and jailed and with difficulty persuaded his father to return to Dordrecht. When he himself received warnings of plots against his life, however, he did not let them bother him.

He was more despairing for his country. If the governing classes lost their nerve, as they seemed to be doing, and failed to subdue the rioting, if they did not act with "foresight and courage," there was real danger of a revolution that would restore the House of Orange. Should this happen, the English republicans would become implacable and the war would go on until utter disaster befell the Dutch.

The revolution did not come, but De Witt did not recognize then or later that one reason was that Princess Mary had no more taste for popular revolution than he did. She wanted her son's restoration to come legally, from the hands of the States of Holland, not from King Mob. The riots remained fitful and sporadic, lacking the organized leadership that De Witt had suspected was behind them, and rioters without leaders do not make a revolution.

Lack of leadership on the part of a ruling group may make the conditions for a revolution more propitious, however. If the Orangist party had been deprived of its born head by the death of William II, neither Cats nor Pauw had taken the part of an Oldenbarnevelt. For that was the choice before the Dutch – to be led either by the Prince of Orange or by the councilor pensionary of Holland.

Pauw, put back in the office of councilor pensionary in his old age, did not have the energy to undertake all the multiple duties of his office, and much of his work had devolved upon De Witt, especially when Pauw fell ill after his return from England. When the councilor pensionary died on February 21, 1653, the question of Holland's leadership could no longer be put off.

Yet the election of a councilor pensionary was a weighty decision and not one to be hurried. The perilous war situation and the troubled conditions at home brooked no delay either, De Witt reminded the States of Holland, and he proposed that the assembly name an acting councilor pensionary for an interim. He did not seek the post for himself, even though it might be anticipated that whoever was named would lead in the running for the regular office. The Dordrecht deputies proposed the appointment of Albert Ruyl, the pensionary of Haarlem, but all the rest fixed their choice upon De Witt. We may take it for granted that they had been impressed by the skill and the diligence with which he had already performed Pauw's duties.

That the Dordrecht deputies, speaking for the government of their town, should not have favored their own pensionary may have been due to a straining of the relationship between him and his "mother city." In The Hague he had ceased to be purely a Dordrechter in his judgments, one who put his city's interests and views without hesitation before all others. Either because he was doing Pauw's work and had therefore become willy-nilly a servant of the whole province, even of the whole state, or because residing regularly at the seat of provincial and national government had made him too familiar with their larger interests to think solely in Dordrecht's terms, he had not supinely accepted instructions from the burgomaster. There had been a sharp and angry clash between them over his failure to support Dordrecht's candidate for the post of bailiff of South Holland – a modest post, but still worth procuring for a fellow-townsman.

When the election of a councilor pensionary was held on July 23, eight names were put before the States of Holland. Seven of the nominees withdrew in favor of De Witt, a striking personal tribute to the impression of competence he had built up during the previous two and half years. He did not accept at once, however, but was given time to go to Dordrecht to consult with the burgomaster and the Old Council, and incidentally with his father and brother.

De Witt did not leap at the appointment with panting eagerness. Was he shaken by the ominous warning that came from his father's old friend and fellow prisoner at Loevestein, Nanning Keyser? "If you accept the office," Keyser told him, "it must be a matter of indifference to you whether you go into your coffin whole or in pieces." Keyser was known to be a timid man and De Witt did not shrink before danger. Still, he told Jacob and Cornelius that he hesitated because of the extreme difficulty of the post, which placed upon its holder enormous burdens of responsibility at a time of utmost peril for the country. They persuaded him to accept nonetheless. We do not know what they said to overcome his reluctance, but there is no doubt that they cited both the importance of the office and his fitness for it.

The magistrates of Dordrecht took longer to give their consent, and then they hedged it with the provision that he remain committed to them; he was given leave only for five years, the term of the councilor pensionary's office.

De Witt returned to The Hague at once to give Their Noble Great Mightinesses his acceptance. He took the oath of office on the morning of July 30. The next day they unanimously granted him an act of indemnity he himself had drafted. It provided the protection of the law for all that he did while in office. But what would that avail if enemies overwhelmed the power of the state by revolution?

The years of apprenticeship were over. De Witt had learned his way in the world of Dutch politics at first hand. He had won the respect and admiration of his friends, and his foes too gave him unwilling respect for his abilities even as they focused their hatred upon him. Now the full responsibility of the most dangerous office in the Dutch state fell upon his shoulders.

3

The first task
1653–1654

It was a most extraordinary post that De Witt took up when he became councilor pensionary of Holland. It corresponded to none other in the political world of the time nor to any since. There was nothing novel in any of the elements that made up the office; it was only the combination of formal powers and informal duties that was unique.

The councilor pensionary of Holland was a *servant* of state, and those foreign diplomats who described him to their courts as the "prime minister" were using the word "minister" in a sense that had not yet been forgotten. The designation was quite accurate in equating him with such figures as Richelieu and Mazarin in France and the *validos* in Spain, for like them he was a man-of-all-work in the guidance of the state; but their master was the king, and his was Their Noble Great Mightinesses the States of Holland. He was unlike the prime minister of our own day because he was not the head of government; it was, on the contrary, during all the years that he served it, a government without a head.

He was, furthermore, a minister of state without a ministry in the modern sense of the word, a department of government. Political tasks and offices in the United Provinces were not distributed according to the principle of distinct function, which had already come into being under the rule of Louis XIV in contemporary France. There was no ministry of foreign affairs, no ministry of treasury, or the like. A few subordinate bodies – notably the Court of Holland and the provincial Chamber of Accounts – had no specifically political tasks.

Assemblies like the States of Holland had the broadest powers of governance over their province. They were both legislature and executive: more correctly, the distinction was not even made between the two. The States of Holland called itself sovereign, and if we hesitate to grant it that status without reservation, it is not so much because the States General acted as a sovereign in relation to other countries as because the power of ultimate decision within the province of Holland itself (as in the other six provinces) did not reside in Their Noble Great Mightinesses but in the "members" of Holland, the eighteen voting towns and the order of Nobility. Yet it did not rest either with each of them taken singly. It was only in their joint capacity that they were sovereign, and at least in principle in all important matters the majority could not override the objection of any one of the members.

Under such circumstances it was immensely difficult to create and carry out policy. Since the emergence of an independent Dutch state that task, which is the specific task of political leadership, had fallen either to the stadholder of the province or to the councilor pensionary, or usually to both of them in tandem. The conflict that tore at the vitals of the Republic during the Twelve Years Truce had taken the form of a clash between the stadholder, Prince Maurice, and the land's advocate, Oldenbarnevelt. Now, thirty-five years later, in the absence of a stadholder, the task of leadership fell of its own weight upon the councilor pensionary of Holland.

The councilor pensionary's post was neatly defined by the name it had borne under Oldenbarnevelt – advocate of Holland – before it was changed to the more innocuous "councilor pensionary" after his fall. He was the upholder of Holland's interest not by arms but by the force of his thought and judgment, given in advice to the States of Holland, which alone had the power of final decision for the province.

Originally the councilor pensionary had been a legal officer, quite literally the "advocate" who spoke in law courts for the State of Holland and advised it on legal matters, especially since many of the deputies were not themselves juridically trained. During the three decades of Oldenbarnevelt's administration the central task of the councilor pensionary had shifted, however, to political guidance of the States of Holland. The councilor pensionary sat in the States of Holland not as a deputy but as a kind of exalted political secretary, presenting matters on the agenda with the relevant documents and drafting the decisions taken in the form of resolutions. He did not simply record votes, as in a modern parliamentary body, but rather incorporated the results of a debate in a resolution, which would then be accepted after a second

36

reading. Furthermore, he did not work with formal motions or bills, but drew together the consensus of opinions in the formulation of resolutions.* Indeed, it was his duty to persuade members if possible to reach such a consensus. The councilor pensionary was not, however, a passive register of opinions; he was also a participant in the debate as the pensionary of the order of Nobility, a parallel post which he held simultaneously. Since the Nobility was the first member to give a judgment on matters before the assembly, a vigorous councilor pensionary was able to set the tone of debate and define its substance.

The work of initiating policy and carrying it into practice for the province fell in very large measure upon De Witt. He did this not in his own name – he did almost nothing in his own name – but as a member of all the important committees of the States of Holland. Some of these were concerned with operations, like the naval affairs committee, which oversaw the three admiralties situated within the province as well as the work of members of the other two admiralties (of Zeeland and Friesland) who were named by Holland. Other committees were concerned with matters essentially of policy, like the committees on relations with individual foreign states. Still other committees were named for *ad hoc* purposes.

The councilor pensionary was the one permanent member of these committees. He kept their records, presented for discussion the relevant materials from the archives or from agents in the field, and drafted proposals to be presented to the whole assembly of Their Noble Great Mightinesses. He would also go into the field himself, particularly when the navy was involved, in the name either of the committee concerned or of the States of Holland.

He had, too, the task of reconciling discordant opinions and bringing the members to a unified purpose and will. It was no easy accomplishment. The members were self-willed and most concerned with the interests of their own towns; and it often required all the arts of persuasion at De Witt's command to break through their stubbornness. As respect for his judgment increased, they became readier to accept it; but they never surrendered their right to be insistent or querulous, and to make up their own mind. They never forgot who was master and who servant, and if they

---

* Resolutions, it may be added, covered everything from permanent laws to decisions on current policy as well as appointments.

became grateful for their councilor pensionary's services, they also came to resist his superiority of intellect and his almost ceaseless pressure on them to act more quickly and decisively.

Over the years he gradually acquired another instrument of influence, control over patronage. It was never outright control; indeed, his formal instructions forbade him to involve himself in matters of appointment to posts in the armed forces or in the civil branch of the state service. In practice, however, it was impossible to enforce so stern a rule of non-interference. His judgment of persons was sought as of policies, and after a while his informal recommendation represented a long step forward toward appointment. Few posts were given upon the basis of mere competence, although De Witt tried to give it its due weight. For the most part, they went to the politically loyal, among whom were obviously members of his own wide network of family relations; but appointment of "friends" never went far enough for their own satisfaction, and always too far for rivals outside that lucky circle.

Many of these posts were in the gift not of Holland but of the States General. That De Witt's judgment carried weight with Their High Mightinesses as well was part and parcel of his larger, essentially informal work of leadership of the Dutch nation as a whole. In the assembly of the States General the role of political secretary was performed by the *griffier*, and De Witt participated in Generality work ("Generality" was used to mean the States General and the parts of government and the territory under its authority) as one of Holland's deputies. In debates it was he who customarily spoke for the principal province, and in committees he was almost always one of Holland's members. As in provincial matters, he did much of his work in Generality business through and on behalf of these committees. Especially in questions of foreign policy, there was usually no clear distinction as to whether he was wearing his Holland or his Generality hat. Envoys of foreign states who conferred with him treated him as the country's foreign minister, although they knew quite well that there was no such official in the Dutch Republic.

Some of these things De Witt had been doing even before his election, when Pauw was away or ill. Some developed over the years, the result partly of the force of his own mind and personality and partly of the compelling need of the state.

The more subtle and elusive aspects of his influence, so much greater than his formal powers, were not fully present in the difficult first year of his office, when his principal task was to bring the war to an end, one way or another, victoriously if possible but more probably bowing to defeat.

There was no honeymoon for De Witt on taking office. He was at once plunged into the grueling task of leading the United Provinces in a war that seemed lost. Within weeks he knew that the chance of salvaging a victory at sea was nil and that the Dutch would have to make the hard choice between a humiliating and painful peace at terms set by the English, and political and economic disaster. For, if the Dutch navy could not protect their merchantmen, their prosperity would be doomed and their very independence endangered. It was a choice for which the Dutch nation was not ready and which De Witt himself made reluctantly. It would be his grim task during his first year as councilor pensionary to persuade them to accept their defeat and to trick them if need be into so doing.

He would have preferred to negotiate peace with the English on equal terms. He had hoped and worked for a victory of the fleet under Martin Tromp. He wanted the admiral to take the offensive and break the English blockade by battle rather than try to sneak the Dutch merchant fleet out to sea in convoy. Although the States General refused to change Tromp's orders to suit De Witt's wishes, Tromp himself moved to gain the advantage by taking his fleet up the coast toward Texel to join Vice Admiral Witte de With's thirty-six ships to his own ninety. But the English caught up with him at Ter Heide before he reached Texel, and he had to fight without reinforcements. The battle raged for three days, from August 8 to 10, moving down along the coast to the mouth of the Maas. The sound of the guns could be heard from the shore, and the result of the battle could be expected within hours. Alas, by the third day, it was news of disaster that arrived. The Dutch fleet had been shattered, and Tromp himself was dead, shot through the heart.

Even now De Witt did not despair. He hoped that God's favor would swing from the English to the Dutch, and meanwhile worked to repair the fleet and restore its command. Witte de With as vice admiral had taken over the flag for the time being, but there were widespread complaints about his high-handed manner. De Witt sought the advice of two respected commanders, John Evertsen and

Michael de Ruyter, although the former was an Orangist and the latter a Zeelander. Both were willing to serve under Witte de With, but the States of Holland decided instead to make a land soldier, Jacob van Wassenaer, lord of Obdam, the provinces's lieutenant admiral and to seek the general naval command for him. De Ruyter, although at nearly forty-seven years of age ready for retirement, agreed to stay on and to serve as Obdam's guide in naval matters. The States General appointed Obdam to the supreme naval command, as Holland had proposed.

De Witt gained from Their High Mightinesses instructions for the new naval commander so broadly phrased that Obdam and De Ruyter could choose almost any naval strategy they wanted, including the blockade of the Thames that Tromp had already tried without success. To win this policy De Witt had to ride roughshod over the opposition of Zeeland, which wanted a policy of convoying with its obvious immediate goal of safeguarding commerce. But a fierce November storm proved the impossibility of keeping the fleet at full strength over the winter. And when it came to rebuilding the navy, De Witt now saw the necessity of numbers and even of ships built for naval service. He accepted only slowly, however, the principle set forth by Tromp before his death that not merely more ships were needed to counter the English but also bigger and stronger ones. Such plans for naval renewal, even if they worked out, could bring fruits only in the long run. Peace in the here and now would have to be the work of diplomacy.

Dutch diplomacy would have to do that work, however, with a double handicap. Not only was it deprived of the successes in warfare that might have provided arguments more eloquent than the best of speeches; it also had to face the unwillingness of the Dutch nation, which had just won an eighty-years-long war of independence, to accept defeat. But it possessed at least one advantage: negotiations had not ceased with the outbreak of war but had continued even while the battles raged. With hindsight we may add another advantage – a masterly if youthful hand was guiding Dutch statecraft.

The belief that the elevation of the child whom the folk called "Our Prince" would work the miracle of reversing the fortunes of war was given practical form only five days after De Witt's election as councilor pensionary. On July 28, Zeeland put before the States General a proposal for "designation" of William III as captain and admiral general. It was a carefully chosen time. Zeeland's deputy, Adrian Veth, was in the chair as "president of the week," and De Witt was in Dordrecht considering whether to accept his election to the councilor pensionaryship. He returned at once to The Hague and immediately after taking his oath of office strode up the stairs to the meeting hall of Their High Mightinesses to fend off the Zeelanders' proposal, which if adopted would shatter the last chance for a negotiated peace.

Veth and his fellow-deputies from Zeeland were deaf to the verbal arguments presented by the Hollanders, and the States of Holland decided to send a "well-reasoned deduction" – the contemporary Dutch term for a formal written argument – to the other provinces. De Witt drafted the deduction in five days. It was the first elaboration of the theory of government without a stadholder and captain general that would come to be known by its adherents as the "True Freedom." It was not an affirmation of outright republicanism, if by that term we mean the explicit principle of government without a crowned head. Indeed, De Witt even avoided calling Cromwell's régime in England a "republic," substituting instead the blander word "government." He argued not against a king or count-duke for the United Provinces, but against the necessity for an "eminent head," a description of the role of a stadholder rather than a title. He was particularly sharp against the presumptive right of the Princes of Orange to be elected to such a position. The governing bodies in the towns and provinces, he held, had the right to choose whomever they wished for all high offices in the state.

Just then, suddenly, the "old form and order" of the Dutch state faced a different danger, not overturn by an Orangist revolution from below but from a peace proposal by the English foe. On July 31, the English Council of State presented to the Dutch ambassadors a proposal to merge the English and Dutch republics "in such manner as they may become one People and one Commonwealth." They would form a federal union in which each country would maintain intact its own domestic laws but its decisions and appointments would require the approval of the other. Cromwell made it clear that his intention was to block restoration of the Prince of Orange, and he even offered to abandon the Navigation Act the Dutch so abhorred, replacing it by a provision that there would be complete equality for all residents of the Anglo-Dutch republic in matters of trade. The flabbergasted Dutch realized that they would be junior partners in such a combination and refused to treat it as anything but a wild scheme. De Witt's friend, the Amsterdammer Conrad van Beuningen, told him the time had come for the Dutch to pay the price of losing the naval war and reduce their own claims. It was better, obviously, to knuckle under even to the Navigation Act than to give up Dutch independence.

De Witt waited until Cromwell turned back from political fantasy to reality before he resumed serious negotiations. Discussion of peace terms was resumed, but now more was said in London to Van Beverningk, Holland's member in the embassy to London, than to the other ambassadors. So at least we must conclude from De Witt's handling of Van Beverningk's private letters to him. Either he burned them or he sent them back to Van Beverningk; in any case, he did not trust them to his archives, where he filed his correspondence with almost never-failing care. We can easily guess what these letters contained, partly from De Witt's replies and partly from unfolding events.

Cromwell shifted his tactics but kept his eyes fixed on the objective of keeping the Orangist party out of power. On November 28, he presented a draft of a treaty of peace to the Dutch negotiators. They found fault with a number of clauses, especially those which gave the advantage to English shipping and trade over Dutch and established England's "dominion of the seas" adjacent to her shores. They also balked at Article XII, which barred the States General in perpetuity from electing William III or any later Prince of Orange as captain or admiral general or stadholder. Cromwell failed to realize that the stadholdership was a purely provincial office, over which the States of each individual province, not the States General, had the right of election.

This exclusion (in seventeenth-century Dutch "*seclusie*" or seclusion) was Cromwell's central demand. Without it he would not grant the peace the Dutch so needed. He was surprised that the dominant party in Holland did not leap at an opportunity to serve their own interest when it coincided with his. De Witt and his friends did not want this policy forced upon them, however, and undertook naval and diplomatic measures to revivify the Dutch war effort. Yet Cromwell's demand was so obviously in line with their policy that their opponents never ceased to believe that it was De Witt who had taken the initiative for the Exclusion clause. They dismissed out of hand as transparent hypocrisy the repeated affirmations that it was Cromwell who came up with the notion and insisted upon it to the bitterest end.

The situation changed a few weeks later just as the envoys, despairing of their mission's success, were preparing to go home. Cromwell took all power into his own hands, dismissing Parliament and having himself proclaimed as Lord Protector. Wanting Dutch recognition of his new title, he modified his peace terms to the extent of putting the exclusion clause into a separate article, and consented to leave out the name of the Prince of Orange provided the substance was accepted. In January 1654, when the envoys sailed home over the storm-torn North Sea, they carried a draft treaty with them.

At The Hague, peace seemed almost at hand until Cromwell insisted upon recognition as Lord Protector. It took all of De Witt's wiles to get such an acknowledgment through the States General. It proved, however, to be the least of his difficulties. Cromwell's assent to a separate article in the treaty with the States General had been made conditional upon an explicit agreement by the States of Holland to exclude the Prince from all high office. If this proviso became known, an uproar could be expected that would probably prevent ratification of the peace treaty as a whole. The first hurdle was crossed when the treaty was signed in London on April 15, the Dutch giving almost everything and getting little beyond mere peace. To avoid a debate in the States of Holland on a provincial Act of Exclusion before the States General ratified the peace, De Witt arranged for Their Noble Great Mightinesses to recess, and Their High Mightinesses gave their assent to the treaty on April 22. The States of Holland were recalled to meet six days later, but the towns were not told of the troubling decision their deputies would be called upon to make.

The meeting was held under a promise of complete secrecy given by each deputy before De Witt told the assembly the rough news from England. Cromwell, he informed the deputies, would not ratify the treaty unless Holland first adopted an act excluding the Prince, and he set a limit of three months for its enactment. The deputies did not dare to take so bold a step without consulting their burgomasters, so that the circle of secrecy had to be extended further. The deputies reassembled on May 1, and four days later did what they had to do. Cromwell's ratification came three days later.

All was not well, however. Word of Holland's action leaked out almost at once, reaching the halls of government and the streets at much the same time. Four provinces – a bare majority – demanded in the States General that Holland reveal its decisions on all matters affecting the country as a whole. The States of Holland rejected the demand: they were answerable for their decisions as a sovereign power only to God. The Orangist provinces retaliated by proposing that the ambassadors in London – who carried the credentials of the States General, not of their individual provinces – be told to refrain from delivering to Cromwell any decision or declaration concerning the Prince of Orange that had been adopted by the States of Holland on its own. Such a refusal, De Witt knew, would be met by the Protector of England with renewal of war. He therefore won over his own province, although not without difficulty, to stand by its policy.

His most immediate problem was to get the Act of Exclusion, which was already in the hands of the two Holland envoys, Van Beverningk and Nieupoort, delivered to Cromwell before the contrary instructions from the States General reached them. First he hinted in his letters that he expected that Cromwell would demand immediate delivery. When Gelderland proposed to demand from the envoys their copy of the resolution of the States of Holland concerning the Prince, the urgency increased. De Witt bought time by promising a satisfactory account in a few days. At last he resorted to a subterfuge. He wrote to Van Beverningk and Nieupoort that they would soon receive instructions from the States General not to deliver the Exclusion Act, and he repeated his hints to "bring the business to a quick end." Finally, he told them to obey the anticipated order from the States General to return the act *if it had not already been delivered*, though he clearly expressed his expectation that it would have already been handed over by then. The two Hollanders, who were no fools, caught his meaning and delivered the troublesome document on June 27.

De Witt had regained the initiative. Peace had been made with England, and it was time to restore harmony at home. Holland's action would have to be explained and defended, and the task was given him of doing so in another "deduction" ampler than that which had rebutted Zeeland's proposal of "designation" of the Prince a year before. It was made all the more necessary because the other provinces gave vent to their wrath at the expense of Van Beverningk. He had been elected (April 30) treasurer general of the Union – in practice war minister of the United Provinces – and Zeeland now revoked its vote until and unless he disavowed his part in the Exclusion affair. There was less trouble with the two Princesses of Orange, Amalia van Solms, Frederick Henry's widow, and Mary Stuart. De Witt led a delegation of the States of Holland that gave them the case for Exclusion. It was the consequence of a war that had been lost, a necessity that had to be swallowed. They denied that it was a necessity but could not prevent it.

Zeeland presented a long statement to the States General in condemnation of Holland's action. It was a careful marshalling of the Orangist arguments. The Exclusion was not a matter for Holland alone, for it affected the foreign policy of the United Provinces as a whole. In any case, Zeeland held, there was an obligation for Holland and the other provinces under the Union of Utrecht to elect the Prince to the offices which he held by quasi-dynastic right. De Witt thereupon himself turned to the preparation of a deduction that he had earlier suggested that his friend Van Beverningk write, although he now sent his draft to him and Nieupoort for their comments. Its first aim was to convey the impression by artful ambiguity that Cromwell had not demanded the Exclusion clause until the rest of the treaty had already been drafted; there was no outright lie but the net effect was almost the same. The deduction went beyond this to an exposition of Holland's side in the conflict with the other provinces.

In reply to the accusation that the province of Holland had violated the monopoly of foreign relations accorded to the States General by the Union of Utrecht, De Witt affirmed Holland's sovereignty within its borders with regard to its own affairs – and what could be more its own affair than whether or not to elect a stadholder, a purely provincial officer? As for the claim that the province was bound by tradition and gratitude to place the Prince of Orange at its head of the offices that had been held by his forefathers, he denied it on both counts. Tradition? It had been no more than political and military convenience that had put them into office. Gratitude? The Princes of Orange had indeed performed many services to the Dutch state, notably in warfare, but they had been amply compensated, as he sought to prove by a detailed listing of the salaries and grants they had received over the past eight decades. Far from recognizing a tie of sentiment that bound the nation and the House of Orange, he denied it.

He went further to refute as well the argument so often heard from the pulpits of Calvinist preachers that God had laid down in the Old Testament the superiority of monarchy as the form of government for sinful and imperfect men. To their biblical texts he responded with others from the same source that painted kings as tyrants. Like the preachers, however, he took for granted the direct applicability of scriptural example. He was a rationalist, to be sure, but one who used reason to argue from texts, not to call their validity into question or to put them into a different historical context than his own age.

With De Witt's deduction and the declarations it was designed to refute there began a long debate over the place of a stadholderate in the Dutch Republic. It was a strangely contorted debate because the terms of the controversy on the opposite sides did not mesh. Although the preachers, trained in theology but not in law, treated the stadholders as if they were biblical kings under a new name, the jurists who supported the Orangist side argued, as we have seen with Zeeland's declaration, from the premises of historical practice and moral obligation, to which they added an affirmation of political utility. In the Dutch Republic, where the seven provinces in the States General were all equal in principle and there was no rule of majority, and similarly within each province, where a multitude of "members" – voting towns, rural districts in Friesland and Groningen, and noble orders – were also equal, a single superior leader, an "eminent head" was needed to reconcile their interests and passions and bring them to unity. De Witt, and after him defenders of the principles of the "True Freedom" for another century and a half, built a republican theory based on refutation of both the preachers' and the jurists' arguments. In our next chapter we shall examine De Witt's republicanism as part of a larger picture of him as a powerfully intelligent man of action who took his theories where he found them, used them for his purpose, but displayed little or no interest in them as such.

The deduction was persuasive to the States of Holland, which adopted it on July 25. On August 6, it was read to the States General by De Witt himself. It was immediately printed in Dutch and distributed widely, not only to the States of the other provinces, to whom it was primarily addressed, but also to notables throughout the country. For foreign readers it was quickly translated into Latin and French.

The French ambassador, Chanut, in a letter to his counterpart in London, made an acute observation that seems to have escaped De Witt's attention but not Cromwell's (the letter was intercepted and transcribed before going on to its addressee). The other provinces, wrote Chanut, had driven Holland to appeal to public opinion, so that "the people are made the judges of their magistrates." An Orangist observer added another, more chilling judgment: the people might also become the executioners of these same magistrates.

The intellectual and psychological demands of the councilor pensionary's office were without question the most taxing put upon anybody in Dutch public life. Whether the ability to meet them without flagging over the years required a balanced, warm home life may be debated in the abstract, but in the case of De Witt all the evidence supports such a judgment.

Only two months short of his twenty-eighth birthday when he took office, he was at the peak of vigor. Even as the urgencies of ending the war with England pressed down upon him, he found time to dance, play the violin, stroll and flirt. He was a full-fledged participant in the social life of The Hague. Nobles and regents mixed easily, although an awareness of who stood higher and who lower in the ladder of prestige was seldom absent. De Witt was inducted into the "Ordre de l'Union de la Joye," a band of good fellowship, both men and women, led by Amélie de Brederode, the eldest daughter of field marshal Brederode. He was sponsored for membership by her younger half-sister, Sophie Marguerite, called "*freule* [Miss] Margaretha of Nassau." The Nassau name came to her because she was the illegitimate daughter of Count John of Nassau–Siegen and Brederode's first wife. Although therefore a distant cousin of the Prince of Orange, she found delight in the company of the young councilor pensionary and they exchanged notes hinting at love written in the high-flown language of cavalier gallantry.

Upon the basis of these letters, a nineteenth-century historian descended from an uncle of De Witt's has suggested that he even proposed marriage to the *freule*. The notion of such a relationship between Jacob de Witt's son and a cousin of William III, however distant, was rejected out of hand by the great Dutch historian Fruin. We may be less certain today just what a young man's heart may drive him to do, but so impulsive an act would not have been in character with the man as we come to know him over the years of his life. There may be indirect confirmation, however, in the urgent suggestions that Jacob de Witt began to make to his son that he looked for a companion among girls of his own class.

Romance was linked to politics when De Witt went to Amsterdam to find someone to take his heart. That was where both the wealth and the influence of the country were concentrated. If he chose a bride from the regent class of the great city, he would enter into a family alliance valuable to him in conducting the affairs of the nation. Not that he was cold-blooded in his quest. The daughter of an administrator of the East India Company, suggested to him by his father, did not win his favor. Margaretha Tulp, whose father was the famed anatomist Nicholas Tulp, turned on the light in his eyes, but she did not respond to his interest. The spark of love proved mutual, however, when he met and courted Wendela Bicker. She was nineteen years of age, the heiress of the late Jan Bicker, who had been not only one of the wealthiest merchants in Amsterdam but also, with his brothers Andrew and Cornelius, a master of its political life for twenty years. The two surviving brothers had been the victims of William II's attempted coup in 1650, like De Witt's own father; but it was of romantic love that he spoke and wrote. His courtship lasted from October 1654 until Wendela accepted his proposal of marriage early in January 1655. It was not a prudish age, and they wrote quite frankly of the joining of bodies no less than of souls.

A contract of marriage was signed by the end of the month, providing Wendela with a substantial dowry of 50,000 guilders. The wedding took place on February 15, and they set up home in the house on West Einde Street that De Witt had rented in 1653 when he had become councilor pensionary. It had been the home of a member of Holland's Nobility and in later centuries would be the residence of the English ambassador. The spare simplicity with which he had lived there as a bachelor gave way to a more elaborate style, but Wendela, for all her wealth, remained a Dutch *huisvrouw*, concerned more with cleanliness and comfort than with ostentation.

With marriage to Wendela, De Witt's financial position began to change. He had inherited a nest egg of less than 10,000 guilders from his mother, but it had been too modest to cover his expenses in settling down in his own residence when he became councilor pensionary, and he had had to call upon his father for financial help. The costs of the wedding, household furnishings and personal gifts to Wendela were far beyond his means, and Jacob again provided him with the funds he needed, although this time not without having to borrow the ready cash he did not have on hand. De Witt therefore would have been in some difficulty in making ends meet if he had not had Wendela's personal wealth for his use. To her dowry was added another 110,000 guilders inherited after Wendela's mother died in 1656.

De Witt began at once a program of prudent but steady expansion of their estate. The bulk of their wealth was invested in government bonds or land. In economic terms, De Witt was in the first instance a civil servant, living on a comfortable but not lavish salary. His (more precisely, Wendela's) independent wealth now made him a rentier and landowner. He had practiced law very briefly and had never been in business, so that he was neither a professional nor a capitalist businessman. But such distinctions would have sounded strange to him; he did not serve narrow personal interests but the broad needs of his country, and saw no conflict between them. He was implacably precise in his honor and honesty, but did not think that these forbade him to borrow money at one rate from individuals to invest in government bonds paying a higher interest. Nor did he scruple, when there was more demand for bonds than the quantity available, to use his influence with the various receivers who issued them to obtain as many as he had cash to pay for. Similarly, he was a careful landlord, demanding his due of tenants though respectful of their rights.

He himself remained a tenant for many years. He and Wendela had shared the house on West Einde Street with cousins, but they soon moved to other rented homes, all some minutes' walk from the Binnenhof. The first of these was a house on the Herengracht, almost at the edge of The Hague where it is joined by the Fluwelen Burgwal.

The couple's life together was a happy one from the beginning. Each found in the other what had been desired. He came home after the intensive toil of each day to relaxation and affection, and she gave her love and warmth unreservedly. She was neither a bluestocking living a life of intellectual independence, nor a domineering wife, like her sister-in-law, Cornelius's wife Maria van

Berckel. She was delighted to run her own home and to live through and for her husband and children. For the fruits of love came steadily through the years, the first a girl named Anna and then more daughters and sons. There were seven in all, five girls and two boys. Most survived, but two daughters died in infancy, and mother and father bore their deaths with stoic acceptance of God's will. De Witt proclaimed himself no "discriminator" against girls, but was pleased when a son came after seven years of marriage.

Beyond the bounds of his own home, De Witt's circle of family affection was strong and tight. His father soon withdrew from active politics into a post as councilor and master of accounts for the domains of Holland. This was largely a sinecure, but he had to reside in The Hague. He therefore moved from Dordrecht to live with his son, in whose household he became a quiet, studious presence. De Witt's sisters loved their younger brother as they always had, but, as he ascended to fame and power, it was they who sought reassurance of affection from the busy councilor pensionary. Sometimes the relationship was made difficult by political conflicts between their husbands and their brother, and they did what they could to smooth matters over. De Witt remained on the closest of terms, personal and political, with his brother Cornelius. They shared political beliefs down to the last "t", but Cornelius was more headstrong, less deft in the handling of people, and readier to take on airs of importance. He accepted as wholly normal his younger brother's dominance, although his wife raged that he was not getting all his due. John was also close to the cousin who shared his name but spelled it "De Wit." This John de Wit was a lively personality, more passionate in expressing the ideas of "True Freedom" than the cool, steady councilor pensionary.

On his wife's side Wendela brought him not only important political connections but also close personal ties with her family. At first they treated him with an easy familiarity mixed with a hint of condescension, but as it became evident that the Bickers were not regaining the political domination lost in 1650 they became readier to defer to the rising eminence of Wendela's husband. Her brother-in-law, the banker Jean Deutz, became a very close friend. The two couples traveled together as tourists to the Spanish Netherlands while the luxury of time given over to mere enjoyment was still available to the ever busier councilor pensionary. Deutz became De Witt's financial adviser in the administration of his personal estate, and his trust in the banker's judgment and probity was total. Wendela had two cousins both named Gerard Bicker, but they were very different personalities. One was the fat, self-indulgent bailiff of Muiden castle, a boastful and cowardly young man whom De Witt treated with distaste and scorn. The other, known as Bicker van Swieten, was an intelligent young man of no particular distinction but a good friend whom the De Witts saw frequently at each other's homes. Politically important as well as personally satisfying was De Witt's tie with Wendela's uncle, Cornelius de Graeff, lord of Zuidpolsbroek. The older man had taken over the leadership of the government of Amsterdam from the Bickers, to whom he was allied by marriage, and De Witt eagerly sought his advice and support. But he also enjoyed Zuidpolsbroek's clearness of mind and warmth of hospitality.

4

The man of thought

For more than two thousand years, ever since Plato found the cure for evil rule in the prescription of a philosopher–king, men in the Western world have been fascinated by the idea that political power, if coupled with the highest intelligence, can bring the good life to mankind. Often those proposed as candidates for such a role do turn out to be rulers blessed with powers of mind that are indeed more than ordinary. All the same, it is difficult to avoid a judgment that a dose of flattery is involved. Would anyone today play the flute sonatas of King Frederick II of Prussia if he had not been Frederick the Great? Would anyone treat the philosophical writings of Lenin with seriousness if he had not been the creator of the Soviet state? Perhaps, but it would seem necessary to find some criterion of intellect independent of politics.

In the case of John de Witt we might think at first glance that we have indeed discovered our philosopher–king (using "king", of course, in the broadest sense of political leader). His intellectual powers were in fact truly extraordinary, at least in one field. His work as a mathematician won the admiration of both Christian Huygens and Isaac Newton, the former of undoubted genius and the latter one of the greatest minds the world has ever known. Modern historians of mathematics, less admiring, still rate him as a gifted amateur. Since there were few professional mathematicians in the seventeenth century, his "amateurism" means very little, but how far he would have gone had he had no political career we can only speculate. We need only observe that in action as well as in other realms of thought De Witt was a clear-minded rationalist. Does he rate then as a great political thinker? An examination of his political writings will show a man in command of the current political theories of his time, but without either originality or depth.

Yet it is worth paying attention to De Witt's political ideas, for they enable us to understand more deeply and precisely the character of his political activity and the ideological commitments of the Dutch nation in the later seventeenth century. It is – or would seem – obvious that he was the outstanding *republican* statesman in the history of the Dutch Republic (Oldenbarnevelt, although the *creator* of the Republic, was less specifically republican). It would seem then almost perverse to call De Witt's republican principles and attitudes into question. There can be no doubt that he was a passionate and stubborn defender of the constitutional form of the Dutch Republic *as he understood and desired it*. Nonetheless, there is a hidden anomaly in his republicanism, deriving from both the ambiguity of the constitution of the United Provinces and the variety of meanings of the word "republican."

To take the latter problem first. We must of course put aside the characteristic American usage of "republican" (with a capital "R") for one of the two principal political parties in the United States. Although that usage derives from the broader generic meanings, it has become quite separate from them and has little to do with the original thrust of the word. We may use the term "republican" in the classical sense, however, to mean commitment to the principle of civic virtue that the good citizen serves his country and does not ask that it serve his private interests. The word then certainly applies to De Witt, but it would apply equally well to good subjects of the king in monarchies. In any case, it is a usage familiar only to philosophers and other learned men. The commonplace definition of "republican" means commitment to government without a monarch at the head of state, and this is what is intended when De Witt is seen as a republican par excellence.

But what did it mean to be a republican in the *Dutch Republic*? The Dutch state had come into being in the late sixteenth century not as the deliberate creation of people who believed in government without a king, but as the unintended result of the rejection of Spanish rule. Only the failure of a series of efforts to replace Philip II with a king or other crowned head willing to govern with, through and for the States had led by the end of the 1580s to recognition that the United Provinces had become a republic. The fact that sovereignty – the power of final decision – had slipped into the hands of the States was acknowledged and made into the basic principle of the Dutch constitution.

The political leadership of the state was assumed by Holland's land advocate, Oldenbarnevelt, and the military leadership by the stadholder of Holland and several other provinces, Maurice of Nassau, the second son of William the Silent (the eldest son, Philip William, had been brought up in Spain as a faithful subject of Philip II). Although the specific issue in the great crisis of the second decade of the next century was the place of religion in the state, the constitutional problem that became central was whether the ultimate sovereignty lay in the individual provinces or in the States General. At no time did Prince Maurice claim power in his own name, which is the essence of monarchy. He acted in the name of the States General, where he had the support of a majority of the provinces. He did not employ his triumph, as we have seen, to transform the Dutch state. But he did take on the political as well as the military leadership of the country, as Frederick Henry and William II continued to do after him. Even in the crisis of 1650, which was constitutionally a replay of 1618, William II had made no overt move toward establishing himself as sovereign in the United Provinces, and there is no hard evidence to confirm the charges that such was his actual purpose. What William II did open up to controversy was the stadholdership.

During the two decades that followed his death and indeed until the disappearance of the Republic of the United Provinces in 1795, the central constitutional question became the stadholdership, its desirability and indeed its very existence. It was not whether the country should be a republic or a monarchy, as in nineteenth-century France. The two sides in Dutch politics become known as *Staatsgezind*, "favoring the States," and *Oranjegezind*, "favoring Orange" (or *Prinsgezind*, "favoring the Prince"). Although there had been no explicit monarchism in the Dutch nation for more than half a century, Orangist writers drew upon the familiar theories of kingship to sustain their arguments in favor of the stadholder as "eminent head" of the state. They did not round out their doctrines with elaboration of the stadholdership as it actually existed, carefully distinguishing it from kingship. They therefore played into the hands of the *Staatsgezind* authors, who argued as if the stadholders were aspirants to a royal crown. Because the participants in the debate knew all too clearly what was intended, no one was disturbed by this twisting of terms, and it is later generations of historians and their readers who have been led astray.

The anomaly of De Witt's republicanism lies not only in this confusion between stadholdership and kingship. It rests too in what we mean when we add the suffix "-ism" to the adjective "republican." To its older meanings it has in recent years added another as indicating an ideology, a primal vision not limited to one place or time but held to be true everywhere and always. In this sense De Witt was anything but a republican ideologist. He did not treat republican government as inherently superior to monarchical, except in the Dutch provinces. In the Deduction of 1654, when he regretted the war that had just been fought with England, he did not discuss the similarity of their governments but their common religion; but this may have been just an argument he thought more persuasive with the Dutch people. When in 1660 King Frederick III of Denmark tightened his royal authority, De Witt was not troubled: the king was a better ally than his council, and that was all that mattered. Eight years later, when the English envoy Sir William Temple portrayed himself as at heart a republican, De Witt replied with gentle reproof. He was himself a republican, he said, because he had been born in Holland and was a servant of the States of Holland. If he had been born in England, he would have been a loyal monarchist. Indeed, if he had lived in the sixteenth century, he might well have remained faithful to his natural lord, Philip II. This suprising statement may have been meant only to remind Temple not to appeal to ideological principles, and it probably did not go so far as to represent his own deeply held beliefs. It was the stadholderate, not monarchy as such, that he opposed.

De Witt became involved in 1661 in the most important exposition of republican thought published during his administration. This was *The Interest of Holland* by Peter de la Court, a lawyer and textile manufacturer in Leiden. De la Court's theoretical work was brought to his attention by mutual friends, and the manuscript of *The Interest of Holland* was sent to him before it was published. It is fairly certain that he added two chapters. They are unlike the others, which are more virulently ideological and narrowly concerned with Holland than with the Dutch Republic as a whole. De Witt toned down De la Court's Machiavellian argument that there was no obligation to keep treaties that had turned against a state's interests, but he sharpened the criticism of Prince William II for his dynastic connections. He deleted an entire sentence in which the author, who was excluded from the regent class in Leiden, found fault with the narrow oligarchies that held power in the towns for their sole benefit.

De la Court came under sharp attack from the clergy for the anticlerical tone and the open Machiavellianism of his book. He consulted De Witt, who did what he could to avert prosecution of the author, though he was annoyed by his aggressive attitude. The situation turned worse after De la Court moved to Amsterdam in 1666. Three years later he brought out a second edition of his book under a new title, *Indication of the Salutary Political Foundations and Maxims of the Republic of Holland and West Friesland.** He boasted of its having been read and added to by notable personages in its first edition, and obtained from the States of Holland a privilege (a form of copyright) for fifteen years. The manuscript had not been read through, however, and it turned out that he had restored to the text some of the offensive passages that De Witt had deleted earlier. After outraged denunciations by the synod of South Holland, the privilege was withdrawn. This did not prevent continued sale of the book, and it was widely believed that De Witt had sponsored its publication and that De la Court was no more than his hired pen. Although its true authorship was known, it was later translated into French and English as the memoirs of John de Witt, and here and there in library catalogues this attribution still remains, uncorrected.

De Witt's name was also connected then and later with that of another writer who discussed political theory, among other things, but one immensely above De la Court in fame and importance, the philosopher Spinoza. It was generally believed that he was a good friend of the councilor pensionary, who visited him at his modest lodgings after he moved to The Hague, asked his advice, and gave him a pension of 200 guilders a year. Spinoza's grand work of political theory, the *Theological and Political Treatise (Tractatus theologico-politicus)*, has been viewed as an advocacy of the principles of the régime of the "True Freedom."

Alas, none of this is true. It was the result of the naiveté of later

---

* West Friesland was the part of Friesland west of the Zuider Zee, politically part of the county – later province – of Holland.

historians and biographers who took too literally the allegations of slanderous pamphleteers for whom the philosopher and the statesman were tarred with the same brush of atheism. There is no evidence that they ever actually met, although Spinoza was admired and protected by other notable regents, Van Beuningen in particular. We may take for granted that De Witt knew of Spinoza, but he never once mentioned him in his correspondence. All that is certain is that Spinoza held the councilor pensionary in high respect.

Yet, even their political conceptions were different. Spinoza was a pantheist who believed in a totally secular human history in which God did not intervene in any way. De Witt on the contrary continued as an orthodox Calvinist to distinguish between biblical and secular history only in favor of the former, as the more certainly true. Spinoza built his picture of the nature of civil government in terms of strict Hobbesian utilitarianism, while De Witt did not diverge from traditional views. Both believed in freedom of citizens, assured by a strong state against threats from clerical persecutors, and neither favored an absolute democracy.

The kind of political theory that De Witt found congenial and useful was exemplified by a three-volume defense of the right of the States of Holland to determine the prayers given in public churches. The *Public Prayer* was written by De Witt's namesake cousin, John de Wit. The occasion was the refusal of many Calvinist preachers to follow orders from the States of Holland in 1663 to use a new prayer formula from which the name of the Prince of Orange had been deleted. The councilor pensionary read his cousin's manuscript and found little to change. It not only asserted the authority of the provincial States over the Reformed church within their territory, but also held that the Princes of Orange were no more than servants of the sovereign States. As a work of theory the *Public Prayer* deserves the oblivion into which it quickly fell. As a defense of the régime of the "True Freedom" it was sharp and strong, and it was as a tract for the times that De Witt valued it.

The fierce hostility of a majority of the Calvinist preachers for De Witt arose not only from their commitment to the House of Orange, but also from their resentment of the protection given by the States of Holland to the school of theologians who accepted the new philosophy of Descartes. They believed, correctly, that the

John de Witt

councilor pensionary was the guiding hand in this policy; they therefore assumed, incorrectly, that he himself was a philosophical Cartesian. Why not, when many of the Cartesian believers were relatives and friends of his, like his cousin, the Dordrecht preacher Andrew Colvius?

The issue of conflict, which tore apart the theological faculty at the University of Leiden for many years, was whether Descartes's philosophy was compatible with orthodox Calvinist theology. There were two problems. The first was that the Cartesian philosophy was a deliberate endeavor to replace the Aristotelian system which Calvin had continued to accept even after his revolt against the Catholic church. The second was that Descartes drew an absolute line of distinction between science and philosophy on the one hand and theology on the other, so that what could be true in one could be false in the other.

Cartesian philosophy had begun to win adherents in the Dutch universities, especially at Leiden, where Descartes had lived. When dissertations defending Cartesian views came up for defense, the orthodox professors of theology were outraged. Disputes over the award of degrees and over appointments to the faculty of theology followed. The struggle came to a head in 1656 when the synod of South Holland demanded that philosophers be barred from applying their principles to theology. The councilor pensionary was drawn in by a professor, Heidanus, one of the innovators who was befriended by a maternal aunt of De Witt's. Heidanus wanted the States of Holland to forbid the synod to decide philosophical matters. De Witt did not want such forthright action but a compromise that should prove satisfactory to both sides. He knew from the history of the quarrel of the Remonstrants and Counter-Remonstrants that theologians' squabbling could easily overflow into political controversies involving the whole nation.

Finally, after efforts to bring the contending parties to a settlement had failed, the States of Holland adopted a decision drawn up by De Witt that imposed one (September 30, 1656). Theologians and philosophers would each have freedom within their own domains, but would not cross into the other's territory. Holy Scripture was reaffirmed as the highest authority, but theologians in interpreting it were to refrain from using philosophical terminology. The philosophers in turn were not to employ arguments that had been particularly offensive to the orthodox

58

theologians; although they were free to philosophize, they should not reach, teach or explain the books of Descartes. The two faculties were to live with each other in friendship, avoiding offense.

It was an extraordinary decison, for it reduced questions of the highest spiritual and intellectual importance ultimately to matters of good will and good manners. De Witt – like Talleyrand a century and a half later – wanted no zeal, and he could not understand why theories should so agitate men. He failed, too, to realize that the boundary between theology and philosophy is not an impermeable wall but a sieve with ideas flowing both ways. The political consequences of this misunderstanding were not negligible. The orthodox preachers were confirmed in their belief that De Witt was a "new Oldenbarnevelt" who used the power of government to push wrong beliefs and even heresies upon them, instead of putting the force of the state at the service of true religion. Neither they nor he had any vision of government that was neutral in matters of religion. As a result, the intensity of religious conviction was added to the passions already present in political struggle. This was a matter of the utmost seriousness since the preachers held a firm grip upon the common people, who in time of crisis could become dangerous to the established order.

Toward other religions – Catholic, Mennonite and Jewish in particular – De Witt displayed a practical tolerance that never went so far as to consider them equal to the Reformed in either truth or the right to the support of government. When the synods demanded that the Catholics be forbidden to practice their faith or that Mennonites and Jews be repressed, he did not try to argue the dominies out of their doctrines. Instead he obtained from the States of Holland renewal of old edicts against false believers and then saw to it that nothing was done in enforcement. Such hypocrisy on behalf of liberty enraged the preachers; they won repeated victories, and each in turn was hollow. Such trickery could be the work only of a henchman of the Devil, against whom all weapons were permissible. In their eyes the councilor pensionary became a moral and political outlaw; to slay him would be not a crime but a deed in God's service.

There was only one field where De Witt was a Cartesian, more or less, but it was one where no popular passions were involved. Mathematics had been his special delight while he was at Leiden

University, although law was his formal subject, and he had won the admiration of Descartes's disciple Frans van Schooten the Younger. Once political controversy had calmed following the end of the war with England in 1654, he found time to return to the treatise upon conic sections that he had drafted in 1649. He reworked it and sent it to Van Schooten, who was professor of mathematics at Leiden. Van Schooten was preparing a second edition of Descartes's *Geometry*, and he asked De Witt for permission to publish it along with the work of the master. He noted that De Witt was not strictly a disciple of Descartes but suggested that he adopt his method and symbolism. De Witt assented, and Van Schooten took upon himself the chore of providing figures, checking calculations and revising it where necessary.

The work went slowly through press at the famed publishing house of Elsevier, and did not finally appear until February 1661, under the title of *The Elements of Curved Lines* (*Elementa Curvarum Linearum*). De Witt was as frankly proud of it as he was reticent in praising his own achievements in the realm of politics. It soon replaced the treatise of Apollonius as a textbook for conic sections, receiving the recommendation of no one less than Newton himself. It remained in use for half a century until differential calculus took the place of analysis for the study of conic sections. Christian Huygens read *The Elements* in manuscript, and told a fellow-mathematician in England that if De Witt had not been taken away from mathematics by his political duties he would not have had his equal as a geometer in his time. This judgment might be suspect because Huygens's father was the secretary of the Prince of Orange, but this son, a mathematician and physicist just below the class of Newton, put more value upon the study of numbers and figures than upon the work of statesmen. Whether, if De Witt had followed the path Huygens clearly preferred, he would have achieved the fame that became his in politics, we cannot say, for his reputation as a pure mathematician has rested upon that single book, and modern historians of mathematics do not place him anywhere near the first rank.

Historians of one branch of applied mathematics, actuarial science, have a far higher estimation of De Witt's work in their field. For them he is one of the founders of the science that connects probability theory with mortality experience and therefore underlies the practice of life insurance. He did not work alone in these studies. He had the guidance of Huygens and John Hudde, an

Amsterdam regent who had also studied with Van Schooten and published a treatise in the second edition of Descartes's *Geometry*. Whether De Witt found time to study the works of the French mathematicians Fermat and Pascal that lay down the foundations of probability theory is uncertain. In any case, his interest seems to have been far more practical than theoretical. What he wanted to know was the comparative value of various kinds of public bonds both for their purchasers and for the issuing authorities. Following the principles set down by Huygens in a study of games of chance published in 1657, he treated the life expectancy of bondholders and their beneficiaries as if they were engaged in a gamble.

This was a question of practical significance, for the States of Holland had a choice between two kinds of bonds to offer the lending public. The first were the redeemable bonds known as *losrenten*, which had no fixed date of redemption but could be paid off at any time at the option of the issuing authority; the second were life annuities known as *lijfrenten* which paid a higher rate of interest but were extinguished upon the death of the last person upon whose life they were written. De Witt, by applying the principles of what is now called mathematical expectation to data drawn from the annuity registers of the States of Holland, came to a surprising conclusion. Life annuities at the interest rate of 7 per cent were actually more favorable for both government and purchaser than the usual redemption bonds at the rate of 4 per cent. In practice redemption bonds had become virtually perpetual bonds, as funds to pay them off were seldom available. Life annuities, on the other hand, paid a significantly higher rate of interest. The comparison was, of course, one between dissimilar advantages, which could be brought together in one ratio only in the world of politics, not of pure profit calculations.

De Witt put his proposal in favor of life annuities at an adequately higher rate of interest to attract purchasers before the States of Holland in 1671 in a treatise called *The Worth of Life Annuities Compared to Redemption Bonds*. It was written in the simplest language he could muster for an audience that knew little mathematics beyond arithmetic. Still, although he persuaded the States of Holland to adopt his scheme and issue both kinds of bonds, the general public outside found the explanation in the treatise, which was published, to be beyond its understanding and it continued to prefer redemption bonds.

De Witt had turned his attention to this question in the course

of his work as the *de facto* finance minister for the province of
Holland and the States General. He had no formal power as such,
but, as in foreign affairs, the tasks of conceiving fiscal policy and,
once it was adopted by the relevant assembly, supervising its
execution, fell to him as councilor pensionary of Holland. Unlike
his French counterpart, Colbert, he did not concern himself deeply
with the operation of the economy as a whole. He had no realization
that the great age of Dutch commercial and maritime expansion
was at an end, but saw the problems that arose as fiscal questions,
to be solved politically, reconciling as much as possible the
divergent interests of towns, provinces and branches of the
economy. When it came to specific economic matters, he was no
expert and called upon those who were to guide him.

Where his power of intellect and his mathematical training gave
him a special advantage was in understanding the complications
and subtleties of public finance. He kept in his pocket a little
notebook in which the current state of the treasury was clearly set
down and where resources were described which could be swiftly
tapped if needed. He was in general not a reformer like Colbert,
but wanted merely efficient application of the existing system. His
objective was tax and bond programs that benefited both
government and people most; even the life annuities proposal, as
we have seen, derived from this political aim, not from an
endeavor to streamline the Dutch fiscal system. His first principle,
the absolute integrity of the credit of Holland and of the Dutch
Republic as a whole, was no novelty on his part but an established
practice.

When the cessation of wars and their enormous drainage of
public resources through taxes and loans finally permitted, he saw
to it that the outstanding bonds were paid off with funds obtained
by issuance of new bonds at a lower rate. Between 1655 and 1663,
the provincial debt of Holland was reduced from 140 to 120 million
guilders. The second English war reversed that favorable trend,
but once it was concluded, De Witt guided a new restoration of
the previous pattern of debt reduction. By 1668, at the beginning
of his fourth term in office, the amount Holland paid annually for
interest on its bonds dropped from almost 7,000,000 guilders to
just under 1,168,000 guilders. The savings were applied at once
to further reduction of the debt. The approach of the war that

finally broke out in 1672 again brought a shift to accumulation of instantly available funds in the treasuries.

As in so much else, De Witt was a man of keen intellect who applied his powers of mind to the work at hand. He was not at all a philosopher at the helm of state, such as Plato dreamed of. The only exception was mathematics, a love which he could seldom indulge. Perhaps he loved it because it yielded certainties that politics could not. But it is doubtful that he achieved such self-knowledge, for he was not given to introspection. Our chapter title is probably wrong, therefore. John de Witt was not a "man of thought," but a thoughtful and extraordinary intelligent man of action.

5

Consolidation of the "True Freedom"
1654–1660

The clash over the Exclusion Act had displayed all too clearly the instabilities and fragilities of stadholderless government. Riots and incipient revolt had plagued the country. Disagreements and harsh clashes in the multiple governments of town, province and country had ripped at the unity of will and purpose that was so necessary for a little, rich country in a world of hungry powers. To restore civil peace, repair the damages of war to the navy and the treasury, protect the interest of the producers of wealth abroad and at home – these required leadership of a high order. The province of Holland had taken that responsibility upon itself in November 1650, but since by its nature leadership is personal it had passed on the task to its councilor pensionary.

For the next six years the most complex and difficult problems De Witt faced lay in the relations of the United Provinces with other countries, but the most urgent and essential consisted in consolidation of the system of "True Freedom" at home. The two fundamental elements of that liberty were the sovereignty of Holland and government without a stadholder.

"Sovereignty" here did not mean the ultimate power of the state in all political questions, as it had already come to signify in general theoretical writings. There was as a matter of fact no legal restriction upon the powers of Their Noble Great Mightinesses, but for the most part that was not at issue. "Natural law" had not yet come to mean the "natural rights" of the individual citizen, as it did in the eighteenth century. What was involved was specific to the Dutch constitutional situation. To the question, "What are the respective rights of the Union and the individual provinces, of the States General and the provincial States?" the proponents of the "True Freedom" answered that the Generality possessed only those powers given to it by the Union of Utrecht of 1579, which ultimately amounted to little more than the waging of war and the making of peace. It did not extend to direct power over the subjects of the provinces, either in taxation, or in criminal and civil justice, or in religion. The doctrine had first become important in the struggle between Oldenbarnevelt and Prince Maurice, when provincial control of religion was at stake. It had been transformed by the crisis of 1650 into an affirmation that the provinces each had a right to choose or refuse to choose a stadholder, that this office was strictly provincial and that it was not required by the terms of the Union of Utrecht.

To define the "True Freedom" as provincial sovereignty and government without a stadholder would be correct but insufficient. It would be to see only the top of political life. Below the top, however, there were numerous consequences of the shift of leadership. Most significant was a new balance of forces. Until the death of William II there had been both collaboration and competition between the Princes of Orange and the province of Holland. Twice competition had become confrontation, but the ordinary pattern had been collaboration. The stadholder had looked after the specific interests of his house and the wider interests of a diverse clientele; the interests of Holland were a complex intermix of the primarily trading needs of its greatest city, Amsterdam, and the varied desires of the other towns, some commercial and some industrial.

No simple line of political cleavage separated these interests: identical groups in rival towns might well go to different sides on large national issues. Lines of differentiation among economic groups were vague and uncertain. From top to bottom the distinctions were immense, yet between adjacent groups they were small, sometimes almost invisible. Virtually the only status that was sharply distinguished was nobility. Its membership was as closed off as that of Venice, for there was no means of creating new nobles, apart from ennoblement by foreign princes. Apart from the linked houses of Orange and Nassau, the upper ranks – dukes and counts – were almost empty; barons and mere "lords" (*heren*) occupied the lower ranks, principally in the inland provinces of Utrecht, Overijssel and Gelderland. The political weight of the nobility varied widely. Large and even predominant in the mainly rural provinces, it was smaller although not negligible in heavily urban Holland and wholly absent in Zeeland except for the Prince of Orange as marquis of Veere and Vlissingen (Flushing).

The nobles participated in political power as members of the provincial States, not individually (except in Zeeland) and not usually by birthright but by election. In Holland the noble order, called the *Ridderschap* ("Knighthood"), chose its members when its ranks were opened by death; it was not by law restricted to the baronage, but few lords were elected. The *Ridderschap* (or Nobility, as we shall call it) was the first member of the States of Holland in precedence, and we have seen that De Witt spoke for them as their pensionary. He bore no hostility to them as a class, served their interests as best he could within the general framework of provincial and national needs, and worked constantly and carefully to gain their support for his policies. This was not always easy, as their military traditions bound them to the Prince of Orange as their commander-in-chief; but when appointments in the army passed into the hands of the civilian authorities in 1651 De Witt acquired a powerful instrument of influence over their decisions, if not their affections.

Far more important than the Nobility were the members of the governments in the towns, those the Dutch called "regents." This was especially so in Holland, which was the economic and political heart of the country. It has been customary for historians to call them a bourgeoisie because they were wealthy, not noble, served the interests of business and were presumably themselves business-men. Wealthy they certainly were, sometimes immensely rich, but more and more of them bought landed estates and called themselves after these manorial possessions. If we treat such "lords" (equivalent to French *seigneurs*) as the lowest stratum of the Nobility, as was usual elsewhere in Europe although not in England, the regents might be considered as such; yet they were not "commoners" either if we use that word to translate the Dutch *gemeente*, for that implied "ordinary people". By De Witt's time many of them, like his own father, had withdrawn from active business life and drew their income from investments in land, houses and government bonds. This had not developed as rapidly in Amsterdam, where regents usually continued to be active in business. If they were members of a "class" in the modern sense, they were certainly not aware of it. And they did not characteristically think of themselves as an "order" either. They too, like the Nobility, held their posts in the town councils by cooptative election by their sitting fellow-regents. Clans broke apart amid recriminations in the perpetual scramble for office; factions formed and re-formed constantly. Family connections – which especially in the smaller towns could include virtually every regent – did not prevent fierce rivalries and infighting among cousins. To muffle such factional strife, the institution of "contracts of correspondence," laying down a fixed and "fair" sequence of offices to be awarded to signatories and their descendents, was coming into practice in De Witt's decades, but did not reach the widespread and flagrant use that marked the eighteenth century. Town councilors served for life but burgomasters were elected for annual terms; they came up from and returned to the town councils. Town pensionaries were formally servants of the councils, therefore technically not regents, but they were recruited from the ranks of the educated and the well-to-do and were not normally distinguished from the regents. Expressing and reconciling the diverse interests of the regents in the towns of Holland, from huge Amsterdam to tiny Schoonhoven, was the core of De Witt's leadership. In serving all, however, he served none exclusively, not even his "father city" of Dordrecht.

The relationship of the regents to those they governed, the "inhabitants" as they were called, was complex and more troublesome. The inhabitants were anything but a cohesive group, alike only in that they did not share in the rule of their cities. The upper stratum, just below the regents, were the burghers, who as *poorters* had inherited or purchased citizenship in the towns. Some were substantial businessmen and professionals, others artisans and shopkeepers. Legally all could become regents, but this was an effective possibility only for the richest and best-educated fortunate enough to marry into the families of established regents. Such movement, socially and economically sideways but politically upwards, became rarer, however, and the Dutch system of aristocratic government was being inexorably transformed into the oligarchy of the following century. Nonetheless the sense of exclusion from political power was not yet sharp among the burghers of this higher stratum.

It was more vivid and bitter among the lesser burghers, who retained memories of the time a century and more earlier when their guilds took part in the election of the town governments. They wanted a voice in the town halls, a share in the offices bestowed by the councils and burgomasters, and policies that protected their particular economic interests. They often saw the regents not as "city fathers" but as petty local tyrants, and they viewed the Princes of Orange as their defenders. Possessing both the ability to read and write and enough property to provide a secure livelihood, they were the core of what would become the democratic movement of the eighteenth century; but at the moment they lacked any coherent or clear program. As members of the town militias they were both the sustainers of order and its potential destroyers. Toward them De Witt felt a supercilious benevolence: their interests were best served, he thought, by docile acceptance of the governance of the regents.

Toward the bulk of the simple folk below the burghers, the manual toilers who lived by their employment and dwelled in hovels, he felt no sympathy whatever. They were the rabble, in a horribly drab Dutch word *het grauw*, "the gray," those who lacked personal identity but formed a faceless class. They did not possess arms like the burghers, but still they were a peril because their passions were hot and they were ready to riot and plunder. They too were worshippers of the House of Orange, but they were a weapon that the Princesses of Orange were reluctant to use. For De Witt, as for all the regents, they were a muttering mass always to be watched and kept down – they were a potential enemy within the Dutch state that, out of hand in a time of crisis, could destroy it.

The countryside remained politically inert throughout De Witt's period. There was no self-government in the villages except for the most local matters, and no voice in provincial government except in the northern provinces. The landowners – the barons and the lords – spoke for the rural communities and did not form a distinct part in Dutch political life. De Witt himself became a "lord" (*heer*) with estates in southeastern Holland in 1660, in order to fulfill a requirement for taking a new office, but he remained as before neither friend nor foe to the countryside.

All the preceding is a definition not so much of the everyday content of Dutch politics in De Witt's time as of its boundary conditions. De Witt's ordinary work was threefold management, in the first instance of the States of Holland, second of the States

General and the relations among the provinces, and finally of the foreign relations of the Republic as a whole.

The rock bottom foundation of his leadership was the guidance of Their Noble Great Mightinesses the States of Holland and West Friesland (to give them their full formal name). The duties assigned to him by the text of his instructions were, as we have seen, limited, but the tasks that flowed to him were much more extensive. Few of these were explicitly defined; they were implicitly granted because of the recognition that he alone was in a position to look at affairs from the perspective of his province overall rather than of any single member. Even as the national leader, although he gave unquestionable priority to the interests of Holland, he preferred to make them mesh with the needs of the other provinces to the greatest extent possible and to create, to use modern terminology, a consensus. "To the greatest extent possible . . . " In the constitutional and political system of the Republic, with its division and subdivision of the decision-making powers, consensus might seem in fact impossible. To achieve it De Witt possessed essentially three tools: the preponderance of Holland, all the greater in the absence of a stadholder; his own qualities of intelligence and knowledge; and his firm hand guiding the "States party."

I have put quotation marks around "States party" to indicate that it was not a party in the present-day sense. For that matter, neither was its antagonist the "Orangist party." The States party was, properly speaking, an assemblage of diverse forces. Some were inspired by republican principle and broad common interests, but others were factions joining forces to gain office. "Republican principle" here means less a doctrine of hostility to monarchy as such than an emphasis upon the powers and rights of the provincial States as against those of the stadholders; now, after the death of William II, it meant determination not to elect his son to his father's offices. "Common interests" means in general favoring commercial and industrial towns over the country; but it would be anachronistic to equate this to the harsh confrontation between industry and agriculture that developed in advanced countries in the nineteenth century. The quest for offices, always fewer in number than the candidates for them, brought into being a rivalry of "ins" and "outs," a pattern that fell far short, however, of the formal organization of political parties in the nineteenth and twentieth centuries. De Witt was the leader of the States party not by any formal authority given or taken, but because it was he who whipped together the coalition of forces – towns, clans, individuals – that in general followed his policies. To create such a political alliance De Witt soon found himself compelled to over-step his formal powers, indeed to violate his instructions, in order to seek the election of friends and supporters to office. Yet he was doing what every high officeholder in the Republic, councilor pensionary or stadholder, had to do because of the ingrained ambiguity of the Dutch political system, if he were to make it work.

Getting his own people into office was most important in Dordrecht, for De Witt's political credibility would drop to nil if he lost the backing of his home city. Yet Dordrecht's support was anything but automatic. Not only were there families in the city that viewed the De Witts as at least a little below them in power and prestige; almost all the members of the government except his immediate family continued to see in him a servant temporarily on detached duty with the province. This was reflected in his support of the city in its continuing competition with Rotterdam, which was better suited by its position near the mouth of the Maas river to serve offshore shipping and trade. He helped Dordrecht keep its privilege as the site of the English staple against Rotterdam's competition. He was less successful when Dordrecht faced Am-sterdam as its rival. As his prestige increased and his control of patronage strengthened, however, Dordrecht's leaders began to defer to him. He used his influence to gain the election of his brother Cornelius as steward of Putten, a district in the islands west of Dordrecht that was under the authority of the States of Holland. Cornelius, a stiff and strong-willed person, did not find easy entry into the government of Dordrecht itself, although his father had repeatedly been burgomaster and his younger brother now held the most important post in the country. He had to stand aside when an alderman was chosen in 1658, receiving instead the less influential post of deputy of the States of Holland.

If Dordrecht's support could be more or less taken as assured, that of Amsterdam could never be treated as certain. Although neither Holland nor the United Provinces as a whole were merely a hinterland for the country's greatest city, as they are so often described, Amsterdam was more than just first among peers. The magnitude both of its wealth and its political role may be measured by two facts: one, that Holland contributed almost 60 percent of the budget of the Union; the other, that Amsterdam contributed a like percentage to the revenues of the province. Virtually nothing of importance could be achieved without or against Amsterdam; but this does not at all mean that Amsterdam had only to speak to have its way. On the contrary, the lesser towns of Holland were as jealous of its preponderance as the outer provinces were of Holland's supremacy. It may be just as rightly said that although no other town carried the same weight in the affairs of state as Amsterdam, virtually nothing of importance could be achieved either without or against a majority of the other towns. The minor members had a formal power of veto, but unlike the larger cities such as Dordrecht and Leiden they could not withstand the pressure of recriminations and threats of future retribution from their more than equal fellow-members.

To work effectively, De Witt needed in Amsterdam the informal connections that in Dutch politics consisted primarily of family ties and personal friendships. The bonds of amity developed as he met and worked with leaders of Amsterdam, but the stronger ties of blood were lacking until 1655 when he married Wendela Bicker. Her paternal uncles, Andrew and Cornelius, had lost their political leadership in 1650 and had not regained it even after the death of William II. Their place at the head of Amsterdam was taken by Wendela's maternal uncle Cornelius de Graeff van Zuidpolsbroek, and it was to him that for the next nine years De Witt looked as both ally and friend. Zuidpolsbroek, a man of sober temperament and sharp intelligence, had a political vision that extended far beyond the walls of his own city. De Witt's relations with him combined the closeness of family affection and the mutual respect of two strong minds; he was De Witt's equal as no one else was.

The other Amsterdammer to whom De Witt had especially close political ties was Van Beuningen, who had been the city's pensionary since 1650. A vehement servant of his city's interests, he held strongly to his opinions and was not put down by the eminence of those who disputed his judgments. He was useful to De Witt when they agreed, but how stubborn an opponent he could be De Witt learned when they disagreed over Dutch policy in the Baltic war that began in 1657. When Van Beuningen, tiring of the strain of his diplomatic missions, gave up his pensionary's post in 1660, De Witt persuaded the new burgomasters elected in February to name his friend, Peter de Groot, in his place. It was a fateful choice, for De Groot, as the son of Hugo Grotius, embodied perhaps as much as any man alive the tradition of resistance to the House of Orange.

De Witt also established a friendship with John Wolfert van Brederode, who as field marshal was the highest commander in the army in the absence of a captain general. Brederode came from a distinguished line that claimed descent from the old counts of Holland. He was married to a sister of Amalia van Solms, but when the House of Orange fell upon bad times he moved swiftly to keep on good terms with the party in power. He helped De Witt to swing the Nobility to acceptance of the Act of Exclusion, kept the army obedient to the civil authority, and expected repayment in the form of favors. A genuine fondness seems to have sprung up between the field marshal and the councilor pensionary, although the baroque language of compliment may deceive us into reading more into their letters than either really meant. After Brederode died in 1655, De Witt showed concern for his family's welfare but withheld from them patronage they requested that no doubt would have been granted to the field marshal himself had he lived longer. Thereafter De Witt retained only one reliable supporter in the Nobility, Obdam, but he kept his hold over the other members by his control of patronage.

The years that immediately followed the conclusion of the peace with England were marked not only by the triumph of De Witt and the States party but no less, if less obviously, by the limited character of their victory. The Orangist party was indestructible, even in its beheaded condition. It was nourished by the sentimental memories of the people and throve on its usefulness to all who opposed the States party – the "Loevestein faction," as they called it – as a focus for their ambitions and endeavors. The best that De Witt could do was to deal with each situation as it arose; what he could not do was to eliminate the opposition.

The controversy over the Exclusion Act died down briefly after its adoption, but was revived when Van Beverningk returned in December to assume the post of treasurer general to which he had already been elected. Friesland, backed by four other provinces, demanded that he first admit his wrongdoing in the Exclusion affair. At De Witt's suggestion, he denied that the initiative for the Exclusion had been conveyed to Cromwell either by himself or, so far as he knew, by any of his colleagues: it had been totally Cromwell's work. Some of the provinces were satisfied and willing to let Van Beverningk take up his office, but Friesland and Groningen held firm. It was not until December 1656 that the States General by a majority vote, with Friesland still stubbornly opposing, approved Van Beverningk's entry into the treasurer-generalship. De Witt eroded the opposition of the other provinces less by the persuasiveness of his arguments than by the effective use of the instrument of patronage. He played upon the conflicts within the Orange camp between the friends of Amalia, of William Frederick, and of the Princess Royal, and arranged for army commands to be given to the sons of Mary's supporters when they backed Van Beverningk's appointment.

What De Witt had not anticipated was Van Beverningk's wobbly reaction to the whole crisis. The councilor pensionary heard that his friend, with whom he had worked so well in the difficult conditions of the struggle over the Act of Exclusion, had swung his support to the opposition. He had been offered, it was said, a high position in the entourage of the Prince of Orange himself. And he was reported to have expressed his dislike for Cromwell with an obscene expletive. It was part of a new Orangist strategy of seeking to disrupt the States party. For the moment, it did not work, for Van Beverningk, reading the signs of the political times correctly, did not break away, as De Witt had feared. Still it was a troubling sign, for it meant that De Witt could not count on holding his party together upon the basis of principle.

No small compensation for this anxiety was the bitter conflict that raged within the House of Orange. The Princesses Mary and Amalia eyed each other with distrust and distaste, but at least they were united in fixing all their dreams of restoration upon the frail person of William III. During these years, the Princesses met the indignity of Exclusion with sullen silence, leaving the arena of politics to the victorious "Loevestein faction" until Providence should turn events around in favor of their son and grandson. Count William Frederick was far more ambivalent in his attitude. He was torn between a commitment to the House of Orange, of which his own family was a junior branch, and a desire to exalt his own status. There was more immediacy to this danger confronting the Princesses than there was to any prospect of the restoration of the young Prince. Indeed, they glimpsed a hidden trap in the proposal to "designate" the Prince as captain general, with William Frederick holding the supreme military command until William came of age. Once in the saddle, would the Count ever willingly dismount?

It became clear in September 1654 that the Count's ambitions would be opposed – by De Witt from one side, by the Princesses from the other – when the proposal was put forward in Overijssel to name a stadholder and captain general for the province. This was, of course, playing tit for tat with Holland. If one province in the exercise of its sovereignty could refrain from filling these high political and military offices, another province by the same powers could fill the posts. Actually, the proposal was part and parcel of a sharp conflict that had brought the province to the verge of civil war. Two factions had formed around the issue of election of a new bailiff in Twente, a district on the eastern frontier under the authority of the States of Overijssel; one candidate was a friend of De Witt's, the other an opponent, although both were noblemen. The social character of the two factions were indentical – a medley of towns and noble cliques. Naked interest and – for a few – political principle divided them. Each group called a meeting of the provincial States, the supporters of the former candidate in Deventer, those of the latter in Zwolle. On October 15, the Zwolle rump assembly named William III as stadholder and captain general, with William Frederick as lieutenant general. The rival "States" at Deventer at once protested to the States General that this action was illegal and asked that troops be sent to defend them. They also turned to their friends in Holland, with whose backing they expected to prevail.

The governing party in Holland was anything but happy at this development. Their problem was how to help the Deventer group and get the Prince's election nullified without touching off armed conflict. The situation simmered until the next summer, when Holland proposed a compromise: William Frederick would give up the lieutenancy general of Overijssel, and the "States" at Deventer would cease to claim sole and whole authority in the province and reunite with the rump at Zwolle. The proposal misfired. The Deventer group stood firmer than ever, while a majority in the States General decided to send a delegation dominated by friends of Zwolle to Overijssel to mediate.

De Witt thereupon sought a different way to impose his

will. An opportunity presented itself due to William Frederick's personal ambition and the fragility of his Orangist loyalty. When Brederode died early in September 1655, the Count wrote at once to De Witt to seek Holland's support for his election as field marshal in Brederode's place. This appeal enabled De Witt as a member of the committee of the States General named to mediate the conflict to put forward a new suggestion: the election of William III as stadholder and captain general would be nullified, and William Frederick would decline the lieutenancy general of Overijssel so as to become eligible as field marshal of the Union. As such, however, he would have to swear to uphold all Dutch treaties, which meant acceptance of the Exclusion. In addition, no field marshal would thereafter be able to hold a provincial stadholdership. Van Beveringk would be allowed to take his office as treasurer general. Thus Holland would achieve its principal aim – to keep William III out of all offices – at the price of giving William Frederick a lesser office, where he would be kept under the thumb of the civilian authority. The proposal was called the "Harmony," a term that was to De Witt's liking because it savored of persuasion and not of force.

The "Harmony" did not at once produce the good relations that the word connoted. It split the Orangist party, making William Frederick an appendage of the States party and the province of Holland; but he gained the highest active military post in the Republic and implicit forgiveness for his part in the events of 1650.

De Witt's friends in Overijssel nonetheless felt the deal to be puzzling and dismaying. The councilor pensionary, who declined to give them his reasons in writing, assured them that if they would come to The Hague he would provide an adequate explanation privately. He had to reconcile the special interests of the Deventer group with the broad needs of "Freedom" throughout the country. When they arrived at The Hague, De Witt's supporters were persuaded; but the disoriented Zwolle group remained baffled by William Frederick's rapprochement with De Witt.

Early in 1657, Friesland tried to get the approval of the States General for election of a field marshal, even without a general settlement. The Hollanders replied with a threat to withhold from an illegally elected commander the obedience of the troops in Friesland in Holland's pay. They followed this step by an even more serious blow to the Count's hopes by proposing formal abolition of the field marshalcy. The States even adopted De Witt's notion of appointing a supreme commander only in wartime, and then not for life but for one or two campaigns. During the recent war De Witt had begun to gain some understanding of navies and naval warfare, but the army remained a closed book to him, a force that he mistrusted and looked upon more as an internal threat than as a defender against foreign enemies.

The political tug-of-war over the military command continued. De Witt realized at last that he could not persuade William Frederick to collaborate wholeheartedly with him, and began to play instead upon the antipathy of the Princesses to their cousin in Friesland. At the same time he strove for the always-vanishing reconciliation that he sought in Overijssel. Finally, in the summer of 1657, an agreement was reached that gave the Deventer party all that it sought except revenge against the Zwolle party. No new field marshal was named, not even in 1658 when the possibility loomed that Dutch land forces might be sent to Denmark to intervene in the Baltic war.

Diplomacy was so intertwined with the domestic affairs of the United Provinces, as we have emphasized already, that neither can be adequately described without a grasp of the other. Yet, in order to see events in their specific context and sequence, it is also necessary to trace Dutch relations with foreign powers separately, crossing over to internal affairs as needed. There is, therefore, an intertwining of separate strands, which seen together form one large fabric.

As the years passed, De Witt's mastery of his function as minister of foreign affairs (it will be recalled that there was no such office, nor indeed any ministry in the modern sense, in the Republic) was strengthened until he was easily the equal of any of his counterparts anywhere in Europe. It was fortunate for the Dutch that they had so skilled and well-informed a guide for their diplomacy, for very few Dutch regents knew much about foreign affairs. Yet, as a small but wealthy country that lived by its foreign trade and so could not escape the buffeting of events in other lands, the Republic needed someone to shape and conduct its policy.

The style of negotiation that De Witt developed was very much his own, for it paralleled that of his political leadership within the country. It relied upon persuasion and candor rather than duplicity and evasion. In spite of his skill in argument, he did not think he could talk other nations into adopting policies contrary to their own interests. His reasoning was realistic, not moral, in character; he did not foresee the time, centuries later, when his country, lacking a big stick to make its point, would plead its cause upon the basis of ethical superiority. His attitude toward "reason of state" – the principle that the end justified the means – was ambiguous. He did not believe that breaking promises was wise policy, but knew that every treaty had its loopholes. His greatest successes in duplicitous diplomacy were garnered at the expense of would-be Machiavellian diplomats who trusted too much to their own wiles. He could get away with trickery with them because he did not practice it all the time and caught them off balance. And he scorned the technique of bribing foreign statesmen, less out of moral revulsion than from a belief that it was money thrown away. Where his realism fell short was in his underestimation of emotional and personal elements in the policies of other countries. Himself implacably self-controlled, he did not see the power of vanity or greed in the behavior of others. One irony of his own conduct of foreign affairs was that he was dependent upon Dutch envoys who were anything but impervious to such moods. Except for a few ambassadors "extraordinary" like Van Beverningk and Van Beuningen, most Dutch diplomats were regents who found life in an embassy easier than the fierce internecine battling of Dutch domestic politics.

Foreign envoys sent to The Hague, on the contrary, were among the best that their countries could muster. It was a tribute to the importance that the Republic possessed among the powers. By negotiating through them rather than through Dutch envoys at their courts, as he preferred to do, De Witt kept the process of negotiating in his own hands. Face-to-face discussion minimized, too, the notorious insecurity of diplomatic correspondence. He easily grasped the principles of code construction but realized that it served not to assure secrecy – what he could break with little trouble, others could too – but to delay reading by the wrong eyes.

The fundamental character of his foreign policy developed out of the situation and the needs of the country. The strategic and commercial necessities of the Dutch, he soon discovered, were far from identical. As a country that lived by its shipping, trading and fishing, the Dutch Republic needed peace. But an active policy of seeking to prevent war among the other powers had the unfortunate consequence of involving the Dutch in their conflicts and even their wars. The notion of collective security had already beguiled thinkers, as it would for centuries ahead, but it was still only a dream. Political realists who wanted peace, such as De Witt, had to make do with the instrument of the balance of power. Equilibrium among the nations was not so much a static condition as an active manipulation of events. It required that some powerful state without the possibility of establishing its own overwhelming political and military predominance – and this was the position of the Dutch – should marshal the forces of the lesser states to prevent "universal monarchy," as formerly of Spain and now potentially of France. Thus it came about that De Witt, who had no love of war for itself, no ambition for glory, found himself directing an active foreign policy that repeatedly led to Dutch involvement in war.

First in priority of consideration among the European powers for the Dutch was their neighbor across the North Sea. The long war of independence against Spain had been successful in no small measure because England had been friendly or at least neutral. The lesson that the Dutch coast and Dutch fishing and shipping were vulnerable to a hostile England had been taught with painful clarity during the recent war. De Witt drew the practical conclusion – rebuilding the Dutch fleet must not halt with peace. Cromwell had gathered in some of the fruits of victory with Holland's "Exclusion" of the Prince of Orange; since even France was beginning to court the favor of the Lord Protector, he had little to fear any more from the friendless roaming Stuart king in exile, "Charles II." Now that the political sine qua non of his political security had been achieved, Cromwell was able to give their head to English merchants for whom getting the advantage over their Dutch competitors was paramount.

An accord was hammered out between the Dutch and the English East India companies within a few months after peace was made. It provided for monetary compensation by the Dutch to the English company, so that Dutch domination of the island empire in the East could grow unimpeded. The accord also granted awards to relatives of the Englishmen who had been executed decades earlier in the abortive revolt of 1623 in the Moluccas whose repression the English called the " Amboina massacre. " The recipients were not satisfied with the compensation they were given, and their demands for more continued after the peace and received verbal support from the English government. It was significant of the scale of relative values, however, that when reports reached Cromwell in the spring of 1655 that the friends of Charles II were about to rise in revolt, he modified his attitude toward the Dutch and courted the councilor pensionary's friendship. The relationship soon began to sour again when Mazarin, needing England to gain the ever-elusive final victory over Spain (to replace the Dutch ally who had fallen away in 1648, we will recall), made an alliance with the regicide ruler in England. De Witt viewed this unnatural alliance with concern: if the two countries, having worsted Spain, should together turn upon the United Provinces, the strategic position of the Dutch would be a nightmare.

Such a combination could not be discounted out of hand. The relationship of the Dutch Republic with France since 1648 had been marked by querulous controversy. Dutch merchant ships were seized by French privateers; Dutch goods imported into France were subjected to discriminatory taxation. During the Anglo-Dutch war Mazarin had been more concerned with strengthening his restored control at home after the Fronde than in risking adventures abroad. Negotiations for a new treaty of friendship with the States General moved at a snail's pace. De Witt for his part wanted no alliance that would drag the Dutch back into war with Spain, and Mazarin aimed at victory over Spain without falling into armed conflict with the United Provinces.

When Cromwell instituted the "New Model of Government" in 1657, an opportunity arose for De Witt to explain the pragmatic, unideological basis of his policy. Nieupoort, who had remained in England as the Dutch ambassador when Van Beveringk returned home in 1654, reported that people expected Cromwell to be proclaimed king. The French ambassador was ready to represent His Most Christian Majesty at coronation ceremonies, but Nieupoort was troubled by twinges of republican principle at the prospect of having to participate in the ritual of monarchy. He asked De Witt what he, as the representative of Their High Mightinesses, should do. The reply was blunt and brief: we have already recognized that Cromwell is the sovereign in the British

Isles; do not balk now at any title he wishes to assume. As it turned out, Cromwell was satisfied with regal powers without the kingly title, and Nieupoort did not have to strain his conscience.

The situation suddenly changed, with consequences far more drastic than De Witt anticipated, when Cromwell died in September 1658, and he was succeeded at once as Lord Protector by his son Richard. No sooner had the news come to The Hague than De Witt went in the middle of the night to George Downing, the English resident, to "condole and congratulate" in the same breath. Richard proved to be a quasi-king with neither a king's proper force of personality nor his natural authority. After little more than a half-year's weak-willed rule, he abdicated the protectorship. De Witt again reminded Nieupoort that the Dutch would recognize whoever held the sovereign power in England. He did not anticipate how far that would stretch his own political principles within a year. The failure of restored parliamentary rule in England soon demonstrated that the army alone had effective power; it was the army's commander, General Monck, who in May 1660 arranged the recall of Charles II to his throne. De Witt speedily mended his fences with the king-to-be who was the uncle of the still-excluded Prince of Orange.

The Republic's relations with France during these years fell into a limbo that was neither amity nor enmity. French hopes of bringing the Dutch back into the war against Spain had been dashed by the death of William II in 1650. No fleeting hope that France might join the Dutch after the outbreak of the war with England in 1652 stirred the ruling party in The Hague to contemplate adding Spain to the country's foes. Little but inconclusive talks occurred. The situation changed early in 1657 when De Ruyter, commanding a Dutch fleet in the Mediterranean, seized two French privateers that turned out to be warships in the royal service. De Witt backed De Ruyter and a contest in retaliatory commercial measures ensued between France and the United Provinces. The interests involved were too slight, however, to warrant outright hostilities, and a compromise was soon arranged. De Witt's concerns had been, first, to assure Dutch honor in the face of French arrogance and, second, to keep French markets open to Dutch merchants on a fair and safe basis.

Honor was the stake in a dispute that broke out one summer Sunday in 1657 in The Hague, but it was the honor not of the States

General but of France and Spain. Strolling in the evening on the Voorhout, the broad avenue lined with trees just to the northwest of the Binnenhof, De Witt came upon the French and Spanish ambassadors in their coaches, each insisting upon the position closest to the center barrier because it implied the precedence of his royal master. A street battle impended between the envoys' followers, with the crowd – a significant portent of changing feelings among the Dutch – ready to come in on the Spaniard's side. De Witt made his way through the crowd but was unable to persuade either envoy to yield to the other. He therefore had a company of Dutch guards brought in to keep the would-be brawlers apart, while a cut was made in the barrier through which the Spaniard rode, continuing parallel to the Frenchman on the other side. The crisis was surmounted, but for a while it had been serious. More was involved than just the ambassadors' vanity. If the French envoy had suffered an open slight, the French–Dutch commercial accord toward which negotiations were laboriously moving forward would probably have failed, but they were able to continue.

When in June 1658 the combined armies of France and England captured the fortified port of Dunkirk from Spain, it became evident that the relationship between the Dutch Republic and France could no longer be left in the uncertain suspense that had marked it during the previous decade. The Spaniards were exhausted and could be expected to acknowledge final defeat before long. If Philip IV refused, the French would probably go on to conquer the whole Spanish Netherlands. If they did, the strategic problem of the Dutch as a land power would become agonizing, for the presence on their frontier of France, now visibly and palpably the strongest military force in Europe, would threaten their independence even more directly than English domination of the North Sea. More than two decades earlier, in 1632, Richelieu had endeavored to remove this obstacle to Dutch–French amity by proposing that the southern Low Countries be made into an independent Belgic republic under a Dutch–French co-protect-orate. Because of the resemblance of the proposed republic to the Swiss confederation, the arrangement was labeled a "cantonment." There was as well a subtle semantic implication here: *cantonner* was the French term for isolating a dangerous situation, and – indeed – the new republic would constitute a danger neither to the Dutch nor the French. In 1635 the Dutch, concerned about possible trade rivalry from a revived Antwerp, had turned down Richelieu's proposal.

The question was now reopened by Mazarin, Richelieu's successor. He called upon Turenne, the great soldier who had learned his craft under his uncle, Prince Frederick Henry, for advice, Turenne being probably better informed about the political situation in the Dutch Republic than any other Frenchman. Turenne brought Count William Adrian van Horne, a Dutch officer in the French army, into the discussion and sent him to Holland to see Beverweert, a member of the House of Orange who had cultivated good relations with the present Dutch government. Van Horne gave Beverweert letters from Turenne to present to De Witt in which a new version of the cantonment proposal was put forward: Turenne indicated that if it were adopted, Louis XIV would withdraw his armies from Flanders. A secret debate ensued in the highest circles of the Dutch Republic, the importance of which cannot be exaggerated.

De Witt himself thought cantonment was a splendid idea, a cure for a nightmare. Instead of replacing the debilitated Spanish rule in the southern Low Countries with the domination of two strong and greedy powers – for he assumed that England would demand a share of the spoils its armies had contributed to winning – there would be only a weak neighbor on the open Dutch frontier to the south. He informed the deputies of Amsterdam to the States of Holland, Gerard Schaep Simonsz and Henry Spiegel, of the French initiative, and wrote to Zuidpolsbroek to seek his uncle's support. Schaep did not share De Witt's eagerness. On the contrary, besides the Amsterdammers' concern lest a free Belgium (to use the anachronistic but convenient modern name) mean an Antwerp free to trade with the world, Schaep argued that France would not really be sated by such a solution, but would sooner or later renew its appetite for a now defenceless southern Netherlands; furthermore, the English would take offence and might resume their war upon the Dutch; finally, the Dutch had moral obligations toward Spain under the treaty of peace of 1648. De Witt was not persuaded by Schaep's arguments, nor was Zuidpolsbroek. There was, however, deep disagreement among the deputies and burgomasters of eight other Holland towns to whom Beverweert had revealed the French proposal, and when they insisted it be put officially before the States of Holland, Zuidpolsbroek concurred.

De Witt saw that what was really at issue was the Dutch policy of virtual neutrality, to which he himself had earlier been attracted. Could the Republic continue to go it alone among the powers of Europe, without a single good friend or reliable ally? he asked Zuidpolsbroek. Something better than a France still bitter at the abandonment of their alliance in 1648 was needed. It could be taken for granted that the English would go on thirsting for the Dutch trade supremacy; and if the French ever combined forces with them the peril to the United Provinces would be immense. Yet it was not possible to avert disaster by switching sides to the Habsburg camp against which the Dutch had fought so long. Such a change would bring loss of support among the Protestant powers as well as probable civil disorders within the Dutch Republic itself. The immediate situation held its perils, for France and England were supporting Sweden in the Baltic war, while the Dutch were helping the Danes. What if the clash of interests spilled over into a more direct confrontation between the great powers? It was essential to keep France's friendship, and cantonment, so De Witt argued, was the best way to hold it.

So the opportunity was not seized and soon passed. Mazarin's interest turned to the growing certainty that Spain would have to make peace before long upon terms favorable to French aspirations. When peace was concluded in the Pyrenees in November 1659, one clause promised the oldest Spanish infanta in marriage to Louis XIV. True, the Spaniards required Maria Teresa (who after her marriage became Marie Thérèse) to foreswear her rights and those of her eventual children to the heritage of the Spanish monarchy. But Mazarin knew that jurists could argue the invalidity of such a renunciation, especially as it had been linked to payment of a dowry in money that Spain at this time did not have. This, together with the knowledge that soldiers can make jurists' arguments irrefutable, made him decide to gamble on obtaining the Low Countries for France rather than merely assuring the safety of France on its northern frontier, which was all that cantonment could yield. Even before the Peace of the Pyrenees was concluded, De Witt found the French growing harsher in their attitude toward the Dutch. Mazarin imposed a freight tax of 50 sous per barrel on foreign ships entering or leaving French ports, adding about one third to freight charges for the trip between the French coast and Holland. It was a tax that the Dutch would continue to resent and resist for years, a constant source of estrangement that became dangerous when added to political differences.

Whether England and France were foe or friend was a question of life and death for the Dutch; and for that very reason, as we have seen, De Witt strove to avoid any ultimate challenge to either of these powers. Once peace had been made with England in 1654, this problem did not dominate his attention on a day-to-day basis: however, two Scandinavian countries, Denmark and Sweden, took their place and presented a similar conundrum.

The existence of the Dutch Republic as an independent nation may not have been at stake in relations with these northern lands, but Dutch prosperity certainly was. From the Baltic and from Norway, which was part of a twin kingdom with Denmark, came essential wares both for the use of the Dutch themselves and for reshipment and resale to western and southern Europe – most of all, grain from Poland, iron and copper from Sweden and naval stores from Sweden and Norway. Denmark mattered not for what little it produced, but for its geographical position. It commanded both banks of the Sound, the passage between the Baltic and North Seas, and extracted a heavy share of its revenues from dues upon shipping passing either way.

The earlier Dutch concern for keeping the Sound dues low or at least equal for all had already been largely solved: in 1649 the Danes had agreed to accept redemption of the dues payable by Dutch vessels in the form of an annual lump-sum payment by the States General. They might fret at this arrangement and seek advantages here or there, but basically the Danes accepted the privileged position of the Republic. Not the least of their reasons was that they kept the Dutch on their side in the traditional rivalry with Sweden.

De Witt would have liked to keep Dutch friendship with both Scandinavian states since the Republic needed both of them. It was, alas, an empty hope. During the English war, the overriding consideration of the Dutch had been to ensure a Danish closure of the Baltic to English shipping, and in this they were successful. But Van Beuningen, who was in Sweden on the first mission of a brilliant diplomatic career, warned De Witt that the cost was

Stockholm's support of England: the best that could be hoped for was Sweden's neutrality in the Anglo-Dutch war. Van Beuningen spoke for Amsterdam, whose interest lay in an active defense of its trade to the Baltic, while De Witt thought it better to keep Dutch commitment to a minimum and looked for a way to prevent Sweden from endangering Dutch interests without becoming involved in armed conflict with that country.

The situation changed in 1654, once the Dutch had made peace with England. The Danes now became more than willing to grant to the victorious English equal rights with the humbled Dutch. Also, a new ruler took control in Sweden. Queen Christina, the able but irascible monarch, abdicated and went to live abroad. She was succeeded by Charles Gustavus of the Palatinate, her German-born cousin who had been brought up in Sweden; he reigned as Charles X Gustavus. He was intent upon winning glory and territory and embarked upon a series of military adventures that embroiled the Baltic for the next six years. In the summer of 1655 he launched an attack upon Poland. The Dutch response was to prepare a strong fleet for the Baltic the next spring to shield the Danes. Yet De Witt continued to hope that diplomacy would ward off the worst – a Swedish alliance with England – and the States General accepted his proposal to send special ambassadors to Stockholm, Copenhagen and Berlin (Brandenburg having become an ally of Poland, from which it held the duchy of Prussia as a fief). The situation became dangerously worse early in January 1656 when the Swedes undertook a land and sea siege of Danzig (now Polish Gdansk). This was the most direct attack upon Dutch interests short of war, for they bought immense quantities of grain at Danzig for their own needs and for reexport. When Brandenburg made a separate peace with Charles X Gustavus, Poland had to struggle on alone. Van Beuningen, now at Copenhagen, saw a victorious Sweden as the main danger for the Republic. He insisted that the Dutch alliance with Denmark be strengthened and that the Swedes be compelled to make a more favorable treaty with the States General than the one in force, dating from 1640. He was indeed willing to risk war with Sweden.

De Witt did not want to go so far, lest war with England and perhaps with France result. In his view, it would be better to help Poland defeat the Swedish besiegers of Danzig; and in early July he obtained a resolution by the States General to send a naval squadron to Danzig to land an auxiliary Dutch force.* The councilor pensionary had to court the favor of Count William Frederick to secure Friesland's vote in favor of this resolution. In this he succeeded, as the dispute over the "Harmony" had subsided.

By the end of July the Dutch squadron of forty-two ships, augmented by nine Danish vessels, arrived at Danzig, and a Dutch officer took command of the resistance against the Swedes on land. The Dutch navy saved Danzig, and the Swedes, intent on pursuing their war in Prussia, felt obliged to buy off the Republic by the treaty of Elbing, in which they promised to respect Danzig's neutrality, renewed the provisions of the earlier treaties of 1640 and 1645 concerning trade and shipping, and granted the Dutch most-favored nation status.

Van Beuningen was opposed to ratification of this treaty. He though the Swedes had given too little and had left loopholes to favor their own trade. De Witt admitted Van Beuningen had a point but did not want to abandon the treaty; instead he proposed to meet Van Beuningen's criticism by seeking "elucidation" of the ambiguous clauses. Holland, followed by the States General, thereupon made ratification of the Elbing treaty dependent upon adequate Swedish elucidations. Van Beuningen remained eager to propel the Danes into an attack upon Sweden, while De Witt stressed the principle of the sanctity of treaties. This was not only a question of morality or of the honor of the States General, important as these were: De Witt deeply distrusted the unpredictable chanciness of war.

A further complication for De Witt himself was that he was not familiar with the details of tolls and tariffs and their implications for trade, and on such matters he had to defer to the authorities in Amsterdam. Such deference did not go so far as overlooking errors in their arithmetical computations. Furthermore, much as he was concerned for the welfare of Dutch merchants, he did not believe the Dutch state could or should protect them from all risk.

De Witt's policy of combining restrained support to Denmark with a firm but fundamentally conciliatory attitude to Sweden, difficult enough to follow in the best of times, was now put to the most severe strain. In mid-June 1657 the king of Denmark,

* In the seventeenth century, such assistance did not constitute an act of war unless the other side wished to consider it as such.

Frederick III, risking all to gain a little, declared war upon Sweden. He called upon the States General for assistance under their treaty of alliance. Without it there could be little hope that he would emerge victorious, for Sweden's military strength was impressively larger than his own. Encouraged by Van Beuningen, who concluded a new treaty of closer alliance with him, he counted upon Dutch help. De Witt did not budge from his basic policy: to bring about a return to peace, with no territorial gain for either side, thus maintaining a balance between the two Scandinavian powers most advantageous to the Republic. The belligerent refusing peace on these terms would be considered the aggressor. There was, however, disagreement over his policy within the United Provinces, aggravated by the ever-present problem of the attitude of England and France, allies now and emboldened by their recent joint conquest of Dunkirk.

A relative stalemate was transformed early in 1658 by a swift reversal of fortunes. Charles X Gustavus, seizing the initiative, crossed the frozen waters of the Sound and conquered all of the Danish islands; Copenhagen alone escaped. De Witt's subtle and complex policy had proved to be a house of cards. The Danes bought peace in March by sacrificing to Sweden all Danish and much Norwegian territory on the Scandinavian peninsula, so that Sweden at last reached not only the Sound but also the open North Sea, creating the territory of the modern Swedish state. Denmark even agreed to bar all foreign warships from passing through the Sound. Thus Swedish control of the Baltic Sea became only a matter of time, a brief time, unless events could be put into reverse.

Yet De Witt did not lose heart or abandon his policy. The States General at his behest offered the Swedes ratification of the Elbing treaty if they granted the desired elucidations; at the same time Dutch naval and military forces were prepared for action. Their opportunity came because Copenhagen had not fallen to the Swedes and the remaining Danish forces rallied in the capital. It came, too, because Charles X Gustavus decided he wanted total, not partial, victory over Denmark and resumed the war in August 1658. His strategy was straightforward – a siege of Copenhagen by land and sea.

The Dutch response was rapid and clear. De Witt abandoned, at least for the moment, the policy of conciliating the Swedes and adopted instead Amsterdam's hostility to Sweden. Obdam was ordered to take his fleet to Denmark, carrying a force of 6,000 soldiers to help in Copenhagen's landward defense. The Dutch fleet met the Swedes in battle early in November but Obdam, still more of a soldier than a sailor, failed to destroy his foe. Dutch troop reinforcements were put ashore, however, and the fleet stayed on station throughout the months of frozen winter, successfully raising the Swedish siege of the Danish capital. The possibility that an English fleet under Sir Edward Montagu might intervene on the Swedish side was deeply disturbing; but Obdam was ordered to hold his position while avoiding a clash with the English if at all possible.

The policy of aiding the Danes was opposed both within Holland and in the other provinces, but De Witt proved as steadfast in the new policy of action as he had been before in that of conciliation. He did not totally abandon his quest for peace, but attempted mediation in collaboration with the English and French envoys at The Hague. He finally overcame their deep distrust of the Republic by accepting the terms set forth in the instructions of the English envoy, Downing, but then the agreement fell apart when Downing received new instructions from the government in London (shortly after the abdication of Protector Richard Cromwell) to withhold his signature and seek new terms, which were highly unsatisfactory from the Dutch point of view since they removed all mention of the Elbing treaty and its elucidations. Yet, all was not lost. A new government took over in London in May, and it reversed the English position, telling Downing to complete the earlier draft agreement, thereafter known as "The Hague Concert."

De Witt had won his diplomatic triumph at last. He pronounced its essential principle: England, France and the United Provinces not only fixed the terms for peace between Denmark and Sweden but also agreed to compel the two warring countries to accept their terms.

De Witt had no sympathy for the Danish king but continued intact, however, the Dutch alliance with Denmark, as well as those with Poland and Brandenburg. The main obstacle to peace remained the intransigence of Charles X Gustavus. The Swedish king not only wanted better terms in a peace treaty but also Danish abandonment of their alliance with the Dutch. Simultaneously the councilor pensionary had to face the wrath of Amsterdam; and he was forced to appeal to Van Beuningen to overcome his city's resistance to The Hague Concert. Van Beuningen used his influence in Amsterdam, and when De Witt succeeded in holding the support of a large majority in the States of Holland, Amsterdam finally acquiesced.

De Witt's situation remained ticklish, since it was all too clear that he was imposing his policy on the States of Holland and the States General, not merely executing their decisions. Suspicions were voiced that he might have gone behind their backs, as in the Exclusion affair, and Amsterdam took the lead in criticizing his conduct. The councilor pensionary in desperation explained his position to Zuidpolsbroek and pleaded with him to make Amsterdam refrain from its policy of compelling Sweden to make peace with Poland as well as with all her other Baltic enemies. This, he argued, would only play into the hands of the foolish and rash Danish king, Frederick III. The stalemate continued; all belligerents stood firm on their claims; the Danes hoped to gain victory by the arms of the Dutch and Charles X Gustavus was as self-confident as ever.

Yet – as so often happens – the accident of unexpected death decided the fortune of war and diplomacy. Charles X Gustavus of Sweden died late in February 1660, and by early May general peace was concluded at Oliva.

De Witt had his diplomatic triumph at last. It resulted in part from his persistence and skill in an extraordinarily complex and volatile situation. But it must also be ascribed to some pure luck, for what would have happened if the Swedish king, equally persistent and skillful – and greedy as well – had lived on, no mere historian can know. But he can be certain that troubled times would have continued.

6

The challenge of Stuart and Orange
1660–1664

The painful fact that Dutch politics was as much determined by events abroad as at home was proved once more by the consequences of the restoration of Charles II as king of Great Britain in 1660. Hatred and fear of the Stuart pretender among the English republicans had been a large element in shaping the war between the Commonwealth and the United Provinces during the previous decade, but after 1654 De Witt had had every reason to believe that he had put limits to the English involvement in Dutch domestic affairs. Ironically, it was Cromwell's death that made possible England's reentry into the political life of the Dutch Republic.

For De Witt the choice between monarchy and republic in England was an empty one. He preferred neither, certainly not on ideological grounds, and saw the country across the North Sea as a rival, an intense competitor, that could be constrained to friendship only by overriding necessity, primarily of a strategic nature. What he did not want in England was revolution and civil disorder, which brought to the surface new forces inexperienced in the larger world and driven by unrealistic dreams. If Charles II could bring back domestic peace to Britain after almost two decades of turmoil, that would redound to the Dutch advantage, provided English ambitions could be kept in check. In the short run, De Witt counted upon the need of the newly restored king to stabilize his régime; he hoped that Charles would not indulge in the adventurism that had marked Cromwell's rule.

To keep England from venturing upon a repetition of the rivalry by arms of the first years of the Commonwealth government, De Witt looked to the other great power of Europe, France. The alliance that Cromwell had formed with Mazarin, which gave

Dunkirk to England and a victory over Spain to France, fell apart with the Restoration, and De Witt hoped that he could play the two kings, cousins though they were, against each other. It was not an idle plan, for the French court was acutely sensitive to the strategic consideration that Britain and the Northern Netherlands if allied against France would form a potential enemy of immense wealth and strength.

Whatever the complexities of the situation, when Charles II was proclaimed king in May, De Witt made the United Provinces play the role of gracious host. A mission of congratulations hastened to the Dutch city of Breda, where the joyful Stuart was staying, even before the first news of his proclamation in London was confirmed. To sweeten their message of welcome, the Hollanders were headed by a member of the House of Orange, Louis of Nassau, lord of Beverweert. But even this friendly gesture was not without ambiguity, for Beverweert, an illegitimate son of Prince Maurice, had quickly come to terms with the régime of the "True Freedom" after 1650. He represented therefore the kind of friendship that De Witt wanted from Charles II, one that accepted the existing leadership in Holland and did not attempt to thrust the Prince of Orange, the nine-year-old William III, upon them by means of external threats or internal disorders.

The good will and amity that Charles proffered to the Dutch, both at Breda and when he later went to The Hague as the guest of Their High Mightinesses, was similarly conditional and ambiguous. Already at Breda he had boasted that together the two countries could lay down the law to the rest of Europe; but the Dutch, he added, must have no friend closer than himself – a claim that implied dependency to those who knew the inner language of diplomacy. At The Hague he basked in the honors paid to him, including a speech of greeting by De Witt on behalf of the States of Holland that must have amused the utterly disillusioned king. The Dutch, De Witt admitted, had come to terms with Cromwell, the supreme foe of the Stuarts, but only under the compulsion of necessity. Now, happily, necessity and true feelings ran the same course. Charles replied with similar flattery and guile. He understood, he said, why the Dutch had done what they had to, but now they dealt with "honorable men." "Honorable men". . . how many times during the next dozen years would De Witt have occasion to remember those words? He mentioned them the following year, and though he did not repeat them thereafter, he could not have forgotten them.

To be sure, Charles II for his part must have always pondered that he had not been able to pin down De Witt regarding the future of William III. The elevation of the Prince of Orange to the offices of his forefathers was what the English king wanted as the price of his friendship, but De Witt would give him nothing but fair words. Trust the good will of the States of Holland, the councilor pensionary told him, but do not press them to act at once.

On his departure, Charles made it plain that he was not abandoning William even though he was putting the interests of his sister, Princess Mary, and of his nephew in the hands of the States of Holland. The time for action would come when Mary called upon the Dutch to prove their good will by deeds. The next day, when the king was about to board the warship that would take him home after his travels, the councilor pensionary spoke with cloying flattery, but his words did not give anything away but verbal honey. Knowing observers were not taken in. The past had not been forgotten, and blunt-spoken Nicholas Stellingwerff, who had been a fellow-prisoner with Jacob de Witt in Loevestein prison in 1650, sourly remarked that the money spent so lavishly on the ceremonies would have been better used to purchase gunpowder and to arm more Dutch ships of war.

De Witt, however, was not willing to cast aside the slenderest chance to keep on good terms with England. A double embassy was named to London, its members chosen to defend the interests involved. The first envoy was Simon van Hoorn, a former burgomaster of Amsterdam and hence a defender of Holland's trade and the régime of the "True Freedom," the second Beverweert, the embodiment of a working compromise between the States party and the House of Orange. De Witt gave them the task of making opposites meet. On the one hand they should maintain intact the freedom of the seas for Dutch shippers and fishermen; on the other, they should sidestep disputes with the English. But it was precisely this freedom which constituted the heart of the rivalry between the English and the Dutch.

That the English were not going to yield any advantage to their Dutch competitors was made crystal clear before the end of the year when Parliament renewed the Navigation Act of 1651, which had been rendered void by the Restoration. Even worse was an act adopted early in 1661 restricting fishing rights within ten miles of the shore to Englishmen. The Dutch bribed some high-ranking English politicians in an effort to forestall the renewal of the Navigation Act, but to no avail: a direct appeal to Charles II proved equally ineffectual.

De Witt saw all too clearly that English deeds made hollow Charles II's protestations of his desire for friendship. When the English ministers complained that the Dutch, by negotiating simultaneously with France for an alliance, were not putting Britain's friendship ahead of all others, as the king had urged them to do at Breda and The Hague, the councilor pensionary commented tartly. As long as England will not make a good treaty with us, he told Van Hoorn, we must do all we can to gain France's friendship. If the English are not concerned enough about relations with us to concede our just conditions for an alliance, then there is no hope of good relations between the two countries.

The negotiations of Van Hoorn and Beverweert continued, but with scant prospect of success. It was a sign of Charles's intransigence and his scorn for the Republic that the new envoy he sent to The Hague in June was Sir George Downing, Cromwell's old minister who had made no secret of his hatred for the Dutch. In that attitude Downing did not change a whit, although he had not scrupled in May 1660 to scramble over to the camp of the restored king, winning a baronetcy as his reward.

Once in the Netherlands, the turncoat proved his loyalty to his new master by arranging for the arrest and transport to England of a number of regicides – members of the court that had condemned Charles I to death – who had escaped to Holland after the Restoration. De Witt had met Downing's demands for their arrest by having them warned in time to get away to safety in Germany. But when several of them returned to Rotterdam, where their wives were living, Downing was ready to frustrate De Witt's maneuvers and forestalled further delay. The councilor pensionary did not dare to resist Downing's direct demand, but he was shamed by what he had to do in the interests of his own country, especially after his efforts to win a pardon for the condemned men had failed and they were hanged. Sarcastic thanks to De Witt from Charles II and his chief minister, Clarendon, embittered him, and in reply he emphasized that he had only done the bidding of his masters, the States of Holland.

The controversy over freedom of the seas remained deadlocked. The discussions in London turned to the demands of the English East India Company, which wanted freedom of trade for itself in the lands halfway around the world, or at least lavish compensation for its losses. De Witt was willing to permit specific issues, such as the English claim to the ownership of the Dutch-occupied island of Pulo Run or for indemnities for the families of the victims of the "Amboina massacre," but he stubbornly opposed establishing commissioners with binding powers for cases that ought to be tried before ordinary courts.

By July of 1662 Van Hoorn reported that people in England were talking of another war against the Dutch, rather than of solving the differences between the two countries by negotiation. What the merchants could not achieve by head-on commercial competition, they could attain, it was thought, by defeating the Dutch in armed combat. Even though the king displayed less bellicosity than the people, the chance of a good settlement dimmed with the revival of the old claims against the Dutch East India Company which the Dutch asserted had been extinguished by the terms of the 1654 peace treaty. It was decided at The Hague to make one last stab at conciliation before calling the ambassadors home. This proved successful, at least in the short run, for Downing worked out the terms of a treaty with De Witt. Charles II informed the Dutch of his approval and Downing returned to England to put the final touches on the accord.

The era of good feelings was exceedingly brief. Negotiations hung fire for a year while a new source of antagonism cropped up, the conflicting claims of the Royal African Company and the Dutch West India company to territory and trading rights on the Guinea coast of Africa. De Witt got Dutch naval preparations under way. In addition to the usual steps of increasing the number of ready warships and piling up stocks of naval supplies, he sent a Dordrecht merchant in his confidence, Herman Ghijsen, to England to spy out the state of the English fleet and of the ports where they were based. Ghijsen's description of twenty-five big warships lying at anchor at Chatham, on the Medway river, a tributary of the Thames, was opportune. During the first English war De Witt had worked out with Tromp a strategy of blockading the Thames, the lifeline of English trade and naval power. If it came to war, the maneuver of seizing the mouth of the Thames could be expanded to destruction of the English fleet upstream. Provided, that is, that the Dutch navy was up to its task as it had not been in 1652–4. Despite the demands of diplomacy and domestic politics, De Witt had worked with steady diligence as virtual navy minister for the past decade to assure that the fleet would be ready when needed.

In the summer of 1664 events began to accelerate, each causing the next almost independently of the initiator's intentions. The first move was taken by Admiral Robert Holmes, commanding the Royal African Company's fleet, who seized the fort and island of Cape Verde, on the Guinea coast. The second move was De Witt's. If no action were taken now, he knew, all the talk would have been in vain. On his proposal the States of Holland decided to have secret orders sent immediately to De Ruyter to take his squadron from the Mediterranean to Cape Verde so as to surprise Holmes and recapture the places he had taken. Everything depended upon swiftness and secrecy. De Ruyter could be depended upon to move swiftly, but how could the orders to him be kept secret? To be valid they had to come from the States General, and it was notorious that nothing that happened in the assembly of Their High Mightinesses remained secret from Downing for long.

De Witt and friendly deputies from other provinces worked out an elaborate and subtle scheme of deception in which the States General would adopt the necessary resolution without being aware of what it was doing. Holland's resolution minus the crucial clause was presented by the States General to the "secret committee" for foreign affairs, where De Witt was the dominating personality. The committee thereupon proposed in general terms that a force of twelve ships be sent to the coast of West Africa to protect the possessions of the West India Company, and a resolution to this effect was adopted on August 9. There was no word in it of any specific orders to De Ruyter.

De Witt then presented such orders to the next meeting of the committee as an amplification of the resolution. His manner was lackadaisical, as if nothing important was under consideration, and he chose a moment when members who could not be trusted happened to be gazing out the window. Then on August 11 he presented the committee's report to the States General while a deputy from Friesland who was in the know was in the chair. He repeated the manner of his presentation, speaking in apparently muddled words while his friends continued to converse as if only minor business was being discussed. The other deputies paid no attention to what the councilor pensionary of Holland was saying in such matter-of-fact fashion, and the resolution was adopted without debate. It was necessary to have it signed, however, by the deputy who had been presiding on August 9, who was *not* in the know. He was therefore handed the resolution along with several others, and he signed them all without reading them. The hardest part of the business had been accomplished: the orders to De Ruyter had been adopted with full legal force, and those who might tell Downing did not realize it. The secretary of the Amsterdam admiralty dispatched the orders to the admiral, and they reached him off Malaga on September 1.

Meanwhile it was necessary to ward off suspicion as long as possible so as to give De Ruyter a head start in his expedition. Downing was instructed to find out what the States General had done, and he confronted De Witt with a point-blank question: had orders been sent to De Ruyter to sail to the coast of Africa? The councilor pensionary replied slyly, telling a literal truth while conveying an opposite meaning. Neither the States of Holland nor the admiralties, he said, had sent De Ruyter orders at which the king of England could take umbrage. As for the States General, Their High Mightinesses did nothing that Downing didn't learn about at once, so what did he have to worry about?

Downing fell into the trap, failing to realize that the orders to De Ruyter came from the States General, not Holland or the admiralties, and that De Witt had not said in so many words that the States General had not sent them. He therefore assured his government that no such orders had been sent. It was late October before rumors began to reach London that the Guinea coast had been lost. War became certain, and De Witt was perceived as the mastermind of the operation and the deception. More than ever the fury and the hatred of the English government were directed at him personally as well as at the government of the Republic.

Gulling Downing had been a masterpiece of Machiavellian artifice, made all the more effective because De Witt was not in the habit of using such dupery. De Witt must have enjoyed this personal triumph over Downing, who was the kind of boastful, false

and cruel character he most despised, but he did not put such
feelings on paper. Much more weighty was the responsibility he
had taken upon himself, together with a few friends. The decision
that made war inevitable had been taken by the States General only
in the most narrowly legalistic sense; it was not only the enemy-to-be
that had been cozened, but the government of his own country.
He had repeated his tactics in the Exclusion crisis a decade earlier,
but had used them more skillfully and swiftly. Such high-handed
manipulation of those who were his masters, in law and in fact,
put him in the highest peril should he fail. Considerations of this
kind did not bother him, however. For one thing, he saw the war
as imposed by the English and not of his own doing. Furthermore,
he was a Machiavellian of the subtlest kind, playing the fox only
when it was absolutely necessary and hence avoiding the reputation
of being a follower of the Florentine. But in the war about to begin
he would have to be a lion, leading his country to triumph, or lose
everything. Leadership, after all, was his fundamental task, and it
is revealing that De Witt had taken as his motto the Latin phrase,
ago quod ago, "What I do, I do well."

The war with Britain that began at the end of 1664 did not bring
the disasters of the first war a dozen years earlier. One reason was
the consolidation of the régime of "True Freedom." In 1652
government without a stadholder had been novel and no new leader
had yet emerged to take his place. Another was the careful
reconstruction of the Dutch navy, not merely in numbers but also
in its adaptation to the changed character of war at sea. But these
two elements, essential as they were, might well have failed had
De Witt not achieved a diplomatic triumph in 1662, the renewal
of the alliance with France that had been shattered by the separate
peace of 1648.

The restoration of Charles II in England had compelled the
Dutch government, and De Witt in particular, to rethink their
attitude toward France. During the previous decade their policy
had been little more than one of benign neglect; there had been
little active quest for change but a desire merely to avoid the
extremes of friendship or hostility. Relations with France no longer
concerned the United Provinces in the same life-or-death way that
did those with Britain. The English ambition to make the North
Sea "British" threatened their very existence as a prosperous and

free nation. France, on the other hand, was a trading partner, contributing more or less to Dutch profits but not imperilling Dutch independence. Unless, of course, the French appetite for the southern Low Countries were gratified and the immense French power were brought right to the Republic's doorstep. Dutch friendship with France, and even more the restoration of the old alliance, therefore depended upon the existence of the barrier formed by the Spanish Netherlands.

With the restoration of the monarchy in England the French government as well had to reconsider its relations with The Hague. It was well and good to prefer an anointed king in London to a republican régime, even one headed by a quasi-royal Protector, but it was something else again when the new king had a nephew in the United Provinces who was an aspirant for the stadholdership. If the youthful William III were restored by the efforts of his royal uncle, it seemed obvious that an Anglo-Dutch alliance would result that, as Charles II himself had said, could lay down the law to Europe. With Spanish preponderance finally shattered, that was a role which the French king wanted for himself. Worse, combined Anglo-Dutch wealth and naval power might even endanger France itself, certainly if it attempted to conquer the Spanish Netherlands.

The reopening of the possibility of an alliance between France and the States General was recognized even before the restoration of Charles II was complete. It was no longer satisfactory to have the Dutch represented in Paris by a sick and aging ambassador, William Boreel, who was disliked by the French court and to boot was at heart an Orangist. Since Boreel was a Zeelander by birth and his province traditionally held the right of nomination to the embassy in Paris, there was no chance of replacing him; instead De Witt arranged for an extraordinary embassy to join Boreel and take over from him the real work of negotiation, as was often done when important matters were involved. Its leader was Van Beuningen, who had just moved from the position of pensionary of Amsterdam to membership on its town council. Van Beuningen was probably the ablest political figure in the Republic after De Witt himself. As a member of the Amsterdam delegation to the States of Holland, he had become a close political friend of the councilor pensionary, but during his embassies to Scandinavia he had displayed his independence of judgment and his unwillingness to be a mere instrument of De Witt's will.

The extraordinary mission did not reach Paris until the beginning of 1661. By this time Charles II had shown himself to be anything but a good friend; the only question was how bad a friend he would turn out to be. The need for French amity was inescapable. Yet Van Beuningen – the other members of his embassy did not play a significant role – soon found himself negotiating with a young king ambitious to prove himself to the whole wide world. The Dutch ambassadors, like everyone else, were taken by surprise when Louis XIV immediately after the death of Mazarin, announced that he would govern personally, without a prime minister. The new foreign minister he named, Hugues de Lionne, was astute and experienced, and had been the real architect of the Peace of the Pyrenees on the French side. The heart of that treaty from the point of view of the Dutch had been the continuation of Spanish sovereignty in the southern Low Countries, preserving the barrier between them and France.

The negotiations for a Franco-Dutch alliance threatened to come stuck on the reef of the discriminatory tonnage tax on foreign – that is, mainly Dutch – ships entering and leaving French ports. Van Beuningen's home city, Amsterdam, abhorred the tax but had to accept De Witt's argument that Louis XIV could not be persuaded to abolish the tax by direct confrontation but only by patient negotiations, if at all. When Louis XIV held firm, the Dutch prepared to swallow the tonnage tax, however unhappily: the need for the French alliance was paramount. Louis for his part made a similar concession by according the Dutch the guarantee for their fisheries which they had made a sine qua non for conclusion of an alliance.

A treaty providing for diplomatic and naval–military support for the United Provinces in the event of a war with England was signed in April 1662. At the same time Louis reduced the tonnage tax by half. Both partners in the alliance had bought it, however, at the price of silence upon the issue that divided them most and in which neither was ready to concede to the other – the fate of the Spanish Netherlands. But Philip IV of Spain was still alive and well, and the disposition of his heritage remained a matter of the future. The two allies might work together for the moment, but the fuse on the bomb that could blow up their uneasy friendship was burning on, however slowly.

The French king sealed the new alliance by calling home from

The Hague an ambassador who had made no effort to please the ruling party in the Republic and sending in his place a supple diplomat, Count Geoffroi d'Estrades, who knew the Dutch well, having served in the States army in his early years. In his instructions to D'Estrades, Louis described the Dutch fear of his acquisition of the Spanish Netherlands as a malady for which the obvious cure was abandonment of these ambitions. It was a cure, he added, that he was unwilling to employ. Instead he thought he could win over De Witt by using a remedy that the French often found efficacious elsewhere, bribery. He authorized D'Estrades to offer De Witt an annual gratification of 20,000 to 25,000 écus – seven to nine times what he was paid as councilor pensionary of Holland!

Soon after D'Estrades arrived at The Hague in January 1663, he told De Witt of Louis XIV's desire to reward his friendship suitably. The councilor pensionary's reply was a courteous but total refusal even to consider the offer of money. When it was renewed at royal instruction, De Witt again turned it down. The French king, who doubted almost everyone's virtue but his own, made one more effort to bring De Witt into his pay. He sent D'Estrades a letter in which he assured his ambassador – and the Dutchman for whose eyes it was also intended – that he had no excessive ambitions for new territory. What he was offering to De Witt was nothing more than a sign of his esteem. The king's words are sufficient, the councilor pensionary replied, turning a rebuff into a compliment. D'Estrades urged Louis XIV to desist from pressing the offer further. De Witt's reputation for absolute personal integrity was no fairy tale told by flatterers but plain fact.

Over the next years, so long as French policy toward the Dutch Republic was built upon support of the States party, the French leaders, Louis XIV and Lionne, indulged repeatedly in extravagant praise of De Witt. D'Estrades, a cynic if there ever was one and properly so if judged by his own character, certainly was not taken in: such words were the cheap coin of court flattery transferred to diplomacy. Louis and his foreign ministers knew full well that they praised for a purpose and that they could switch over to vilification in a moment if they were thwarted. Yet, underneath their exaggeration, there seems to have been an element of authentic admiration for De Witt's abilities.

As for the object of their praises, he took them at their true value. He would be a friend of France so long as he thought it to the Dutch advantage, and he preferred not to be the enemy of so powerful a country if it could be avoided. But, during these years, he began to acquire a reputation as a docile instrument of France that would cling to him for the rest of his life.

He was quite aware that the alliance with France rested upon a quaking quagmire of ambiguity so long as there was no settlement of their differences over the future of the Spanish Netherlands. The old saw, *Gallus amicus non vicinus*, "the Frenchman for a friend but not a neighbor," still held true. At the very time De Witt was fending off the blandishments of Louis XIV, he sent Ghijsen, the Dordrecht merchant who was to go a-spying to England a year later, on a more innocuous mission into the Spanish Netherlands. Ghijsen examined the situation of the country and assessed what problems would arise for the Dutch if it passed into French hands. He affirmed the correctness of Amsterdam's fears that Antwerp was better placed for trade and that, once in French hands, it could no longer be barred from seagoing shipping, in spite of the ban imposed by the Treaty of Münster. There were many in the country who even hoped for incorporation into France, for then the Dutch could not maintain the closure of the Scheldt.

A Dutch military engineer followed Ghijsen to the Spanish Netherlands on a mission of explicit espionage, to discover the state of its defenses. His report was that they were in disrepair. The energies that had held France at bay for a decade after the Peace of Münster had been dissipated; the country was a barrier that would have to be defended by outsiders if attacked by France.

De Witt saw all too clearly, however, that military confrontation with France was the last and worst of all options for the Dutch. Every other feasible way to meet the peril had to be tried, or at least considered. De Witt had no doubt that the best solution was cantonment, making the southern Netherlands into an independent country. The plan had foundered in 1633 and again in its brief revival by Mazarin in 1658. Now, three months after D'Estrades's arrival, it was resurrected.

Late in March De Witt made a hurried early-morning visit to the French ambassador to tell him an extraordinary tale. During the previous night two men cloaked to the ears had come to his home. They identified themselves as deputies in the States of Flanders, sent in utter secrecy by six of the principal towns. They reported that the people in the Spanish Netherlands were ready to expel the Spaniards and create a new Republic after the model of the Swiss cantons, provided that the Dutch would support them. Here was an opportunity to revive the cantonment scheme.

The proposal was so perfectly matched to De Witt's hopes, indeed, that historians have accused him of concocting the whole episode in order to draw out Louis XIV's reactions. If so, it was to no avail, for the French king sent no response whatever. De Witt finally admitted to D'Estrades that the Flemish deputies had not returned; he now thought that they might have been agents of the Spanish ambassador, Gamarra, who wanted to embarrass him.

Was the whole tale therefore trumped up? It cannot be argued that De Witt would tell no lies under any circumstances, although he repeatedly affirmed that it was better to tell the truth if possible. Yet one hard fact would seem to confirm his truthfulness in the affair. If Louis XIV had responded favorably, and that was beyond all doubt what De Witt sincerely desired, then he would have been found out if no Flemish deputies showed up for negotiations. His own guess that the Spanish ambassador was trying to explode the new alliance by an act of provocation was probably correct. That would have been right in line with Gamarra's methods.

No sooner had the cantonment idea fizzled out than rumors began to spread that the Spanish princess who was marrying the emperor would be given the southern Netherlands as a dowry. If this happened, Louis XIV could be expected to invade the country, which he had hoped to acquire after the death of Philip IV, on the basis of the claims of his queen, an elder half-sister of Leopold's bride. Fears that the worst was about to happen seized the Dutch public, although De Witt remained skeptical. The rumors provided him, however, with the occasion to try another tack for solving the problem of the future of the Spanish Netherlands. It was to the interest of both France and the United Provinces, he told D'Estrades, to prevent any surprise at their expense by making arrangements in advance to partition the southern Low Countries if and when it would be proper to do so. Holland would secure the assent of the States General, using if need be the hard methods of compulsion that had worked during the Exclusion crisis of 1654 and the recent Baltic war.

This was venturing far out on thin ice, and it was probably at this time that De Witt was called upon, probably by the Delegated

Councilors, the standing executive committee of the States of Holland, to evaluate the various alternatives available to the Dutch, weighing their advantages and disadvantages and their probabilities of success. He drew up a memorandum which remains a model of political analysis, systematic, deeply informed and cool.

The problem the Dutch faced, he showed, was that the better the option, the less likely it was that it could be achieved. Cantonment would be best, but there was very little reason to expect it to happen. The same was true of transfer of the southern Low Countries to the Austrian Habsburgs as a dowry; it would give the United Provinces a safe neighbor, but was very improbable. An armed alliance between the United Provinces, Great Britain and the Empire to defend the Low Countries was undesirable, for it could bring on a war that would put the Dutch in the greatest peril. In any event, the French might have legitimate claims upon the Spanish inheritance. Then the best the Dutch could hope to do would be to persuade Louis XIV to accept partition, allowing the United Provinces to take the regions of Flanders and Brabant just south of the Republic's border. France would then become a next-door neighbor, but at least there would be a buffer zone to absorb the first blow of an attack. Even this the king was unlikely to grant unless he faced a league between the Dutch, the Habsburg states and others (meaning England, with which the United Provinces was sliding into war) which could mass power greater than his own. De Witt favored a line of partition running from Ostend in the west to near Maastricht in the east, which could be advantageous from both a military and a commercial point of view. But if Louis could not be persuaded to accept either cantonment or partition, the Dutch would have to turn to the other options, however difficult.

It was a bleak picture that De Witt painted, but it embodied facts that could not be denied. The Dutch would have to work along the lines he sketched, moving from one option to another as circumstances dictated, but never out of grave peril. It would take political leadership that was both subtle and strong, carrying along the Dutch government assemblies in policies that they did not fully understand and often keenly disliked. The only alternative, the one that the Orangist party urged as a panacea, was to throw the country into the arms of Charles II, elevating his nephew to the stadholdership and the captaincy general on the assumption that this would win the English king's friendship and alliance against France.

The partition proposal met swift opposition from Amsterdam, as always alert to the danger of losing its trade to Antwerp. De Witt thereupon revived the cantonment notion, the best solution if the most difficult to achieve. Louis XIV toyed with the idea, but repeated his assertion that his queen's renunciation of her rights was invalid and demanded territorial compensation if she abandoned them. The discussion went on, although De Witt informed only the States of Holland of their course, not the States General. A counter-proposal from Their Noble Great Mightinesses the States of Holland tried to inveigle Louis XIV into a commitment not to invade the Spanish Netherlands while Philip IV lived, under any pretext or claim whatsoever. Afterwards, France and the United Provinces should act together, without any other power participating, to encourage or if necessary to impose cantonment. A treaty to this effect should be worked out just between the province of Holland and France; once it was agreed upon, Holland would present it to the States General.

The all-inclusive restriction upon French claims was important because a new complication had entered the discussion in July. This was a different "legitimate claim" upon the Spanish Netherlands than the asserted invalidity of the French queen's renunciation. The French court had come to realize that there were too many contradictions among the clauses of the Treaty of the Pyrenees for it to provide a sure legal basis for French acquisition of the Spanish heritage. Instead an obscure law in force in Brabant and other parts of the Spanish Netherlands applying to the estates of a widower who remarried was applied to the situation of the king of Spain. This "right of devolution," as it was called, provided that in such a case, ownership of the estate passed ("devolved," in the legal phrase) to his children by his first marriage, and he retained only a right to the income. Under this principle, the heritage of Philip IV in the Spanish Netherlands belonged to Marie Thérèse, the French queen, for she had been born to his first wife and Carlos, his sole male heir, to his second.

As soon as D'Estrades informed De Witt that the southern Netherlands might be claimed upon this basis, the councilor pensionary stressed the primary legal argument in rebuttal of the French claim over the next four years – that the law of devolution applied to the estates of private persons, not to countries and rulers. Did Louis XIV want to force the Dutch into an alliance with Spain? De Witt asked D'Estrades.

Although the distinction between the king as a public and a private person ("the king's two bodies") was a favorite theme of medieval and early modern political theorists, the actual practice in royal successions had been frankly proprietary, the same rules controlling the heritage of kings and subjects. Indeed, in Spain the monarch was called the "king proprietor," and only in France and a few other countries were special laws in force for the royal succession.

De Witt was not content with his perfunctory affirmation of the inapplicability of the law of devolution to the case of the rulership of the Spanish Netherlands (technically, the king ruled as duke, count or lord in each of its ten provinces). To determine what the precedents actually were, De Witt studied the history of Brabant and the collections of its laws and customs. His conclusion was that the law of devolution applied only to private persons and had not even been used for fiefs held of the crown since the late fifteenth century. If the king of France was going to employ the law of devolution as the basis of his claim to the succession, he would have to prove his consort's case. Louis XIV's reply, in a rejoinder prepared by French legal experts, was that there had been no applicable case since the late fifteenth century, so that the queen's rights stood intact.

The future of the alliance between the United Provinces and France, concluded only the previous year, was now at stake. The evasion of the issue that had made possible the conclusion of the alliance of 1662 was no longer feasible. The two chief protagonists were hardening their positions. De Witt warned D'Estrades that the Dutch would not capitulate to the king's ambitions, and the ambassador, transmitting the message to Louis XIV, warned his master that the councilor pensionary was not easily led and would do what he thought necessary for the interests of his country and his own reputation.

Even before these sharp words reached him, the French king had been provoked by De Witt's threat of a Dutch alliance with Spain. If the Republic took that step, he would retaliate by making an alliance with England, "which I can do from one evening to the next." His admiration for De Witt vanished into thin air. It was

De Witt who needed his friendship, not the other way round, he boasted. It was up to the councilor pensionary and his masters to make their choice. It was the Dutch, not he, who rejected cantonment, which would have solved all problems between the two countries.

De Witt now sought to persuade the leaders of Amsterdam and other towns in Holland to approve terms acceptable to Louis XIV, but in vain. Worse, Gamarra found receptive ears when he resumed his arguments for a defensive league of the seventeen provinces of the Low Countries, that is, both the Spanish and Dutch Netherlands. Finally, in April 1664, Louis XIV informed De Witt through D'Estrades that he had decided to keep his options open and not sacrifice his future opportunities for the present alliance with the Dutch.

As the threat of war with England loomed ever larger for the Dutch, their need for the French alliance became all the greater. The last hope of keeping it intact was entrusted to Van Beuningen, although during his embassy in 1660–1 Louis XIV had found the Amsterdammer unpleasantly outspoken in his suspicions of French aspirations. He hastened to France after De Ruyter had been sent to the African coast. Van Beuningen soon became unpleasantly aware of the French expectation that the Dutch would fail Louis XIV utterly when the time came for him to act upon the queen's rights.

The war with England began with no certainty that France would in fact honor its alliance with the United Provinces. And without French help the odds on a Dutch victory would be greatly reduced. If the Dutch were defeated, "True Freedom," government by the States without a stadholder, could be expected to topple. De Witt's task was now, above all things, to prevent a repetition of the humiliation of the Peace of Westminster ten years before.

For all the immense and perilous perplexities of the Dutch political situation, there was one battle that De Witt did not have to fight. His leadership as councilor pensionary was taken for granted. When he had been reelected for a new five-year term in 1658, he had not only requested permission of the burgomasters and council of Dordrecht to accept but he had also indicated his readiness to return to his post as pensionary of Dordrecht if they called him back. On his second reelection in 1663 he did not even discuss a possible return, and the council gave him leave for as long as he would be elected councilor pensionary. The States of Holland for their part expanded the powers entrusted to him in his instructions to correspond more closely to those which he actually exercised. They also gave him an act of indemnity for whatever he would do in office and renewed the promise made in 1658 that whenever he retired he would have a seat in one of the courts of justice of the province. His salary had been supplemented in 1660 when he was given the two remunerative sinecures that had been held by Cats since his resignation in 1651.

De Witt continued to guide the States party in the towns and the provinces. Dordrecht gave him trouble because he had ties to both factions that struggled for control of the town; it presented, in fact, the scene of a little internecine war in which almost all those involved were related to all the others. De Witt did his b it to calm the angry combatants, while helping those most closel y allied to him as much as he could. Eventually compromises were achieved, but some of the ill will toward him and his brother Cornelius persisted. Amsterdam, stubbornly self-willed as always, was nonetheless on good terms with De Witt so long as Zuidpolsbroek lived, but on his death in 1664 leadership passed to a young and vigorous man, Gillis Valckenier, who was less ready than Zuidpolsbroek had been to work things out in informal discussions with the councilor pensionary.

Relations with the lesser provinces ran fairly smoothly during these years, with the exception of Holland's sister province Zeeland. There the commitment to the cause of the Prince of Orange was strong, and De Witt found in Zeeland's councilor pensionary, Adrian Veth, both a regular correspondent and a stubborn opponent when it came to discussions of the future of William III.

The claims of the Prince of Orange to high office had become the paramount political issue within the Republic with the restoration of Charles II in England. No longer could De Witt and the adherents of the "True Freedom" assume that they could forever hold off the partisans of the Prince of Orange and perhaps finally dispel the bad dream of his restoration. The councilor pensionary henceforth faced a problem that would perplex and bedevil him to his very last days. Something would have to be yielded to the insistence of the English king that friendship with him required giving the offices of his forefathers to the Prince of Orange: but how much could be sacrificed without destroying the dominance of the "True Freedom"? De Witt's thoughts ran in the direction of eventually giving military command to William III when he came of age, but refusing him the political leadership embodied in the stadholderate. This was not as desirable as total exclusion, but at least it accorded with the long tradition of the subordination of the captaincy general to the civil authority. If this were to be done without endangering the independence of the Dutch Republic, however, it was essential that the Prince be spiritually formed during the crucial years of his youth, just beginning, in these traditions, and that he be taken from the hands of the friends of England who dominated his little court.

It was also essential that the broad, deep but still inchoate forces of Orangism in the country should be prevented from imposing William upon the government either by legal means, outvoting the States party in town councils and States assemblies, or by the weapon of popular riot that was the sole effective way for the mass of the population to influence the regents. Princess Mary had been most reluctant to call upon the latter instrument of political struggle, both because it was the very epitome of all that she despised and feared in her homeland and because she knew that if employed without achieving a victory it could lead to the outlawry of her party and perhaps even to the expulsion of the Prince from the United Provinces. This was a view shared by Princess Amalia, who agreed with her daughter-in-law in little else. Both looked instead solely to the influence of Charles II to bring about William III's advancement.

The Orangists' trust in the king of England to make their cause his own – indeed, to make it inseparable from it – was misplaced. They had been steadfast in their support of the Stuart pretender during the decade of his exile, and they expected him to be as firm for William, in simple recognition of kinship. It was their mistake, wrote the chronicler Abraham de Wicquefort, to act "as if kings had relatives and took any interest into consideration but their own." The Orangist partisans failed to read the meaning of Charles's decision to send Downing, who had been Cromwell's envoy in The Hague, back to the United Provinces to speak for him. Downing may have been a turncoat, but he was absolutely

faithful to his own passionate hatred of the Dutch. He gladly
served Charles II when the king continued the Protector's policy
of international aggrandizement. For Charles his nephew's cause
was not only subordinate to his own interests; it was also an
instrument in advancing them. Yet the unrelenting trust of the
Orangists in the monarch across the North Sea became a fundamental fact of Dutch politics for the next dozen years.

The leadership of the Orangist party fell by the force of events
into the hands of the Princess Royal, Mary Stuart. Her principal
rivals, the Princess Dowager, Amalia van Solms, and Count
William Frederick, the stadholder in Friesland, had to work with
her at least for the moment. They all put first the "designation"
of the Prince of Orange. This meant his election at once to one
or all of the offices held by his father, in particular the captaincy
general, although his mother and grandmother both preferred not
to have William Frederick named as his lieutenant.

The situation was brought to a head when the Nijmegen quarter
of Gelderland voted a resolution urging William's election as
captain general by the States General, with two field marshals
serving as his lieutenants. When Mary called upon De Witt to
support the proposal, the councilor pensionary explained in detail
to her a line of policy that he had only hinted at when Charles II
had been in The Hague. He did not rule out the Prince's eventual
election as captain general but emphasized that it had to be a freely
bestowed gift of the Dutch sovereigns. The Prince would first have
to learn to love the Dutch Republic and to know its institutions
and customs. He would be eligible when he would become of age
and showed his ability; to Mary this meant denying her son his
birthright. De Witt also warned her not to attempt to use the other
provinces to force a decision upon Holland; that would be to repeat
the mistake of William II. He suggested that she accept the
proposal which he had discussed with Zuidpolsbroek, that the
States of Holland take responsibility for the education of the Prince
in a spirit that would prepare him for office, while at the same time
providing him with an annual pension.

Mary did not reply at once. At the end of July, however, she
informed the States of Holland that she was going to England to
see her brother and asked them to make William a "Child of State"
to be educated for readiness to assume his father's offices – the
stadholdership therefore no less than the captaincy general – when

he came of age. De Witt had won. A commission was named, with the councilor pensionary as its key member, to undertake the education of the Prince. At the same time Mary was asked to use her good offices during her visit to England on behalf of an alliance between the United Provinces and Great Britain.

Mary had chosen to play first the strongest card in Dutch politics, the province of Holland. But the other provinces, and notably Zeeland, were not ready to accept inferior status when it came to the Prince of Orange. The States of Zeeland almost at once adopted a resolution calling for William's designation as both captain general and stadholder. The Hollanders at first thought the initiative had come from Charles II, but in fact it was Mary who was behind the action of the Middelburg assembly. She wanted the issue settled before she left for England. She would use Holland but not rely on its sole generosity. She was right. De Witt had told Oudart, Charles II's private secretary, that the States of Holland would not allow their hand to be forced.

His boast was more easily spoken than achieved, however. Early in September a deputation came to The Hague from the States of Zeeland to urge the sister assembly in Holland to designate William III as their common stadholder and captain general, as had been done with all previous Princes of Orange. The States of Holland split, with the Nobility and two towns favoring acceptance and several others wanting no action. The Zeeland proposal helped Mary all the same. When Charles II indicated that he was not demanding as much for his nephew as the Zeelanders wanted, the States of Holland voted on September 15 to grant Mary's request to undertake the education of her son "as a worthy pledge and instrument of great hope." The next day they removed the Act of Exclusion from the law books of Holland. The great compromise seemed to be working, and Mary, having accepted Holland's decision to make her son a "Child of State" – more specifically, a child of Holland – sailed to England.

De Witt now sought to use Charles II's prestige against his domestic opponents who had always blamed him for the Act of Exclusion. Through Beverweert he asked for the return of the original document of the act that had been transmitted to Cromwell. This Charles II willingly did. He had one of the secretaries of state check the papers of Cromwell and the others involved and what they found confirmed that Cromwell had taken the initiative in the

Exclusion affair. Charles II nonetheless refused to issue a formal statement that De Witt and the Dutch ambassadors in 1654 had not been the authors of the Exclusion, although he was ready to let the secretary of state issue a declaration to this effect. De Witt was disappointed. It was only a royal declaration that would brand as untrue the old tale of the responsibility of Van Beverningk and himself, the councilor pensionary informed Beverweert.

De Witt's attention now shifted to the formation of the committee responsible for the education of the Prince of Orange. Just before her departure, Mary sent her nominations for its members. They were all Hollanders, including De Witt himself, Zuidpolsbroek and Beverweert as well as three others. There was fury in the Orangist camp at the absence of any members from Leiden, where the Prince had been living, or from Zeeland, which had taken the initiative for the "designation," or anyone representing Amalia van Solms. The States of Zeeland protested their exclusion to Mary, but Amalia demanded that the States of Holland name a wholly different committee. Mary's nominees nonetheless were formally appointed on October 4. In practice the committee meant De Witt, on whom the principal direct tasks of education would fall.

The committee began its preparatory work at once, reporting its decisions to Mary through Beverweert, who remained in London. Its first problem was political, to beat off the insistent demands of the Princess Dowager that, as co-guardian of the Prince, she share in the nomination of the members of the committee. Mary stood by her own nominations and also approved the plan of education drawn up by the committee. The Prince would be taught not only the rights and customs of the country but also the character and humor of its people – which meant the ideology of the "True Freedom." He would be taken from Leiden, which was permeated with Orangist feeling, to reside at The Hague in the Binnenhof. William of Nassau–Zuilestein would be replaced as the Prince's governor by someone acceptable to the States of Holland.

Mary balked at the dismissal of Zuilestein, and De Witt at once reminded her that Holland had not yet agreed to pay for the Prince's upkeep, which had been draining the limited resources of the House of Orange. Essentially she had to decide between letting her son be formed as a Dutchman in the tradition of the Republic, and keeping him an Englishman of her own stock and loyalties at her own expense.

It was a decision Mary never had to make. She came down with smallpox just before year's end and died on January 3, 1661 (December 24, 1660 in the "Old Style" dating used in England). Her testament was a bomb that destroyed the collaboration between the House of Orange and De Witt that had evolved since her brother's restoration. Charles II was named to succeed her as her son's guardian, with the injunction to use his influence on his nephew's behalf. De Witt made a last-minute attempt to salvage the principle of compromise. If Charles II and Amalia unconditionally and unreservedly granted the States of Holland the education of the Prince of Orange, the committee would continue with its work; otherwise Holland would drop the whole business and let the king and the Princess Dowager settle their dispute by themselves. For De Witt it was essential that the Prince's education be kept out of the king's hands. The committee must be able to work on its own without Charles II's involvement.

The hardening of the English attitude was indicated by the surprising inability of the lord chancellor to find the original documents of the Exclusion affair which De Witt knew would prove his own good faith in it. It was clear, as De Witt heard through private channels, that there was every intention of using these papers against him when the right time came. Evidence against him was being assembled. By the end of March the committee saw nothing left for it to do and proposed its own dissolution if the Prince's guardians did not accept Holland's terms. Downing's return to The Hague augured badly and, at the end of September, the States of Holland laid down all responsibility for the Prince's education and disbanded the committee.

The Orangist movement fell into disarray such as had prevailed before 1660, but the hope persisted that with the aid of the king across the water it would be possible, sooner or later, to put the Prince into office. De Witt himself saw that the exclusion of William III could not be maintained forever, but was satisfied if the moment of decision could be put off into the distant future.

This policy was made easier because Charles II soon lost interest in his nephew's cause, which Amalia now had to uphold alone. She recognized that it was useless to put her reliance upon a ruler who was moving to open enmity with the Dutch and realized that it was therefore necessary to cultivate the ruling party in Holland. She expected no gain for her grandson from the impending war between England and the Dutch Republic.

7

The humbling of the foe
1665–1667

De Ruyter reached the Guinea coast in October 1664. With the advantage of surprise he accomplished the mission of reconquest during the next five months. The English responded with a surprise attack of their own. On December 29 an English force pounced on a Dutch convoy of merchantmen returning from Smyrna as it passed before Cadiz, but the minuscule squadron of defenders won the day. In England orders went out to seize all Dutch ships in English harbors, or found at sea, and more than 130 were taken. The formal declaration of war against the United Provinces did not come until March 4, 1665, almost as an afterthought.

De Witt and the country he led were ready for the great challenge. During the decade since 1654 the navy had been built up in numbers and quality by the steady exertions of the councilor pensionary and the admiralties. As during the previous war with England, he was determined to use the fleet with strategic boldness. The English heard from a spy as early as 1662 that De Witt had conceived a plan to throttle their commercial and naval power by a blockade of the Thames. They might have taken this warning more seriously had they known what Herman Ghijsen was up to when he had gone on his own spying mission in May 1664 to Rochester and Chatham. But before such a grand stroke of war could be attempted, the Dutch would have to establish their dominance in the North Sea. This would not be easy to achieve, however, for Charles II had not neglected his navy and his brother, the duke of York, was a lord high admiral of energy and resolution.

De Witt took the preparation of the Dutch fleet into his own hands as much as possible. He was the principal member of the naval committee of the States General, which went to Texel with full powers to take all necessary steps and to give final orders to the admirals. He put these duties ahead of his ordinary work in

The Hague, which he confidently left to his cousin Nicholas Vivien, who as Dordrecht's pensionary-deputy replaced him in his absence. Complicated and difficult as the political situation was to become during the next two and a half years, De Witt remained convinced that even the deftest manipulations of politics, domestic or foreign, would fail unless the English were defeated at sea. In wartime war became not the master of politics but its paramount instrument.

For the sake of effective conduct of the war, De Witt was willing to innovate. Getting crews in adequate numbers was difficult. The sailors did not sign up until they had run out of all their money, and then they held out for higher pay as the admiralties competed with each other in the wages they offered. De Witt was dismayed, yet he was not wholly unsympathetic to the sailors' plight. He favored putting them on year-round duty rather than paying off the bulk of the crews in the autumn. He was moved less by considerations of compassion, however, than by the desire to have the fleet readier to sail in the spring, as well as by his calculations that the cost would be no greater.

He proposed a kind of maritime conscription of the coastal villages, which would be required to furnish crews in exchange for tax relief. He admitted that this would be a violation of one of the traditional liberties of the Dutch, but it was one made necessary by the defense of these very liberties, and he added that, in fairness, the inland towns should be placed under similar compulsion, and that the obligation should fall upon all, not just upon the poor. His proposal, however far-seeing, was rejected out of hand by the States of Holland. Crews continued to be recruited as volunteers, if men driven by the direst poverty can be so described.

De Witt was more successful with another innovation, but one without broad political consequences. He chafed at the extreme caution of the pilots who would bring out the ships anchored in the Texel roadstead at the head of the Zuider Zee only through the channel called the Land's Deep and then only when the winds blew from the north or northeast. They distrusted the alternate channels, the Slenk and the Spaniards' Gate, as too shallow. In May De Witt ordered the fleet to sail through the Land's Deep even when the wind was somewhat unfavorable, but first he sounded the channel himself. Two months later, after the fleet had returned for repairs following a lost battle, he decided to see for himself whether the Spaniards' Gate could be used. He went out in a rowboat and watched while the sailors sounded the channel with the lead, discovering that it was now deep enough for even the biggest ships. There was general astonishment at the landlubber who beat the experts at their own game, but also no little resentment.

The most important problem, however, was the leadership of the fleet. It was still under the command of Obdam, who had been kept in command despite his failures during the Baltic war because there had been no politically reliable admiral at hand to replace him. De Ruyter, whom De Witt had come to trust and admire, was far away, first off Africa and then in March 1665 sent to the Antilles. When Obdam dawdled in bringing out the fleet, De Witt called for an end to delays. Obdam took the remark as implying he was a coward and angrily told the councilor pensionary he would return from battle covered either with laurel or cypress, triumphant or dead. It was not Obdam's courage that De Witt doubted but his competence. He suggested that the States General send deputies to sea with the fleet who, acting with full powers from Their High Mightinesses, could stiffen the resolve of the tactical commanders and compel them to act as one. He proposed to go himself as one of the deputies. Both suggestions were turned down. Obdam carried strict orders but no intrusive deputies with him as he sailed across the North Sea to confront the enemy.

On June 13, the two fleets met off Lowestoft. The Dutch lost sixteen ships sunk or taken, and the rest fled back across the North Sea. Obdam, true to his promise, had died when his flagship blew up during single combat with the duke of York's flagship. Had De Witt been with him, he too would have sunk beneath the waves and this book would end here. Or, more likely, it would never have been written, for the most significant achievements of the councilor pensionary's career still lay before him. How the war would have gone if he had died at Lowestoft, no one can tell with certainty, although it is hard to see how the Dutch could have held out without De Witt's implacable determination and exceptional intelligence. History fortunately records what happened, not what might have been, and we may go on with our tale.

Two days later De Witt went to Texel again to join other members of the naval committee in their work of rebuilding and reequipping the fleet. On the way he displayed the same contempt for personal danger that he had shown in Middelburg more than a decade before, while still only Dordrecht's pensionary. Traveling by land along the shore to Den Helder, he saw the English fleet on the horizon and two English frigates chasing nine Dutch ships close to land. When the Dutch vessels ran aground, he boarded one and sailed to safety after the ships had floated off with the tide.

At Texel there was a clash of wills between, on the one side, the vice admiral, Martin Tromp's son Cornelius, and the council of war he headed, and on the other the naval committee led by De Witt, over the treatment of captains accused of disobeying orders and fleeing during the battle. The council of war did not want to condemn fellow-officers to death, as the civil authorities demanded: finally, given explicit orders to proceed, it condemned three to death and punished five others with dishonorable discharge or exile. For De Witt, a legal trial was one thing, lynch justice another. He was outraged when a mob in Den Briel assaulted the elderly admiral John Evertsen after he came ashore, even though he had fought well. Disregarding Evertsen's passionate Orangism, De Witt arranged Evertsen's honorable retirement.

Called back to The Hague after almost a month's absence, De Witt continued to assert the priority of winning at sea over managing the business of politics at home. With Obdam's death and De Ruyter's absence in the Caribbean, Tromp became the only feasible candidate for the fleet command, despite his headstrong tactics (his Orangism was less of a problem). De Witt's proposal for sending commissioners from the States General with the fleet now won approval. Three deputies were named, De Witt, Rutger Huygens of Gelderland and John Boreel of Zeeland. Tromp accepted the unprecedented arrangement coolly but without open protest. The task of the commissioners was to restrain Tromp's impetuosity while at the same time spurring his captains to greater boldness. This task in reality fell to De Witt, for his fellow-commissioners left the work to him "alone and absolutely," as he admitted to his sister Johanna. This was one of the very rare occasions when he dropped the mask of humble servant of the States of Holland and boasted of his own prowess.

Luckily, before the fragile collaboration of De Witt and Tromp could be tested in the flames of combat, a better solution for the problem of the naval command presented itself in August 1665 with the return of De Ruyter. At De Witt's suggestion, the States General named him in place of Tromp; the States of Holland appointed him as the province's own lieutenant admiral, although he was a Zeelander. Tromp, bitter at his demotion, threatened to resign, but was commanded by the States of Holland to remain as second in command or face trial, and he chose to stay.

Within a few days the fleet sailed out from Texel roadstead, using the Spaniards' Gate. The fleet commissioners were present when the new admiral called a council of all his captains. De Witt and Huygens, to display the supremacy of Their High Mightinesses whom they represented in their persons, drew laughter when they appeared in elaborate costumes all covered with gold and silver. Boreel alone escaped the mockery because he wore the ordinary black garb of Dutch regents, as De Witt had always done ashore. It was a mistake of judgment De Witt did not repeat, and he and his fellow-deputies lived simply in cramped quarters in a single cabin. Huygens, who at nearly eighty years of age was twice as old as De Witt, coped best with the discomforts. The councilor pensionary, a prey to seasickness, slept in a special hammock hanging from a large sphere that had been devised for him by the scientist Christian Huygens. De Witt was all too evidently a landlubber, but De Ruyter was pleased to see how quickly he learned about ships and their sailing, and their collaboration became easy and close.

During the next month De Witt experienced the fickleness of the sea, its relaxing charm when the weather was fair and its fierceness in a storm. The fleet sailed to the coast of Norway to convoy home a gaggle of merchantmen that had been pursued by the English into the neutral port of Bergen. At first contrary winds kept the Dutch warships out to sea, and De Witt enjoyed watching porpoises at play and a surfacing whale. When the wind changed, the merchant ships escaped and began the return home under escort. On the way a great storm blew up for four days and scattered the convoy. Although De Ruyter's flagship, the *Delffland*, proved to be a rough-sailing vessel, De Witt stood for hours on the poopdeck, watching with the lookout for strayed ships and encouraging the sailors with fair words. When the storm subsided, it became clear that many ships had been lost.

More than ever, De Witt was determined to remain with the fleet, no matter how vigorous the entreaties from Vivien and others to return to take in hand the pressing political problems. The first need, he replied, was to prepare the fleet so that an encounter with the English would not result in disaster worse than that inflicted by the storm. He could be spared at home, where others could easily do his political work, but was needed where he was. The sailors, even the flag officers, were better at carrying out orders than at conceiving complex plans in an ever-changing situation. Decisions had to be taken quickly and without hesitation. Both his fellow-deputies and De Ruyter wanted him to stay.

There was no doubt an element of supreme self-confidence, perhaps of vanity, in these remarks, but they touched upon one of the most subtle problems of the relationship between political authority and military command. It was the tradition on land that the sovereign commanded his armies in person, although it was rare that any king was himself a great captain: Frederick the Great a century later and then Napoleon I were the great exceptions, and even with them the question of whether battle served politics, or the reverse, was never really solved. In any case, never before – and, indeed, never again – was the attempt made to bring together political and military decision-making at sea, even though not in a single hand. It says much for the wisdom and character of De Ruyter, the greatest sailor of his age, that he worked so well with De Witt, a landsman and a politician, and that they became firm friends.

There may be another, less obvious element in De Witt's persistent refusal to come back to The Hague. "The winds are beyond our power and control," he admitted, confirming that *l'homme propose, mais Dieu dispose* (man proposes, but God disposes). What he did not say to Vivien, and may not even have worked out in his own mind, was that political affairs are the responsibility of man, but in their own puzzling complexity escape control no less than the great wager of battle. It was easier, paradoxically, for him to act fearlessly and accept immense risks in combat, where the decision was God's, than in the perplexing unpredictability of matters of state. Politics was an "uncertain element" no less than the sea.

A second storm did not shatter De Witt's dream of destroying the enemy. He kept the fleet out until early November despite the reluctance of the admirals to face the worsening weather. He continued to hanker after battle, but the English avoided confrontation. Boreel, insistent that the fleet be brought in, lost his patience and his temper in a midnight argument with De Witt, but got his way.

The naval war had not gone anywhere near as well as the councilor pensionary had hoped, but at least it was the war which he had expected and for which he had prepared. What he had not anticipated was that it provided an opportunity for a land invasion by a German princeling that made Dutchmen hang their heads with shame before it fizzled out. The invader was a "priest in armor," Bernhard von Galen, bishop of Münster. A hard-fisted ruler of his principality, Galen saw in the Anglo-Dutch war an opportunity to make good his ambition not only to expel the Dutch garrisons in the lower Rhineland but also to seize the towns he claimed in neighboring Overijssel. He snapped up an offer of an offensive alliance brought him by the English resident in Brussels, Sir William Temple. England, able to fight the Dutch only at sea, would furnish him with subsidies for an army of invasion of the Republic.

The forces that would have to withstand the invasion were anything but ready. Many companies of troops had been sent aboard the fleet to serve as marines, but the problem lay far deeper. The army of the States, built up by Princes Maurice and Frederick Henry into a model for Europe, had fallen on hard days of neglect after the conclusion of peace with Spain (at Galen's city of Münster!). The régime of the "True Freedom" had no territorial ambitions beyond the Dutch frontiers and saw the army's task as purely defensive. The number of soldiers was reduced, their training neglected, and their arms were inadequate. It was a mercenary army – as were all contemporary armies – but few Dutchmen served in the ranks and the officers were a medley of Dutchmen, Frenchmen, Scots and Englishmen (and not all of these latter had left the States' service with the declaration of war by their king, since they did not fight troops of their own nationality). Worse if anything was the absence of able leadership. De Witt and the regents of Holland had not given their full trust to any of the principal commanders since the death of Brederode in 1655. For the councilor pensionary, the army had become less an instrument of national policy, like the navy, than a potential subverter of the civil authority, as in the never-forgotten summer of 1650. The very mercenary character of the army brought a kind of reassurance. It served for pay, and the principal paymaster was the States of Holland. Furthermore, if the army had to be expanded, De Witt was confident that the heavy purses of Holland could quickly secure all needed troops. He had no sense for the work of a commander in organizing and giving spirit to a combat army; what he remembered of the Princes of Orange was less their achievement in that field than their political ambitions.

Yet it was to the House of Orange that, in the face of imminent invasion, he turned for a commanding general. John Maurice, count of Nassau–Siegen, was a cousin of the Prince of Orange, but like Beverweert he had early come to terms with the new order of the "True Freedom." He had made his reputation as a fine administrator while governor of Dutch Brazil before its reconquest by the Portuguese. Now, however, he was past sixty years of age, becoming lethargic, and he had not commanded troops in battle for two decades.

He had little more than a month to prepare for defense against the invasion, which came in late September. A small number of cavalry and infantry regiments that had just been paid off by the prince–bishop of Osnabrück, Ernst August of the House of Brunswick–Lüneburg, were taken into the Dutch service. An alliance had been signed with the dukes of that House just as Galen issued an ultimatum to the States General.

Galen did not even wait for its rejection to send his troops into the eastern provinces of Overijssel and Twente, making deep penetrations during the first two weeks. Further north, an attempt was made to capture the bridgehead on the Ems river where the English might land troops but it failed. John Maurice was able to do no more than hold out on the west bank of the IJssel river while the bigger fortified towns fought off the invaders. The chronicle writer Lieuwe van Aitzema scornfully wrote that the Republic of the United Provinces, whose heraldic symbol was a lion, had been "bitten by a mouse." There was laughter at the French court over the embarrassment of the Dutch, but Louis XIV held faithful to his alliance with them.

De Witt sent reassurances and encouragement even before he came ashore from the fleet in November. The hopes of the councilor pensionary lay in what could be accomplished together with a French army of assistance commanded by General Pradel which had just arrived in the United Provinces. Alas, the French soldiers, ill supplied by the hard-pressed Dutch, were more active in stealing from the Dutch peasants than in fighting the enemy. John Maurice proved to be exasperatingly sluggish, despite De Witt's repeated pleas for blows against Galen even in mid-winter. It was not the military operations of the States army and its French auxiliaries that compelled Galen to withdraw from the Netherlands but the failure of the English to send their promised subsidies in time. A church mouse is proverbially poor, and Galen could no longer pay his little army. De Witt hoped that the Dutch troops who moved across the IJssel would be able to carry the war into Galen's own territory, but they were themselves short of supplies and stopped at the frontier.

De Witt got a dressing down from D'Estrades, the French ambassador who was a soldier no less than a diplomat, for the inadequacies of the Dutch land forces. What the States army needed most of all was vigorous, experienced command. There was no suitable Dutchman for the chief post of command, and the great French marshal, Turenne, who had not yet forsaken his Huguenot faith, was approached. He preferred, however, to remain in the service of Louis XIV, who admired and cosseted him. De Witt had to make do with John Maurice. Fortunately, there was no need to test his flagging abilities again, for diplomacy patched up a peace with Galen in April. The bishop stayed neutral during the remaining years of the Anglo-Dutch war, but he did not forget his initial successes against the Dutch Republic and the possibility of repeating them on a far larger scale if and when the States General lost French support. De Witt did not take to heart the warning that the brief success of the puny invasion represented. The army drifted out of his immediate concerns and returned to its drowsy existence as the neglected sluggard of the Dutch defenses. Only the question of its command gnawed at De Witt's attention, and this mainly because of political dangers represented by William III as its eventual captain general.

De Witt concentrated his endeavors upon the continuing war with England. The swirling events of the naval struggle and the intricate proceedings of politics, domestic and foreign, coincided in time, each profoundly affecting the other, but, for the sake of clarity, we continue our tale by telling first the story of the war and then that of politics. Needless to say, these events were not experienced with such perfect discontinuity by the participants and least of all by De Witt, who had to cope with urgent crises of all kinds as they came, all helter-skelter.

The navy fought with one huge advantage, the participation of the French fleet. For Louis XIV declared war upon England in January 1666 in belated fulfilment of his alliance with the States General. Twenty to thirty French ships would usefully fill out the Dutch fleet, but De Witt was determined that the Dutch navy should be rebuilt to such strength that it could face the enemy alone and defeat him. Nor would he concede its command to a French admiral, however much the king of France would press the claims of royal precedence. The commanding admiral would be De Ruyter, who had been so impressive the year before that the councilor pensionary saw no need for a deputation of commissioners to accompany him in the 1666 operations. The naval committee, with De Witt as usual its workhorse and impelling spirit, confined its activity to preparing the fleet and to giving general instructions for its use. These were presented to De Ruyter by De Witt on June 2 aboard the new flagship, significantly given the name *De Zeven Provinciën* ("The Seven Provinces"). He should seek out and attack the enemy, with the French squadron under the duke of Beaufort if it came in time, but otherwise with the Dutch forces alone. It was well that this proviso was included, for Beaufort brought his squadron up from the Mediterranean with such deliberate dawdling – ordered by Louis XIV, who wished to give the least possible offence to Charles II – that he did not join up with De Ruyter until a year later.

The Dutch fleet sailed off to battle on June 7 and met the enemy on June 11 off North Foreland. Four days long the two fleets, both well-prepared and well-commanded, fought each other until finally the mauled English drew off, taking advantage of a fog. Their losses were much heavier than those of the Dutch, although not so great as the four-to-one ratio reported to De Witt. Still this "Four Days Battle," as it has gone down in history, was the greatest victory that the Dutch had ever gained over the English. Even so, it was not sufficient to bring the war to an end. The English had been badly hurt but not reduced to helplessness, and many of the Dutch vessels needed to have their damage repaired before they could put to sea once more. De Witt made this his first task, and by July 3 the whole fleet numbered eighty-eight fighting ships.

The councilor pensionary, his great strategic plan for bringing the war to an end always in mind, now had De Ruyter seek not just battle but a landing in the Thames river estuary that would shatter the English hope of eventual victory. He pressed De Ruyter very hard not to fear the shoals of the King's Channel and to act quickly, before the English rebuilt their fleet. Once away from the domineering presence of the councilor pensionary, the admirals and the pilots balked before the dreaded perils of the mouth of the Thames.

When another battle began on August 4, it was fought on the open North Sea, so that the distant thunder of cannons could be heard even in The Hague. This time the English had the better of the Dutch in a battle that ran into the next day. De Witt was more certain than ever that the best way to defeat and destroy the English fleet was at its bases within the Thames estuary. Had this been done in June after the Four Days Battle, no Two Days Battle to undo that victory would have occurred. If the sea was the "uncertain element," the strategy of a landing could tame it.

De Ruyter brought his battered fleet into the shelter of the Scheldt for repairs. De Witt, accompanied only by a fellow-member of the naval committee from Utrecht, raced down to the shore of Zeeland to urge on the work of refitting. Impatient to reach the admiral, they took a yacht that used the searoad instead of the safer but slower inner waterways. They came within sight of the English fleet off Schouwen, but the councilor pensionary denied that they had been in danger: they had a small, flat-bottomed ship that could run in through the shallows where the English would not dare go.

When they boarded De Ruyter's flagship, they discovered that the true crisis in the fleet was not material damage – that was fairly small – but a sharp clash between De Ruyter and Tromp. The admiral accused his second-in-command of having sailed away when his chief was engaged in the principal action of the battle. De Witt, despite his detestation of Tromp's politics and personality, did not want to lose his undoubted naval talents. He pounded with words at the two flag officers until they signed a settlement, but this did not stick. Tromp insisted on complaining directly to Their High Mightinesses that it was De Ruyter who had left his fellow-admirals in the lurch. Their Noble Great Mightinesses the States of Holland angrily dismissed Tromp from their service, though De Witt had succeeded in patching up a fresh reconciliation. Tromp thereupon resigned his commission from the States General as a captain, going ashore and abandoning his command in the middle of the war. His place as lieutenant admiral was given to Baron William Joseph van Gendt, a nobleman from Gelderland who was the colonel of the marine regiment and worked well with both De Ruyter and De Witt. The councilor pensionary was astounded and pleased when the change was accomplished with only brief minor disturbances among the sailors, among whom Tromp was immensely popular.

De Witt's eagerness for a decision by battle continued undiminished. Early in September he urged De Ruyter to attack the English ships which were refitting in Sole Bay. Before the assault could be made, sickness struck heavily at the Dutch fleet, disabling De Ruyter himself, and the ships were called back to port. Yet the finger of God touched now on land no less dramatically and decisively than in the clash of ships. In mid-September the Great Fire ravaged London. De Witt, eager for a chance to play a "bit of mischief" on the English confounded by the conflagration, went out as a one-man delegation to see De Ruyter aboard his flagship. He found the admiral so weakened by tertian fever that he had to be sent ashore to recover. The fleet command passed to vice admiral Aert van Nes, but under the direction of De Witt. For several weeks the fleet continued to seek out the English, but their ships remained safe within the Thames. De Witt had to put off to 1667 his dream of a victory so decisive that Charles II could not evade making peace.

The councilor pensionary sent out spies to detect the weak places in the English defenses, but kept what he had in mind as a secret shared only with his brother and a few other confidants. The fleet was brought to combat strength again, but De Witt knew that the enterprise he was planning required the utmost of skill and determination for its success. He would entrust it to no single admiral, not even to De Ruyter who had regained his health. He himself could not go with the fleet, because the expected French invasion of the Spanish Netherlands – the great complication in all his diplomatic calculations – required his presence in The Hague. Instead Cornelius de Witt was named as a one-man delegation to the fleet by States General. The councilor pensionary's brother would be his other self aboard the flagship, for even if he lacked John's insight and imagination, he matched him in strength of will, and he knew his brother's goal.

The fleet that sailed out of Texel roadstead on June 6 was not as large as that which had gone into battle on the open sea during the years just past, but it was strong in what mattered – the number of big, heavily-gunned ships. It was now safe to reveal the planned operation to the war council, and they heard that their task would be to go first to the mouth of the Maas to take on troops and supplies, then cross the North Sea, sail into the Thames up to the Medway – a broad tributary on the southern bank of the estuary – to destroy the English warships at anchor there, and then go upstream to burn the great dockyards at Chatham. It was an extraordinarily risky operation, worse even than the meeting of fleets in battle on the high seas, for if the English were prepared they could snap a tight trap upon the attackers. But the gain from success would be even greater: the English will to continue the war would be shattered and Charles would have to consent to the treaty of peace that was being negotiated at Breda. The councilor pensionary knew that his plan was in the best of hands. De Ruyter was a master of naval warfare, skilled, sober and bold, and brother Cornelius would break all resistance from lesser officers readier to die than to accept such responsibility.

De Ruyter took his force into the King's Channel on June 17. On the 20th, Sheerness Fort, commanding the mouth of the Medway, was taken by combined naval attack and land assault. Two days later the main Dutch force moved into the Medway, broke the great chain above Gillingham, and captured the *Royal Charles*, the very ship on which the king had sailed home from Scheveningen seven years before. Other ships lying in the Thames were burned at anchor. But the Dutch landing forces were unable to make their way to Chatham, and the dockyards stayed intact. Then the fleet withdrew.

Even with De Ruyter caution came to the fore, to the disappointment of the councilor pensionary, who had wanted the victory to be made double-tight by inflicting further damage upon the English. He regretted that the war council headed by De Ruyter was unwilling to take the risks that the country was ready to accept. (It may be doubted that "the country" had any such will, but De Witt, ordinarily so careful to paint himself as the mere servant of the States of Holland, forgot himself and indulged in that identification of self and country more customary in monarchs.)

The raid into the Medway was one of the supreme achievements in the annals of naval warfare, in its way the equivalent of Trafalgar. It was a masterpiece of conception and execution, and John de Witt was the master craftsman without whom it would never have been attempted. Once the pain of defeat was stilled, even the English came to honor the brilliance of the operation.

The raid was also a perfect example of war at the service of politics. It achieved its political purpose to the full. Peace was made at Breda on July 31,* and the councilor pensionary exulted that his brother had been "the best plenipotentiary." But even now there was a price that would have to be paid, sooner or later. The English people had been frightened and the English king humiliated. De Witt knew, even as he rejoiced in the victory, that they would somehow have to be turned from enemies into friends.

* The details of the negotiation of the Peace of Breda are given in the following chapter.

8

A snarling peace
1665–1667

The peace signed at Breda required for its accomplishment all the feats of naval warfare recounted in the pages just past. Yet all the prowess of sailors, admirals and the superb navy minister that De Witt had shown himself to be during these years would have gone for nothing if he had not also been a master of diplomacy and domestic politics. We must therefore now retrace our steps to the year 1665 and tell the story of the other side of the war.

During the second English war the aims of both sides remained little changed during the two and a half years of fighting. The central purpose of Charles II and his nation was to establish sovereignty over the adjacent seas in order to garner for themselves the profit of fishing, shipping and trade, at the expense chiefly of the Dutch. For these intended victims the aim of the war was simple in the extreme – to thwart the purposes of the foe, to restore the status quo ante bellum. De Witt put the situation plainly and forcefully to D'Estrades some months after the war began. If the English are envious of Dutch trade and the opulence it produces, he said, let them compete with us as traders. If they try to deprive us of our livelihood by means of war, we will fight to the very end.

Yet Charles II was able to shift the center of attention from English ambitions to Dutch recalcitrance and to paint himself as desirous of peace and De Witt as the principal obstacle to its achievement. He picked up the theme of the Prince of Orange's advancement which he had put aside so soon after the death of Princess Mary and let the Dutch think all they had to do in order to bring the war to an end and to make eternal friends of the English was to name William III stadholder and captain general. If the Dutch took him at his word, he would gain control of their state, and their ability to contest the English claim of maritime supremacy would cease to exist. If they refused to give William these offices, then he could incite the Orangist party to oppose and even overthrow the régime of the "True Freedom." Either way, he would be able to shift the burden of responsibility for the continuation of the war away from himself and perhaps persuade Louis XIV to refuse his support to the Dutch, as the presumed aggressors.

In this hope he could work upon the ambiguities in the position of France. Louis XIV was the ally of the States General, but he was not really the enemy of Charles II. For him the alliance of 1662 was directed against Spain, the old common foe of France and the United Provinces. But he did not wish to face a combination of English and Dutch power, which the restoration of William III would create, and hence he felt compelled to support the régime of the "True Freedom" despite his distaste for its republican character. De Witt and his friends for their part confronted a similar hard choice. France was a prospective foe of the worst kind if it established itself in the southern Netherlands, yet its friendship, or at least its neutrality, was indispensable during the war with Britain. The interplay among the sides in this triangular relationship, with its consequences for the internal politics of the Republic, dominated developments. Other powers, notably the German princes and the Scandinavian kings, fished in troubled waters. By themselves they made little difference but as they linked up with one or the other of the principal protagonists they changed the balance of forces a little, although never fundamentally.

Once he saw that the Dutch would fight, and fight hard, Charles moved to play his trump card: restoration of William III. He could not count upon Amalia von Solms, the natural leader of the Orangist party since the death of Princess Mary, for she did not trust the king of England and wanted her grandson restored by the action of the Dutch sovereigns, not by the gift of the foe. In her own way, she was a Dutch patriot. Like John Maurice, she was allied with the elector of Brandenburg, her son-in-law, but he was not an enemy of the United Provinces and she felt no conflict of loyalties on that side. Charles found a willing instrument for arousing Orangism against De Witt within the Prince's little court, however. He was Buat, a French colonel in the States' service, who had been the commander of William II's guards and remained part of the entourage of his posthumous son. The young prince felt for his governor, Zuilestein, the love of a son for a surrogate father, and for Buat, William had the delighted adoration of a teen-ager for a dashing soldier, who in turn idolized him as "my little master."

Charles II made first contact with Buat through Nicholas Oudart, the secretary of the Prince of Orange's council; but when Oudart was arrested and expelled, his place in the conspiracy was taken by Sir Gabriel Sylvius, a personal secretary of the king himself. Sylvius met with Buat in Paris in September 1665, giving him a letter with peace proposals that stressed the king's interest in his nephew's promotion rather than the commercial competition between the two belligerents. For Buat the negotiations with Sylvius that followed were a flirtation with personal disaster, for he was serving the cause of the wartime enemy. But he was an essentially unpolitical man who was thinking only of the interests of his beloved "little master," not of those of the Dutch nation, and certainly not of Dutch merchants and fishermen. To make matters worse for this dabbler in politics, Sylvius was a clumsy diplomat with little sense of the realities of Dutch political life.

The plans of this brace of incompetents nonetheless almost succeeded during the first months of their enterprise, while De Witt was absent with the fleet. Charles II told a Dutch ambassador who had remained in London after the outbreak of war (the automatic internment and expulsion of enemy diplomats when war was declared had not yet come into practice) that he would gladly talk terms of peace if the States General sent a special ambassador to him and kept the French out of the business. At Amalia's request, two deputies from Overijssel proposed that Their High Mightinesses respond by naming William III, not quite fifteen years of age, as the extraordinary ambassador and, to sweeten the Dutch response even more, elect him captain general at the same time. In the absence of the councilor pensionary, the proposal won wide support. But, before its proponents could drive it through the States General, De Witt returned from the fleet in early November and rallied the States party to prevent its adoption. One of the Overijssel deputies was certain it would have won if the "Schoolmaster" had stayed away another month. This pattern of maneuver and counteraction would continue to the end of the war. Charles would trumpet his readiness to grant peace if only the Dutch elevated William, and De Witt would have to remind his countrymen how much more the king really wanted.

Two leading regents in Rotterdam, John Kievit (who was Tromp's brother-in-law) and Ewout van der Horst, were recruited by Buat for the operation against De Witt. They met Sylvius when he secretly slipped into Holland, and agreed with him that the Orangist cause needed a more vigorous leader than Amalia. Their candidate was none other than Van Beverningk, the very man who shared with De Witt the greatest responsibility for the success of the Exclusion of the Prince in 1654, but who had just resigned his post as treasurer general, a visible sign of his estrangement from the councilor pensionary. Van Beverningk, who was at Cleves negotiating the treaty of peace with Galen, feared a trap, however. He insisted that he would see the English representative there, Sir Walter Vane, only if Charles II indicated in advance his readiness to accept a reasonable and honorable peace, which meant abandoning his claim to maritime sovereignty. He became even more distrustful when he learned from De Witt that the councilor pensionary had established contact with the English government through Buat.

This channel of communication had been opened in November, after De Witt's return. Buat came to him to present the English peace overture and the councilor pensionary, with the approval of the States General, allowed Buat to continue his correspondence with the English government. De Witt correctly suspected, however, that the English wished to play up their own willingness to make peace and thereby arouse the populace and many regents against a government that insisted on fighting a costly and bloody war that seemed unnecessary. He also feared that Charles II sought to feed French suspicions that the Dutch might be negotiating separately, betraying their alliance with Louis XIV.

De Witt had every reason to be uneasy about the French king's intentions. In the very first month of the war, Louis's foreign minister, Lionne, told Van Beuningen, who was in France as ambassador extraordinary, that the Dutch might in fact be the aggressors, as Charles II claimed, and if that were proved to be true Louis XIV would not be bound by this alliance to come to their aid. Worse, Lionne went on to make the reasons for French reluctance clear as purest crystal. The true problem, he said, was the Spanish Netherlands. If Louis came to the support of the Dutch, he would make an enemy of England; and when he acted to gain what rightfully belonged to him in the southern Netherlands,

England and the Dutch Republic would join forces to oppose him – all because the Dutch felt they needed a barrier between themselves and France instead of trusting to the king's friendship.

This report frightened the leaders of the States party. It was a horrendous choice that they faced: either to permit Louis to go into the Spanish Netherlands and then sit upon the doorstep of the United Provinces, or, in order to thwart the French king's progress, to make peace with Charles II upon his terms, with all that that meant for Dutch independence. But De Witt for the moment avoided both Scylla and Charybdis. He continued to base Dutch policy upon continuation of the alliance with France, neither conceding Louis's claims upon the Spanish Netherlands nor closing the door upon them. He gambled upon the French king's unwillingness to see the Prince of Orange in power, hoping that it would be enough to outweigh his craving for the southern Netherlands.

De Witt read the king's mind correctly, at least for the time being. Louis XIV committed himself to support of the established government in the United Provinces and to De Witt personally. He hoped that somehow he might win over the councilor pensionary, and through him the whole Dutch government, to abandon their insistence upon a barrier between their countries. The king might laud De Witt to the skies, but he was not, in his own words, bewitched by the Dutchman's eloquence. All during 1665 he continued to prefer to attempt mediation between the two contending parties rather than declare outright for the United Provinces, as the Dutch demanded. Finally, on January 26, 1666, Louis XIV officially declared war upon Charles II. He had, as we have seen, already sent auxiliaries to help in the Dutch defence against Münster. With the new year, therefore, De Witt could turn to his task of guiding the Republic's diplomacy, secure in the knowledge that the most important condition for its success had been achieved.

The diplomatic initiative remained Charles II's. He continued the Sylvius–Buat operation, that strange combination of negotiations with the existing government in the United Provinces and simultaneous intrigues to overthrow it. It was no easy matter for De Witt to ward off the danger that Sylvius and Buat would succeed, either by imposing the Prince of Orange, or by compelling acceptance of English terms, or by estranging France and the

Republic. French suspicions could be stilled, or at least kept below the dangerous level, by informing D'Estrades of what was going on. But otherwise De Witt had to wait for and respond to the approaches from England.

He refused to see Sylvius in person, although he tolerated his presence in Holland. He did not fend off personal meetings with Buat, who spoke for Sylvius and his masters in England. In February 1666, Buat brought to the councilor pensionary a proposal for peace which he said he had discussed with Van Beverningk. The terms would have constituted a partial Dutch defeat: an indemnity of £200,000 to be paid to Charles II, which was tantamount to accepting that they had been the aggressors; a compromise with regard to trade; and assurance that the Republic's allies – which meant France, of course – would also be reasonable. De Witt, all along reporting to the States of Holland and to D'Estrades, insisted upon less ambiguous proposals. He also warned Buat to stop attempting to arouse opposition against the Dutch government. He did not respond to Buat's assurance that the king of England wanted his friendship, knowing the councilor pensionary to be an "honorable man" (*galant homme*); if he smiled within, he did not move his lips.

Buat soon discovered that for Charles II his own interests were paramount, and that he vacillated when it came to advancement of the Prince of Orange. He could not understand why the English king did not respond positively to an offer that would make him master in the United Provinces and thereby the greatest monarch in the world. Sylvius's written reply was indeed so disconcerting that Zuilestein told Buat to throw it into the fire. Buat shifted his hopes to a strategy far more dangerous for the future of the Prince of Orange, and certainly for himself, than his service as an intermediary between the English king and the councilor pensionary. He boasted to Sylvius that if the Dutch lost the expected naval battle, then De Witt and his friends could be ousted from power. This constituted treason on two scores, courting the defeat of the nation to whose defense he was sworn, and seeking the overthrow of the established government. He had chosen his time badly, moreover, for the first great clash at sea in 1666 was the Four Days Battle. De Witt, far from going under, was more solidly in control than ever.

Yet, by a quirk of consequences, Buat gained the support of

Charles II for his strategy. On royal instruction Sylvius sent two letters to Buat. The first was to be shown to De Witt, and it renewed the king's assertion of his desire for peace. The second was marked "for yourself" (*pour vous même*), and it told Buat to move strongly in organizing the plot to bring down De Witt, if need be by force. The first letter was buttressed by one which the former Scottish consul in Amsterdam, Sir William Davidson, wrote to De Witt from London. The king, so said Sir William, was sorry to see the spilling of Christian blood continue. It was time to begin negotiations for peace, but without the participation of France. He offered to be the channel of communications between the councilor pensionary and the king. If Charles II had been serious, Davidson would have been a far more reliable and intelligent intermediary than Buat. De Witt replied at once that the Dutch would discuss concrete terms for peace, but under no circumstances apart from their ally France.

De Witt's reply was courteous if firm, but it left unmentioned an event that had happened two days before which put the whole prospect of negotiations into doubt. On the morning of August 18, Buat received the two letters from Sylvius as well as one from the Earl of Arlington, the English secretary of state who directed the affair. He went to the councilor pensionary to show him the letters meant for De Witt's eyes. It was not until he got home that Buat made the harrowing discovery that he had left the letter marked "for yourself" in De Witt's hands together with the others. When he went back to ask for its return, De Witt told him it was already being examined by the Delegated Councilors, the standing committee of the States of Holland.

This may have been a hint that he should flee. In any event, nine hours passed before officers of the Delegated Councilors came to take Buat to the States of Holland, who examined him and then put him under arrest. Buat had been a madcap soldier, but he was not so heedless of his life that he would not have used what may well have been a proffered opportunity for flight unless he had more important work to do, even at the cost of his own head. De Witt later thought he had used the time to burn or conceal other letters affirming his treasonous activities, for one such, even more incriminating, was found, filling out the picture of his plot to overthrow the established party in Holland and put William III in power.

Arrests of a number of those involved were made, but Kievit and Van der Horst escaped to England. De Witt was sure that other persons of more importance than these two were implicated, but Buat, the gallant soldier who had played at politics and lost, did not name them at his trial. He was innocent, he told his judges; he had acted only out of love for the Prince of Orange, who loved him. He was found guilty and beheaded on October 11. To say that he was innocent in a sense different from what he had meant – that he was guileless in the cynical world of politics – is not to mock his memory. No man who laid down his life for his "little master," as he did, deserves less than our sympathy, if not our approval. He was guilty of treason, and Louis XIV also insisted that he be put to death as proof that the Dutch were not breaking their alliance with France.

Buat's death served the cause of his master better than his clumsy conspiracy had done. He became an instant martyr whose blood Calvinist preachers compared with that of Jesus on the cross. The hatred of the Orangist populace intensified against the councilor pensionary who was blamed for all the hardships and sufferings of a war that he would not bring to an end. As for those who stood behind Buat, we can only guess at their identity. They may have included Fagel, the pensionary of Haarlem, or even Van Beverningk, for whom De Witt was now more of a rival than a friend, but such an imputation is only an inference of possibility, no more, from their past and later conduct.

One name we cannot doubt, although we cannot prove it. This was Zuilestein, who at least advised Buat. Zuilestein, the Prince's uncle and his governor, was as totally devoted to William as Buat had been, but far wilier. He knew that De Witt had made his dismissal from the Prince's governorship a sine qua non of the program for education of William as "Child of State" proposed in 1660, and he realized that the councilor pensionary was now proposing to revive that educational program. If he had been joined with Buat in the conspiracy, he had also almost certainly been acting without the knowledge of either William or Amalia van Solms. The Princess Dowager was Orange to the heart, not Stuart, and she distrusted Charles II as much as she disliked him. William III had much to learn about his royal uncle, but he had already learned to put his own interests foremost. There is no evidence that he wanted to owe his advancement to his country's defeat.

The collapse of the Sylvius–Buat conspiracy left Charles II with only naval operations and traditional diplomacy as instruments for combatting the Dutch. He must have writhed when he heard from Davidson, who had gone to Brussels, that De Witt was supposed to have said that "Charles Stuart's three crowns are staggering and trembling and that he [De Witt] will make him an example for all other kings." The councilor pensionary's position was firmer than ever. Yet he could not simply reject out of hand the peace proposals that the king put forward, especially through Danish and Swedish mediators. The immediate question was where negotiations should be held. The one place that De Witt ruled out was The Hague, which Charles II had proposed, because it would provide the English with an easy opportunity to arouse the populace and stir up the municipal and provincial assemblies against the leadership in the saddle in The Hague. The councilor pensionary preferred either London or Paris, or even Dover, but finally the town of Breda in States Brabant was accepted for the negotiation while the naval war continued unabated, as we saw in the previous chapter.

Although the usual delegation of eight members – two from Holland and one from each of the other provinces – was named to go to Breda, only a working delegation of three actually went early in May to engage in the negotiation while the others waited until the treaty should be ready for their signature. The leader of the delegation was Van Beverningk, the ablest negotiator the Dutch possessed. He kept in constant touch with De Witt, reporting the dogged efforts of the English negotiators to win at the conference table what they had not been able to attain on the high seas. To his face the French diplomats urged acceptance of many of the English demands, threatening otherwise to make a separate peace with England (they did not need to remind him that this would be playing upon the Dutch the trick they had inflicted upon the French in 1648). He suspected that the French and English ministers were working behind his back for such a settlement without – and against – the Dutch. The French, Van Beverningk thought, wanted to have a free hand for the invasion of the Spanish Netherlands everyone knew was coming in the wake of the death of Philip IV in 1665.

De Witt was indignant at such indications that the French might play false with their obligations under the alliance of 1662, but hardly surprised. Even after the declaration of war by Louis XIV in 1666, the relations between the United Provinces and France had swung between the extremes of mutual protestations of friendship and private expressions of antipathy and distrust. Even in the midst of a difficult war, De Witt was unwilling to concede the price that Louis XIV persistently demanded for his alliance – support for, or at least assent to, his making good his queen's claims in the Spanish Netherlands. The French king and his foreign minister plied De Witt and Van Beuningen, who conducted the negotiations with France at Saint-Germain, with assurances that nothing would be done without consultation with the States General. But Louis would not yield on the fundamental issue of his queen's hereditary rights; he might moderate the extent to which he would enforce them, but he would not abandon them. They were set forth in the famous *Treatise on the Queen's Rights* (*Traité des Droits de la Reine*), which argued their legal basis in the law of devolution. The king had it presented officially to the States General as well as to other powers in May 1666. Troubled as he was by Dutch imperviousness to his arguments, he had no choice for the moment but to support the government of De Witt.

The councilor pensionary for his part attempted to persuade the French monarch that it was to his interest to take only a part of what he claimed rather than the whole and to retain the friendship and alliance of the United Provinces. He presented to D'Estrades possible arrangements, either revival of the cantonment which he always considered the best of all, or a partition that would leave at least some buffer between their two countries. But by 1667 the king of France had already decided to take what was in his mind rightfully his (his queen's, to be more precise), whatever the Dutch did. At the same time he was anxious lest the Dutch become reconciled with the English and with them form the core of an alliance – Sweden, the German Protestant princelings and even the Emperor were possible entrants – to thwart him. Already the king was torn by two opposite concerns, one to gain glory in war and to establish his preeminence among the monarchs of Europe, the other to avoid any coalition being formed that could withstand or even defeat him. De Witt's efforts were aimed at using the threat of such a coalition to induce the king to reduce his demands so that the need for the coalition would cease. What De Witt found difficult to get around was that moderation on the part of Louis

XIV would seem to the world to be a retreat before the potential coalition and hence a blot on his glory.

The councilor pensionary therefore had little choice but to follow through on both options, and meanwhile to refuse reiterated Spanish demands for open and effective support of their resistance. England, he reminded Van Beverningk, had once offered the States General much better terms than what the French thought the Dutch should accept, provided that they broke their alliance with Louis XIV. If France turned away from the Dutch, as the French ministers threatened, he expected that they could get the English to make peace quickly, especially because they also were troubled by the impending French invasion of the southern Netherlands. When Van Beverningk informed him that the English wanted amnesty for Kievit, Van der Horst and others implicated in the Buat–Sylvius conspiracy, and that the chief negotiators were backing this demand, De Witt became steely hard in his opposition. The king of England might lavish his hospitality upon them in his own country, but they were traitors in their homeland. The States General could not grant such terms (because they were subjects of the province of Holland, not of the Generality), and the States of Holland would not. De Witt was equally firm in rejecting and thwarting English attempts to infilter spies into Dutch territory under various pretexts of quasi-diplomatic status.

The Breda negotiations were transformed by the Dutch success of the raid into the Medway. It was the "great compeller of peace" that would break English arrogance and stubbornness, was De Witt's correct prophecy. The English agreed to major improvements in the status of Dutch shipping and trade, even relaxing the Navigation Act to permit the Dutch to ship to England goods which came from Germany and other countries as well as their own. The Dutch retained Surinam and the English New Netherland, renamed New York and New Jersey. De Witt was jubilant but wary. Everything had to be put down in black and white, with utmost formality, so as to be beyond all doubt or equivocation, to which he found the English exasperatingly prone. The completed document was ready by July 10, although it was not signed until July 31. The formal ratifications did not come for another month, during which time De Witt kept the Dutch fleet at sea and on the alert.

The Peace of Breda enabled both countries to turn their

attention to the new situation caused by the French invasion (called the "War of Devolution" in our history books), which had begun in May. It may have been a "snarling peace," as an astute English observer remarked, but England and the Dutch Republic were no longer at war with each other and could even become future allies. In any event, De Witt had won his essential aim since the beginning of the war, to thwart the effort of the English to gain ascendancy in trade and shipping by means of force.

The conclusion of the peace was followed within a few weeks by a momentous decision of the States of Holland, known as the "Eternal Edict". It gave, and it took away. On the one hand it gave Holland's support for naming the Prince of Orange at once to the Council of State and holding open to him eventual appointment as captain and admiral general; on the other, it abolished the stadholderate in Holland and refused the province's approval for the election as captain general of anyone who was a stadholder in another province. The edict constituted a recognition that the "True Freedom" of the States party still dominated the political life of the country; but also that the Orangist party had survived the debacle of the Buat–Sylvius conspiracy and was an ineradicable part of the political commitment of a formidable part of the Dutch nation.

In March 1666, months before Buat's arrest and execution, the States of Holland had made an important gesture of rapprochement with the House of Orange. On March 31, they voted to name William a "Child of State," renewing the concept that had been agreed upon in 1660 but never put into effect. De Witt found Amalia easier to persuade than many in his own party. True believers in the "True Freedom" were puzzled and dismayed. Weren't they now doing exactly what they had been denouncing ever since the death of William II? a friend in Amsterdam asked the councilor pensionary. The councilor pensionary replied with candid acknowledgment of political necessity. There was so much support for the Prince not only in the other provinces but even in the States of Holland and indeed in Amsterdam itself, that a last-ditch stand against his appointment was a wise compromise. Its purpose was to take the young Prince out of the hands of those who were instruments of Charles II. Their expulsion was an essential precondition for the success of his plan.

A little more than a week later a committee was named to take over the Prince's education, and De Witt became its leading member. He drafted a plan of instruction based upon that which he had made in October 1660, and it was put into effect at once. Zuilestein, the Prince's governor who was married to an English noblewoman, was dismissed; his salary would continue unless he made trouble. He was replaced by Baron van Gendt of Gelderland, a political friend of the councilor pensionary. Others in the Prince's entourage, including an English nobleman who had been appointed by Charles II, were also turned out.

The loss of Zuilestein left the young William deeply shocked and hurt. Fatherless since birth, he was very close to his governor, and he pleaded with the members of the States of Holland and with De Witt personally to be allowed to retain him. He turned too to the French ambassador, who had been a personal friend of William II, but D'Estrades told him he had to accept what had been done. This he now did, receiving the educational committee with haughty courtesy and a demand that they see to the proper administration of his estate, which had been in his grandmother's hands. He did not balk at the education which was given him by his new tutors, nor at its supervision by De Witt. It may be doubted that he looked upon the councilor pensionary of Holland as a new father, as he told D'Estrades he would (if we are to believe that not always truthful diplomat), but he worked easily with him, especially during the weekly tutoring sessions in the science of politics with emphasis upon concrete examples.

His relationship to De Witt became psychologically and politically ambiguous. On the one hand he realized he was learning politics at the hands of a master, and for that he would be always grateful; on the other, he did not cease to see De Witt as a foe who kept from him what was rightfully his. William learned to depend upon himself, to hold his emotions under control, in a way to be like De Witt himself despite the enormous distance of rank between a regent of Holland – although one who was his province's supreme servant – and a prince who was the nephew and cousin of kings. His education as Child of State lasted for two years. When it began William III was still a child: when it ended, he was a man ready to stand on his own feet, hardened emotionally but – as De Witt wanted – Dutch in his knowledge and feelings. The Prince of Orange who in the not distant future would lead the United

Provinces for three decades was shaped by De Witt no less, although in different ways, than by his family and friends.

In the summer of 1667, as the war with England neared its close, De Witt took the next step toward safely integrating the Prince into the national life of the Dutch Republic. He did not resist the campaign for appointment of William III to high military office but sought rather to guide and control it. The new "Harmony" which he proposed to the States of Holland on July 2 would not give the young man a command as yet, but John Maurice would be named first field marshal and the Holsteiner Paulus Wirtz would become second field marshal; the Prince of Tarente, a French Protestant soldier, would serve as general of cavalry, as he had done the year before. William was not excluded, however. He would be given a seat on the Council of State, where, although it was not explicitly stated, he would be groomed for the captaincy general.

Yet De Witt had not abandoned the principles of the "True Freedom." He was only bending them in the interest of expediency and in a way which he thought would safeguard the republican future of the nation. The Prince of Orange might become captain general, the supreme military servant of the country, but not its leader as stadholder. The political office would be incompatible with the captaincy general; and all magistrates and officeholders in Holland were to be nominated and elected only by their town councils and the States of Holland, without intervention by the Prince of Orange, as had been usual before 1650. All present and future members of municipal and provincial government and any captain and admiral general would have to swear to uphold this edict.

De Witt had to explain his reasons for the "Harmony" to the same Amsterdam friend who had called the "Child of State" proposal into question the year before. It was not the best that could be conceived, merely the best under the circumstances. If Holland had been united, it could have imposed its will upon the other provinces. But there was too much internal strife in Holland to make that ideal solution possible. Furthermore, the proposal had not come from him but from others, and it had not been feasible or wise to reject it. What had been done was to include in it a principle – the incompatibility of the captaincy general and the stadholdership – that protected freedom.

The "Harmony" did not have smooth sailing through the States of Holland. Amalia van Solms favored it, but she could not prevent some of the towns from refusing their approval. Finally it was pushed through after a delegation visited the recalcitrant towns and persuaded them to go along with the majority. When the final draft of the proposal was presented to the States of Holland early in August, it had been stiffened by inclusion of a clause specifically abolishing the stadholderate in the province. The Prince would be considered for election as captain and admiral general when he reached twenty-three years of age, but only if there was a need for his services. If he was not elected to these posts, the other provinces would have the right to name him their stadholder. The measure was adopted on August 5, and was soon dubbed the "Eternal Edict" because its provisions had no limitations of time.

By an irony of twisted attribution, the Eternal Edict became in the public mind the work of De Witt himself. Its actual authors were Fagel and Valckenier, who had been members of the delegation to the towns. The former had been known for his strong ties with the House of Orange, and the latter was the self-willed leader of Amsterdam who was a member of the education committee but played his own game politically. Valckenier's aim in the Eternal Edict has never been satisfactorily explained, but Fagel's is clear. He wanted to cover up a flirtation with the Buat–Sylvius conspiracy by becoming "more royalist than the king," even stricter in outward republicanism than the councilor pensionary himself. Yet at the same time he salvaged the prospect of military command for William, leaving the attainment of political office by the Prince of Orange to future events. But all of this remained hidden from the world at large and even from most of the leading regents in Holland.

Fervent believers in the "True Freedom" lauded De Witt to the skies for his salutary measure in defense of republican principles, while the Orangists cursed him for his culminating deviltry against "Our Prince." Almost no one saw it as he did himself, as a compromise that would save the country from being torn apart. Far from being the implacable republican of legend, utterly inflexible in the maintenance of the exclusion of the House of Orange, he knew how to bend before the wind and yet not break. But he had never learned, and never would, how to reach and mold public opinion, the broad judgment of the often ill-informed country.

In any event, the edict was "eternal" only in its formal provisions. It could last only as long as the "True Freedom," and that depended upon the success of the constant struggle of the States party in general, and of De Witt himself most of all. There is a story about his cousin Nicholas Vivien at the meeting of the States of Holland when the Eternal Edict was adopted. In his hand was a knife with which he poked at the leather binding of a book. What are you doing, cousin? De Witt asked. I'm trying to find out how well parchment stands up to steel, was the reply. Alas, the historian, bound to truth that rests upon sources, must report that this tale can only be traced back to the early nineteenth century. The story with its vivid enactment of a political verity had been told of other men and other occasions. We may nonetheless repeat the Italian epigram, *Se non è vero, è ben trovato*, "If it isn't true, it's a good story." It would be nice to know whether, if it was true, De Witt laughed.

The councilor pensionary spoke very much to the point when he urged William III to accept the edict. It embodied the expectation that he would one day become commander of the army. The stadholderate had been abolished because his father had put the very existence of the Dutch state in peril. It was reassuring to see that the son did not share his father's faults of character, but the captaincy general would still not be given to him until he had proved himself. When he married, it would have to be to someone of the same religion so that the preachers would not remonstrate. His bride would have to have rank equal to his own, but her family must not be known for its hostility to the Republic. An unwise marriage had led to William II's ruinous policy. The sixteen-year-old apparently did not reply sarcastically that he himself was the fruit of that marriage, but simply said that he understood. He added thanks to Their Noble Great Mightinesses for their care of his person and their own interests. There may well have been sarcasm in these last words, even though they were the proper ones for the occasion.

9

The reversal of alliances
1667–1670

It was widely recognized that the Peace of Breda was an extraordinary achievement and that it was De Witt's. Few observers realized, however, that it had not solved but only increased the number and complexity of the problems he faced. What he had really won was the chance to work for their solution, for if the war had been lost and ended in capitulation, as in 1654, then he certainly would have been toppled from power by his own masters in the States of Holland or, worse, by riot and rebellion. What he had not gained, however, was the initiative. This remained in the hands of Louis XIV and Charles II; De Witt could only wait and respond to what they did. In warfare there may be an advantage to an active defense, as military analysts have argued; in political life, and especially in the relations between states, he who acts first sets the shape for events and enhances his opportunities to gain his way.

The single largest event on the stage of Europe after Breda was the War of Devolution. The French generals methodically moved their armies forward, forcing the Spaniards before them and taking their towns one by one in a succession of easy sieges. But the Spaniards did not turn tail and run, so that by the end of summer it was evident that the French were certain of victory but that it would not be theirs during 1667. The time the Spaniards had bought would enable those who wanted to prevent the conquest of the southern Netherlands by France to put together an alliance big and strong enough to awe the king of France into halting his invasion. The heart of such a league would have to be Britain and the United Provinces; no other state or group of states possessed the wealth and the power to make it possible. This was recognized by those, like the Austrian diplomat Lisola, who wanted not merely the cessation of the war but the humbling of Louis XIV and the destruction in advance of any French "universal monarchy."

De Witt did not share the larger vision of Lisola, no more than did Lisola's own master, Emperor Leopold I. The councilor pensionary wanted both to save the buffer between France and the United Provinces in the southern Netherlands and to retain the alliance with France. He wanted to use Britain as part of the front that would thwart Louis XIV and yet not make the Dutch Republic utterly dependent upon Charles II, certainly not at the price of making his nephew William III stadholder and captain general. Least of all did he want the Republic to embrace the offensive-defensive league sought by Spain, not out of vestigial hatred inherited from the days of the war of independence but because he thought the old enemy too weak to be a worthwhile friend. The Dutch diplomatic situation seemed to be a problem without a solution, or perhaps with too many solutions, all of which, to use a phrase that came easily to De Witt's pen, were "cures worse than the malady."

Yet the councilor pensionary found a way out of his dilemma. It was not necessary to conclude an alliance with Britain in order to tame the acquisitive zeal of Louis XIV; nothing more was required than the threat of such an alliance, in the face of which the French king would surely settle for the conquests he had made during the first year of the war. That would provide the Dutch with the barrier they needed, not as wide as they would have liked but sufficient to keep the immensity of French power at a distance. Louis would have much, if not all, of what he wanted, and he would continue to respect his alliance with the United Provinces, which De Witt did not cease to consider the best foundation for Dutch foreign policy provided that the king did not screw the cost up to an unacceptable level. Charles II could then be kept at arm's length, and the Orangist party at home held in check. It was a brilliant conception, and it had a chance of working, because it played upon the cautious side of Louis XIV, who yearned for glory without danger.

De Witt played his game with his customary skill. When D'Estrades came back to The Hague from Breda, where he had been one of the French negotiators, the councilor pensionary confronted him with a difficult choice for the French monarch: the Dutch would support his stated conditions for peace (at the moment his actual conquests or an equivalent elsewhere) if he consented to halt military operations while the Spaniards were considering them. Otherwise, the Dutch would be compelled to respond positively to the Spanish demands for an offensive–defensive alliance.

That they were capable of moving toward such a fateful shift of friendships was demonstrated by the approval given by the States of Holland to a Spanish request to the States General for a loan of 1,000,000 guilders, with two forts and three towns in northern Flanders as pledges. While it was being considered by the States General, the queen regent of Spain decided that the Republic required too high a price, the effective loss of territory which the Dutch ought rather be defending. A furious De Witt told the Spanish envoys that their expectation of aid from the Emperor, many German princes, as well as England and the States General, was vain. Their government could look for other friends if it was so foolish, he warned. But he had no new policy to propose to his own masters, merely a continuation of the attempt to persuade and threaten France into a compromise.

Louis XIV, warned by Turenne against risking too much, set down peace terms: the county of Franche-Comté, which the Spanish king held as a fief of the Empire, and the duchy of Luxemburg, together with some of the towns and districts he had conquered, as an equivalent for the rest of what he held in the southern Netherlands. While the terms were being considered, he would accept a truce until the end of March. What he would not accept was abandonment of all future claims to the Spanish monarchy.

Lionne, Louis's foreign minister, sent a warning to De Witt through D'Estrades. If the Dutch insisted that the French king acknowledge the validity of the queen's renunciation, then there would be no point in continued negotiations. The king went further. He told his ambassador that approval of the loan to Spain, with its provision for sending Dutch auxiliary troops to the Spanish Netherlands, would be treated as not just breaking the alliance with him but as forming an open alliance against him.

The suspicions of Louis XIV turned to wrath when Van Beuningen, returning from his extraordinary embassy to France, urged upon the secret committee of the States General that a league be formed with England, the Emperor and Sweden, to halt the

French conquests. The chances for such a grand alliance had improved with the flight from England of Clarendon, the chief minister of Charles II, to escape trial on accusations of traitorous collusion with France. His replacement was Arlington, who sent the English resident at Brussels, Temple, to The Hague on an unofficial visit to discuss with De Witt what could be done to save the Spanish Netherlands. Temple, who had made the alliance with Galen three years before, had become persuaded that the principal danger to British interests lay in French conquest of the southern Netherlands. Arlington, and Charles II himself, tried to coax from John Meerman, the new extraordinary ambassador in London from the States General, a forthright statement of the common Dutch–English interest in Flanders, but Meerman warily suspected that the king was trying to trap the Dutch into a war with France while the English stayed on the sidelines.

De Witt's plan of diplomatic jugglery was adopted by the States of Holland on December 10 for submission to the States General. It sought a more limited league than the grand alliance proposed by Van Beuningen: only the Scandinavian states, Brandenburg and the dukes of Brunswick would be invited to join with the aim of achieving a compromise peace. If possible, De Witt added in a letter of explanation to Meerman, the king of England should be brought in, but never at the price of giving him a foothold in the Low Countries, for as a neighbor he would be no better than Louis XIV.

Spanish dissatisfaction with the plan helped build willingness at the French court to give it serious consideration for the territorial gains it assured France. Louis therefore sent to The Hague a German diplomat who was in his pay and whose advice he valued, Count William Egon von Fürstenberg (that he was also the principal minister of the Elector of Cologne did not matter, for the elector was an ally of France). Fürstenberg arrived from Saint-Germain on December 18 with the king's new conditions: he would halt his military operations only if the Spaniards first accepted the terms he had set. Ten days later, just before Fürstenberg's departure, De Witt worked out a version of the proposed compromise that Fürstenberg thought reasonable, less than the councilor pensionary wanted – which included the queen's renunciation – but including agreement that the king would leave it to the Dutch to gain the "equivalent" for him within three months. If the queen regent refused, the Dutch would support the French with their arms. There was no mention of the French queen's renunciation.

These provisions were set down in a resolution adopted by the States of Holland on January 14, with one important addition: if Louis XIV refused to accept the terms for peace he himself had already declared, or resumed military operations in Flanders, then the States General (to whom, of course, the final decision belonged) would use force to impose peace upon the king, with the goal not just of achieving the terms he had refused but restoration of the prewar frontiers. Without the addition, the plan would have been no more than a pious hope; with it, the Dutch admitted willingness not merely to quit the alliance with France, but to go over to outright enmity. With this policy De Witt walked on the knife edge of uncertainty. Yet it did not seem totally hopeless, for there were signs that England might fall into line.

On December 30, Temple had returned, on his way from Brussels to London, and he discussed with De Witt what could be done. Temple painted Charles II as determined to choose sides and ready to ally with France if the Dutch hesitated. His reward from Louis XIV would be Dunkirk, Nieuwpoort and Ostend, the ports of Flanders, and if he joined in conquest of the Dutch Republic the province of Zeeland as well. Temple was impressed by De Witt's ability and sincerity, but the councilor pensionary's suspicions were not stilled by the Englishman's eloquence and charm.

With good reason. Charles II had been negotiating all along for an Anglo-French alliance, but Louis XIV had not been willing to pay the high price in subsidies that Charles wanted, and he did not want to change sides unless the Dutch first broke the alliance he had made with them in 1662. Charles thereupon sent Temple back to The Hague with formal status as an extraordinary envoy, empowered to conclude a treaty. He presented terms for an alliance that went even further in readiness to act against France than De Witt had suggested. The councilor pensionary preferred to stick with the terms he had agreed upon with Fürstenberg, but he could not hold back. He told Temple to his face that the English alliance was little better than the French, for Charles II and his ministers were notoriously fickle. If they abandoned the Dutch, the situation of the United Provinces in the face of a revengeful France would be disastrous. He spoke with obvious melancholy and reluctance, and Temple gave him the dubious reassurance that if his own masters went over to the French side, he would have no part of it. The Englishman thought De Witt was reassured, but we may wonder how much this piece of diplomatic ingenuousness impressed him.

De Witt obtained one worthwhile concession from Temple. This was to put the provision for possible joint action against France, upon which Temple had insisted, in a separate secret article appended to the treaty. He wrote it in the registers of the States of Holland himself instead of letting his trusted chief clerk do so, as was usual. The text of the treaty was hurried through the States General without the customary second reading and without prior consultation with the provincial assemblies, again on Temple's insistence. Only the first deputy of each province was shown the secret articles. The final treaty text was approved by Their High Mightinesses on January 23, just a week after Temple's arrival. The next day the States General approved inclusion of Sweden, and the treaty has therefore gone down in history as the Triple Alliance of 1668.

Sweden accepted the place that De Witt had originally planned for Brandenburg, but Elector Frederick William had grown suspicious of the councilor pensionary's willingness to support France against Spain (for so he read the meaning of De Witt's effort to compel Spain to accept a partial defeat), and he wanted a subsidy for Brandenburg to be paid by the States General, not by the impecunious Spanish. The Swedish envoy at The Hague had been satisfied with such an arrangement, and his masters in Stockholm were hungry for some subsidy to eke out their revenues.

Irony of ironies, the world saw the Triple Alliance as De Witt's supreme victory, even as he graciously acknowledged it was one that Temple shared. He did not display abroad his own gnawing doubts and fears that he was being trapped, and with him his country. What good would it do? It was necessary instead to make it work within the confines of the policy he had developed all along. If he succeeded, the kudos would be truly deserved; if not, larger things were at stake than his reputation.

There were observers who must have known better, because over the years they had suggested to the English court precisely such a league as a way of destroying De Witt by turning the king of France against him. That Charles II needed any lessons in diplomatic trickery may be easily doubted, for he was a greater master of devious politics than his would-be teachers.

By this success in drawing the States General into an alliance which De Witt had suggested but did not in reality want, Charles II solved a number of difficult problems. Within Britain he won instant popularity with a public that was becoming restive about the French king's conquests in the southern Netherlands, and thus he weakened the sour memory of the defeat suffered at the hands of the Dutch less than a year before. In the United Provinces he showed himself a friend of the country and hence strengthened the arguments for the elevation of his princely nephew to his forefathers' offices. As for France, he did not really cut himself off from continued negotiations with his cousin Louis XIV. There was, of course, the danger that Louis XIV might doggedly pursue a victory in the field, but all the indications pointed to his being, for the moment, satisfied. Aggrandized but not sated, the French king would in all probability take revenge upon the Republic in the future, but then – needing the alliance of the British monarch – he might be willing to pay the subsidies he had hitherto judged too costly. In that case, the friendless Dutch could be humbled, reduced to a helpless dependency on England and France. And the councilor pensionary of Holland, who had earned Charles's hatred as few men other than the regicides who had sent his father to death had done, could be overthrown and destroyed. The English king seems not to have pondered at length upon the peril that victory over the Dutch would bring to the English, once the French were masters of the Low Countries.

Some of this De Witt knew, but not how far it went. He did not waste time on speculation, however, but set to work at once to salvage his policy. The very day the treaty was adopted he wrote to Fürstenberg that the Triple Alliance merely embodied the terms they had agreed upon in December, with some slight modifications, glibly sliding over the provisions of the secret article for possible use of force against France. The next day, Temple and he visited D'Estrades to explain what had been done. D'Estrades warned them that Louis XIV was a proud king and that if they "thought to prescribe his laws and force him to compliance," there would result "a war of forty years." (His timing was only a little short, for the Peace of Utrecht came forty-five years later!) Through Wicquefort, who reported on events to Lionne, De Witt tried to reassure the French foreign minister. The terms of the new alliance could have been phrased less harshly, De Witt admitted, but the content was to the king's advantage.

The French court was not unwilling to accept such reassurances, all the more because an invasion of Franche-Comté was about to begin. The conciliatory French attitude swiftly evaporated when the content of the secret articles was leaked to them. Just where and when this first happened is not clear, whether at London by the king of England's ministers or elsewhere, but a cold fury was felt at Saint-Germain. Van Beuningen, who had rushed back to the French court to save the day, reported that Louis XIV did not want to appear before the world as negotiating peace from fear of a projected anti-French league.

If the French court looked askance at the Triple Alliance because it put limits upon victory, the Spanish found it distasteful because it did not compel Louis XIV to disgorge his conquests. Worse, it provided that force would be used against Spain if it did not accept the territorial provisions agreed upon with France. Yet De Witt had to win Spanish acceptance of the treaty and of peace with France. The queen regent in Madrid and her governor general in Brussels balked, but eventually acquiesced. Early in April the States General approved a loan to the Brussels government of 2,000,000 guilders, with six small towns and fortresses as security.

Meanwhile Louis XIV agreed to open peace talks at Aachen, offering the Spaniards a choice between what he had conquered or its "equivalent" in other border territories. When the peace was finally concluded on May 2, Castel Rodrigo, the Spanish governor general, chose to have Franche-Comté returned to Spain, leaving France in possession of a chain of fortified towns that had been taken by the French armies all along the southern boundary of the Spanish Netherlands. It was a clever if surprising move, for if it increased the peril to the rest of the Spanish Netherlands, it also did the same to the United Provinces. The Peace of Aachen (Aix-la-Chapelle) was the completion of the Triple Alliance, but it did not bring the assured peace that De Witt desired.

Barely a month after the conclusion of peace, tragedy struck at De Witt with a force that shook this normally cool, self-controlled man to his very marrow. He and Wendela had been living since 1661 in a rented house at the north end of the Vijverberg close by the Binnenhof, and their family continued to grow with the steady regularity of almost perfect fertility. There were three more daughters and at last two sons, while one pregnancy ended in miscarriage. Two of the daughters died just out of babyhood, old enough to have toddled their way into their parents' close love, and De Witt felt the loss of a seven-year-old "little daughter" with a pain relieved somewhat by his belief that God had taken her into eternal joy with Himself. Proud that he did not "discriminate" between the sexes, he was delighted all the same that the arrival of sons removed a "defect" in the family.

Both Wendela and his oldest daughter, Anna, could express their love for him during the long, dangerous absence aboard the fleet in 1665 in moving and (in Anna's case) amusing letters. Wendela, apologizing for her awkward style, wrote eloquently of her longing for her husband. Anna penned her letter in a childish French that she boasted of learning: "Je langi for après mo cheir papa et je voudree bien que papa fut de retour" ("I miss my dear daddy very much and wish so much he were home again.")

The three older girls suffered from skeletal weakness due to too rapid growth, probably a genetic fault in the Bicker line, and in the late spring of 1668 they were sent to Oirschot in States Brabant to seek a cure at the hands of a famed "miracle doctor," Arnoldus Fey. This was not recourse to a quack, for "Master" Fey not only had the respect of eminent scientists of his own day but also that of modern historians of medicine for his therapy. While the girls remained at Oirschot under Fey's care and the eye of the family maid, their parents visited Wendela's sister in Amsterdam. On their return to The Hague, their youngest daughter, Elisabeth (the second of that name), fell ill and died. Not long afterwards, Wendela herself, while visiting her other sister at Soestdijk, came down with a fever and returned home by canalboat. De Witt, noting improvement, allowed the girls to stay in Oirschot in anticipation of their enjoyment of the fair at nearby Den Bosch. Wendela suddenly became much worse. She pleaded for a chance to see her daughters at least one last time, but before they could be brought back in haste, she died shortly after midnight on July 1.

The next day the shattered De Witt wrote to a cousin on his mother's side residing in Den Bosch, and a few days later informed Van Beuningen in Paris and Meerman in London in a few dry words that conveyed nothing of what he felt. Writing to Van Beverningk, once so close a friend, he let go a little, thanking him for his "affection and compassion in my present affliction." Relatives and friends were surprised at the intensity of his grief, so out of line with his usual composure and emotional reticence. Temple wrote from London with words that spoke of genuine feeling, not the set phrases of condolences sent by other leading statesmen. De Witt was thankful for Temple's words, for, as he admitted in a letter to Lionne, his friends kept him from stumbling. A year and a half later his own condolences to a relative in Amsterdam whose husband died after a long illness, by its reflection that she had had time to prepare herself with "good Christian thoughts", hinted that he himself had been taken unawares and unprepared when his beloved wife, still in her early thirties, had been wrested from him.

For a while friends thought De Witt's work as councilor pensionary suffered, and a certain unsteadiness and uncertainty in his conduct of affairs may be due not only to the knotted state of Dutch foreign policy after the Triple Alliance, but also to his personal tragedy. Gradually, however, his fortitude of spirit asserted itself, although his devotion to his family – children and brother in particular – became if anything stronger than ever. At Fey's request, the girls were sent back to Oirschot for further treatment, and by the end of August they were pronounced cured. The wealth the children inherited from their mother, their share of the famed Bicker fortunes, was administered by their father. He paid more attention than ever to their education, delighting in Anna's rapid progress in her studies and urging her to keep an eye on the more elementary studies of her brother John which continued while they visited in Amsterdam. Anna was a lively and bright teen-ager, the delight of her father's eye.

De Witt was a strict if loving parent. He was therefore unprepared when Anna fell in love a year later with someone he thought unfitted for her. The affair could not be smiled away as puppy-love, for her sweetheart asked for her hand in marriage. It was not her age that worried De Witt, although she was just past sixteen; a girl of that age was considered old enough to wed. De Witt's concern was the swain. He thought the young man utterly unsuitable because he was an idler who would no doubt look to the councilor pensionary, the highest official in the government of Holland, to sponsor him for office. De Witt, writing to Wendela's two brothers-in-law for advice, admitted he already faced too much criticism for what he did on behalf of his relatives. If the suitor had come from a good family and had been a citizen of some

Holland town, that would not have mattered. But De Witt had known the father very well and the mother somewhat, and they had been such that, even if their son had inherited the best of their qualities, "I would rather take my children to the church to see them put into their graves" than married to a person of such temperament. The young man's conduct thus far indicated that he took after his parents, and De Witt was determined to exclude him from the family. We do not know the name of this suitor whom De Witt found so repellent. He probably was a member of the little international community at The Hague, hangers-on often on the make.

De Witt's letter still stuns with its harshness, all the more because it came from one whom the world thought was himself icy in temperament. There is in the letter the anger of a father who saw a beloved daughter throwing away her chance for a happy life, the scorn of a patrician for an upstart without redeeming qualities of diligence and intelligence, and, not least, a quality of all-or-nothing judgment (the grave rather than such a marriage!) that was absent in his politics. We may think De Witt a class-bound bigot or a far-seeing parent, but we glimpse in either case an almost insane intensity when someone he loved was touched and a willingness to face the worst that reminds us of the protagonists in the great French tragedies of Corneille that we know he read. We do not know what words were spoken between daughter and father, but Anna gave up her suitor and remained at home, which was now the house that still stands on the Kneuterdijk, just a block away from the Binnenhof.

While life was putting De Witt the husband and father to the hardest strains, he went on with his daily tasks of political leadership. Preserving the fragile peace made at Aachen a few weeks before Wendela's death required all his ability for concentration, but he seems to have sought respite from the demands of high office when the time came for his reelection as councilor pensionary later in July. At least Wicquefort, who was working closely with him, tells us that he sounded out the leaders of the States of Holland about allowing him to return to his old post as pensionary of Dordrecht, only to be told that he could not be spared. What the archives do report is that he was reelected with a doubled salary of 6,000 guilders a year retroactive to his first election in 1653. He therefore received 45,000 guilders in bonds, and the Nobles added another 15,000 for his services to them as pensionary of their order. The Dordrecht deputies had proposed that he be rewarded with 100,000 guilders, but he persuaded them to desist.

The financial grant was a tribute to his immense labors and extraordinary services, which left the regents of Holland with a sense that he was indispensable. Yet De Witt, in his letter of thanks to Valckenier, who had taken the original initiative for the added remuneration a year before in the town council of Amsterdam, recognized that even at this time he had not won complete assent of all the regents of Holland for his policies. Still his leadership of the province was stronger than ever, although it had to be constantly tended to.

Valckenier soon drew away from him, forming with Van Beuningen and Van Beverningk what has been described as a "middle party" between the States party and the Orangists. They were not so much a party, however, even in the loose seventeenth-century meaning of the term, as a group that was moving from allegiance to the "True Freedom" toward acceptance of the necessity to bring the Prince of Orange fully into the political as well as military leadership of the country. To some degree they were driven by jealousy of De Witt's fame and his monopoly of guidance of the Republic's policies, but Valckenier and Van Beuningen were certainly more narrowly concerned with Amsterdam's interests than De Witt, while Van Beverningk had been a restless member of the councilor pensionary's party ever since the difficulties over his election as treasurer general in the wake of the Exclusion crisis of 1654.

In 1669 Valckenier defeated a faction favorable to De Witt in the election of the four burgomasters of Amsterdam; one of the four chosen was Van Beuningen. The attack upon the councilor pensionary's influence was made even more explicit with a proposal that the States General establish a new office of Secretary of State to conduct the foreign policy of the Republic. The post was destined for Van Beuningen, but the proposal, which would have stripped De Witt of his most important duties, was defeated. The next year Valckenier chose to be reelected himself as burgomaster, although he had dominated the policies of Amsterdam whether in or out of office since the death of Zuidpolsbroek. De Witt avoided direct confrontation with him even when the Amsterdammer took a different tack in the vital matter of the election of the Prince of Orange to the Council of State. Holding the States of Holland in line when he could not be sure of Amsterdam's support, or all the more when the preeminent city opposed him outright, was extremely difficult.

Thus the ground under De Witt's feet became unsteady just as he faced the complexities and uncertainties of the diplomatic situation after the Peace of Aachen. Nonetheless he managed to improve the quality of regular Dutch diplomatic representation in France and England, which had sunk to an appallingly low level in recent years. It was possible to make do with able extraordinary envoys like Van Beuningen in Paris and Meerman in London, but they did not usually have the time to build up a body of friends who could tell them what was going on behind the scenes.

Van Beuningen, who had stayed on in Paris for a few months after the peace to tie up loose threads, insisted finally on going home late in September 1668; and William Boreel, the ailing ordinary ambassador whom he had effectually replaced, died at about the same time. Not until May two years later was Boreel's post finally filled, when it was given to Peter de Groot, the ambassador in Stockholm, who was both a close personal and political friend of De Witt's. During that long period the only official Dutch representative at the French court was a chargé d'affaires, to whom negotiations could not be entrusted. All important matters of discussion had to be handled at The Hague. But there D'Estrades had been recalled, and it was not until February 1669 that a new ambassador came. He was the able, soft-spoken Pomponne, who like De Groot had been his country's ambassador in Stockholm. If anyone would be able to restore confidence and friendship between France and the United Provinces, it would be Pomponne. He was a realist but not a cynic or an easy deceiver; a faithful servant of his king, he appreciated that other countries had their own interests and that good relations resulted from the meshing of the interests of one's own country and those of other states; in a word, in vision and character he was much like De Witt himself.

The situation with regard to England was somewhat better. The ordinary ambassador there was John Boreel, the son of William Boreel, who had died in Paris, and like his father both in his passionate Orangism and in his inadequacy for the high office he held. But at least he did not protest when De Witt neglected him and did his business in tandem with Meerman; protocol required only that Boreel write to the *griffier* of the States General, not to the councilor pensionary of Holland, as most envoys of the United Provinces did on an informal basis. It was a good sign when Charles II decided to send Temple to The Hague to take Downing's place, and with the rank of ambassador (Downing had only been a resident). De Witt found Temple personally very much to his liking; but where Pomponne did not ask to be trusted as a friend, Temple treated his relationship to De Witt as one of man to man, friend to friend, not just official personage to official personage. De Witt did not drop his guard, however much he responded to Temple's guileless appeal. As the leader of Dutch foreign policy, he knew that he was an officer of state, not a private person.

He had good reason to look beyond Temple, whose personal honor he did not question, to his master, for he did question the Englishman's copious assurances that the English king was sincere and steady in his friendship. Charles II had in fact resumed negotiations with Louis XIV and begun rearming his navy at the very time the Dutch were reducing theirs. Louis for his part sent Croissy, the brother of his Dutch-hating minister Colbert, to London with instructions to make an offensive–defensive alliance against the United Provinces if possible, holding over Charles's head the threat of renewal of friendship with the Dutch by agreement on the future of the Low Countries. It was not an empty threat, and the negotiations in London did not go smoothly.

Van Beuningen on his return did not hold out much hope for the resumption of good relations between the Dutch Republic and France. He gave so secret a report to the States General that it was not even entered in its records, but which nonetheless reached the ears of the public and aroused deep fears of what was coming. The peace just made would not last long, he argued; Louis XIV would resume the conquest of the Low Countries whenever the sickly young king of Spain (another Charles II, who began his reign in 1665 at the age of four) died, and would stir up enemies against the United Provinces on their borders, foment dissension and disorder within the country, and attack their commerce by heavy taxation upon their ships and goods. He urged the States General to take reprisals against the high tariff imposed on Dutch goods by Colbert in 1667 by putting similar taxes upon French goods imported into the Republic.

Although Van Beuningen took the lead in Dutch resistance to Colbert's "little war of money" against the Dutch, he was in perfect agreement with the French minister that these measures, which taken as a system we now call "mercantilism," had as their primary purpose to further the king's general policy. Although he was an Amsterdammer to the core, devoted to the commercial interests of his city, he did not make the mistake of historians of later centuries who assumed, out of dogma or ignorance, that it was the tariff conflict that was the source of the hostility between French and the Dutch Republic. Again agreeing with Colbert, he took it for granted that if the political differences between the States General and Louis XIV were settled, it would not be difficult to achieve agreement on matters of trade. In all of this he was supported by De Witt, who repeatedly turned to him for guidance when facing matters of commercial policy beyond his own understanding.

Pomponne's first task on his arrival was to counter the gloomy picture of French intentions painted by Van Beuningen. His master could offer the Dutch friendship, but not at the price of abandoning the eventual rights of his queen and her children in the Low Countries. On the contrary, the Dutch would have to pay a price, abandonment of the Triple Alliance, at once. No less significant, French policy no longer treated the advancement of the Prince of Orange as necessarily harmful to its interests, although Pomponne did not tell De Witt so.

When the two men met, it was a striking confrontation of intelligence and candor without the slightly cloying quality of Temple's affirmations of good will. To the councilor pensionary's declaration that the principle of keeping France at a distance from the Dutch borders was fundamental and unchangeable, the ambassador replied that the loss of France's friendship would be worse and that the Dutch should accept a "decision of Heaven" that they could not alter. Within a month, Pomponne came to the conclusion that the Dutch could not be cured of their "sickness." He stayed on at The Hague, reporting how De Witt coped with the rising fortunes of the Prince of Orange and other matters of moment, conducting no negotiations of substance but available if they should become necessary because the talks in London yielded no result.

As for the Triple Alliance, although it had become the core of

De Witt's diplomatic policy, the loyalty of its other members to it was brittle as glass. De Groot had been sent to Stockholm in April 1668 to stiffen the Swedes' resolve, but he discovered at once that for them the promised subsidy was all that mattered, and they would turn to France without compunction if it was not paid. Spain finally agreed to accept the promise made on its behalf, but by the time De Groot departed for his new mission to Paris a year later it had still not made the first payment.

The Spanish queen mother wanted the Triple Alliance extended first to include Spain as a full-fledged member, but when in February 1669 the Triple Alliance powers agreed upon the forces they would commit to the defense of the Spanish Netherlands, she withdrew a demand De Witt considered intolerable. Although the Spanish ambassador at The Hague informed the councilor pensionary that he was authorized to pay the 380,000 reichstaler promised to Sweden, the queen regent wanted the promise of the allies to dispatch military aid as soon as they were informed of an attack, without making any judgment of their own as to whether it constituted a *casus belli*. Again she desisted, and at the end of January 1670, two years after the conclusion of the alliance, the promise to pay Sweden was at last honored, and the first installment of 200,000 reichstaler was remitted early in March to the Bank of Amsterdam for transfer to Sweden. Only then was the Triple Alliance actually in full force.

It was, however, little more than its own ghost. France and England had moved forward, although not without much acrimonious bargaining, in their negotiations for an alliance of their own in place of the Triple Alliance and directed against the United Provinces. De Witt, aware as he was of the catastrophic implications of such a realignment of forces, nonetheless had to conduct Dutch policy without the help of competent envoys in either the French or the English capitals, not at least until De Groot's arrival in Paris, by which time the work of undermining the Triple Alliance was almost complete. John Boreel, the regular ambassador in London, was useless; he learned little of what was going on. In April 1669, De Witt received a warning of what was afoot, but it came from a Swedish diplomat friendly to the Dutch, Esaias von Pufendorf, who was returning home by way of The Hague. French ministers, trying to persuade the Swedish government to drop out of the Triple Alliance, had told him that England would certainly do so, and they had shown him letters in which Croissy reported giving bribes to some of the English king's ministers.

De Witt thereupon called on Temple "as a friend, not as a minister," to seek an explanation. The reply may have honored Temple as a friend, but it casts a strange light upon him as a diplomat. The story may only be a French trick to put us at odds, he told the councilor pensionary; but if it is true, I too have been deceived and I will have no further part in destroying what I have helped to build for the good of our two countries and all Christendom.

De Witt then made light of his own anxieties. When he had first taken office fifteen years before, he had been quite suspicious; now he was less so. But not so much less that he did not express wonder that Charles II raised a fuss about "such a trifle" as the transfer of Surinam to the Dutch, as provided in the Treaty of Breda, or why he supported the English East India Company against its Dutch rival with such passion, when their disputes were "fitter for merchants than ministers."

It was a remarkable exchange. The Englishman who served a cynical master spoke from his heart with obvious sincerity (and had been chosen because he would); and the Dutchman instructed the man he accepted as a friend in the impersonal principle of the paramount interest of one's country ("reason of state" in the jargon of seventeenth-century political writers).

Temple was indeed being deceived. The negotiations between Croissy and the English ministers were going so swimmingly by the autumn of 1669 that even Boreel began to wonder why they got on so well. Yet, he assured De Witt that the Triple Alliance was intact and that the worst to be feared was English neutrality if it came to a French assault upon the United Provinces. This was a judgment that De Witt himself was beginning to make. He was now himself the victim of his belief in the impersonal supremacy of national strategic interests, which – he held – must deter Charles II from feeding the nightmare monster of French control of the Low Countries and the high seas.

The English monarch was confident, however, that he could tame the French lion and use him. By this time the terms of an Anglo-French treaty had been virtually agreed upon, specifically its provision for a joint offensive war against the Dutch Republic. Final conclusion was delayed only by disagreement over the time when Charles II would publicly proclaim his conversion to Catholicism and over the size of the French subsidies (the king of England could be as greedy as the Swedes, although on a far grander scale). Louis XIV for his part no longer felt the need to keep the Dutch card in reserve if the negotiations with England did not succeed, and he could give free rein to his sense of betrayal by the Dutch, and especially by De Witt personally. He ceased to see a difference between the councilor pensionary, who still pressed Pomponne for conciliation, and Van Beuningen, who did not conceal that he thought France was becoming the Republic's greatest enemy.

By the spring of 1670, with no French armies on the move, Dutch anxieties were calmed. They were suddenly revived, however, when it was announced that the duchess of Orléans, the beloved surviving sister of Charles II, would visit him at Dover. De Witt was able finally to persuade the States General that someone more suited for his diplomatic duties than Boreel was needed at London, and Van Beuningen was persuaded to accept once more the post of extraordinary ambassador, a role he loathed.

When Van Beuningen reached London early in June, the alliance between France and England was complete. The preamble of the Treaty of Dover gave plain voice to the anger of monarchs against a republic that committed the double crimes of ingratitude toward allies to whom it owed its foundation, and insolence in setting itself up as the judge over all other rulers. The war upon the United Provinces was fixed for 1671, and its aim would be to dismember the Republic, with "what was possible" being done for the Prince of Orange. It also provided for Charles II's announcement, immediately upon the declaration of war, that he was embracing the faith of Rome.

William III had so far declined his royal uncle's urgent invitation to visit his mother's homeland, and therefore had not been present in Dover during the days when the doom of his own country was being arranged: he was too busy at home promoting his own career. From the time of the adoption of the "Eternal Edict," the Prince had grown from boy to man very much on his own. He threw off the last of the apron strings that tied him to his cautious grandmother, with her deep respect for legality; but he also sidestepped the dependence on Charles II that such intimates as Zuilestein thought was his surest path to power. He built upon the opportunities available to him under existing conditions without calling into play the instrument of popular violence that Buat (and behind him, we may be sure, Zuilestein) had in vain counted upon during the war years. He made skillful use of the persistent fidelity of the outer provinces, most of all Zeeland; the rivalries within Holland, where dissident towns were jealous of De Witt's preeminence; and the readiness, even eagerness, of the order of Nobility in Holland to accept him as their natural leader. He built up his own position without making a premature direct challenge to the dominance of De Witt and the States party.

The "Harmony" worked out as part of the political package with the "Eternal Edict" turned out to be misnamed. The struggle between the Orangists and the States party over the Prince's advancement continued without interruption, the former pressing for all that was possible as soon as possible and the latter giving no more than they had to. The Orangist leaders, who included not only the elder members of the Prince's family, Amalia van Solms and Zuilestein in particular, but also the principal regents in the Orangist towns and provinces, pressed for William's immediate "designation" to the military offices left open to him. Until he came of age, of course, someone else would have to perform his duties.

De Witt rejected such "designation" because it would limit the eventual freedom of choice of the States in the election of a captain general. The States of Holland warned the other provinces that they must accept that the Prince would not receive high military office until he reached twenty-three years of age in November 1673, although he would be given a seat in the Council of State at once. Otherwise, Holland would go ahead with appointment of a commander of the troops in its pay.

The threat of the breakup of the military unity of the Republic worked, and by mid-January 1668 Holland's proposal was adopted by a majority of the provinces in the States General. Two field marshals were named, John Maurice and Paulus Wirtz. Wirtz, who although formally second in rank became in practice the commander of the whole army, soon discovered that the army was ill-trained and ill-equipped, and that the troops, devoted to the Prince of Orange, saw him as a usurper.

William, even while he continued to enjoy De Witt's tutorship in the craft of politics, began to practice what he was learning to his own advantage. In September 1668, he left The Hague with the announced purpose of a hunting trip to States Brabant near Zeeland, but turned up unexpectedly in Middelbürg to assume in person the post of First Noble of Zeeland. This position had traditionally gone to the Prince of Orange as marquis of Veere and Flushing, and the States of Zeeland had confirmed it as his in 1660. The trip had been long planned with Amalia's approval, as she admitted to De Witt, and the secrecy had been necessary to prevent the councilor pensionary from rallying his friends in Zeeland to prevent William's success. What made the political stroke more painful, apart from its indication that the Prince was not reluctant to act boldly, was that he named the most reckless of all his friends, Odijk, to act as his deputy.

This episode reveals a significant peculiarity in the relationship between William III and his companions. They were hotheads, as ready to risk their all for their beloved Prince as to indulge in threats to the life of the hated councilor pensionary, and they had little sense of what was politically practicable at any given moment. He was at one and the same time ambitious and cautious, inscrutable if need be, but fundamentally Dutch in his commitments.

During 1669, William watched as the Orangist provinces failed to break down Holland's insistence upon enforcing the principles of the "Eternal Edict." The situation took a new turn the next year when he decided to accept the military offices open to him under the "Harmony," without putting aside his ultimate political ambitions. De Witt now had to face the certainty that William would be elected to the Council of State, but he held out briefly for giving him only an advisory, not a conclusive vote. He gave way on this in order to gain a more important provision, the reaffirmation of the incompatibility of military and political office. He steered the election through the States of Holland (formally, approval of such action by the States General), vanquishing last-ditch resistance of the towns whose commitment to the "True Freedom" was less flexible than his own.

On June 2, the Prince took his seat in the Council of State. It was a victory well worth the delay of this trip to England to see his royal uncle. It was no more than a small breach in the dike of the "True Freedom," but whether the trickle would turn into a torrent would be determined by events. There was now no doubt that the Prince of Orange would play an increasing role in the life of the Dutch Republic, but what was still to be decided was the relationship between him and the councilor pensionary, whether uneasy collaboration or open enmity.

10

Against the tide
1670–1672

For the two years that followed the conclusion of the Treaty of Dover, history seemed to play cruelly with De Witt, like a cat toying with a mouse before it suddenly kills it. He could dart this way and that, but he could never break out of the fatal circle of his dilemma. His intelligence, his strength of will, his courage yielded no solution to the problem of how to win the war against Europe's mightiest monarch that was surely coming.

The picture would have been even bleaker if he had realized that Charles II intended not merely to practice a profitable neutrality while Louis XIV invaded the United Provinces but would join in the attack. But the knowledge would not have changed what he had to do: to seek such allies as Dutch money or fear for their own security could recruit; to build up the Republic's army and navy; and to hold on to power within the country against the rising fortunes of the Prince of Orange, whom he still saw as doing the bidding of the king of England. Rational calculation could offer no hope in such a situation; only belief in a God of Hosts who decided the course of battle even against the odds of human expectations could give solace.

The first task remained to achieve whatever was possible in restoring good relations with France and England. When Van Beuningen reached London as extraordinary ambassador on June 7, a week after the conclusion of the Treaty of Dover, neither he nor De Witt realized the full significance of what had been concluded in the meeting of Charles II and his sister, the duchess of Orléans. Van Beuningen, the very soul of suspiciousness when at the French court, was at first hopeful in England, especially after the sudden death of the duchess upon her return to France. If, as some thought, she had been poisoned, would that not spoil relations between Charles and Louis? An autopsy brought reassurance that she had died a natural death, and the two kings were intent upon keeping their league against the Dutch intact. It was not Van Beuningen but the chargé d'affairs in Paris, Rumpf, who first sent a warning that Charles II had gone over to the French side, although he did not learn how complete that transfer of alliances had been.

De Witt did whatever he could to court the favor of the English monarch, so long as it did not endanger fundamental Dutch interests. When Temple asked for the arrest of Cornet George Joyce, who a quarter of a century before had turned King Charles I over to the parliamentary army and was now living in exile in Rotterdam, the councilor pensionary acceded, but he insisted it be done in strict accordance with Dutch laws. He warned the authorities in Rotterdam of the danger in offending Charles II, but they responded by permitting Joyce to flee to safety and oblivion. De Witt refused pointblank a request for a pardon for Kievit, and he would not support expulsion of three Scots preachers resident in Holland unless evidence was given that they were guilty of rebellion, not merely of religious nonconformity.

He was more forthcoming about meeting English complaints against offensive pamphlets and such public "insults" as celebrating the naval victories in the late war with tapestries and paintings and by permitting paid visits to the *Royal Charles*, the English flagship captured in the Medway. A painting in the Dordrecht city hall that depicted the victory was moved to a room where the public was not admitted, and visits to the ship were halted. De Witt nonetheless privately treated the English complaints with disdain, especially because Charles permitted his own subjects to speak and print worse things against the Dutch.

The peril from France was more obvious, but the Dutch leaders did not fully grasp the objective of the flattery which the French began to bestow upon the Prince of Orange. It was realized that Louis XIV was no longer an upholder of the States party, but not that his anxiety about William's elevation had been lessened because he regarded the Prince as so subservient to Charles II that he presented no danger to the French king who was his uncle's ally. De Groot, who became the new Dutch ambassador in France, reached Paris in September, and De Witt continued to pin a thin hope of restoring French friendship upon Louis's presumed desire not to see the Prince of Orange in power. But it remained an argument of desperation to which the French court closed its ears. (Over the decades to come, when William III became his most implacable foe, Louis seems to have avoided thinking back to this miscalculation. Of course he had assumed that he would be triumphant in the war against the Dutch Republic, and then William would have been under the thumb of the victors. It took a long time for Louis to learn that a statesman ought not and dare not count too confidently upon military victory.) Dutch fears that a French army marching northward would attack the United Provinces proved unfounded; its target turned out to be the duke of Lorraine, Charles IV, who persisted in seeking to build up with Dutch support an army of 13,000 men to be available for use against France.

Dutch anxiety was also aroused and less easily stilled when the duke of Buckingham arrived in France in August. Rumpf learned that his purpose was to conduct negotiations for an offensive–defensive alliance (he failed to realize that this was a sham negotiation to fool Protestants like Buckingham who would accept a war against the Dutch but not the king's conversion to Catholicism, promised in the Dover Treaty, of which they were not told).

De Witt found the report incredible and beseeched Van Beuningen to discover the truth in England. Arlington, the chief minister of Charles II, found it easy to reassure Van Beuningen that there was nothing to worry about. The English, he admitted, sought to gain some advantage over the Dutch, but they did not want a war to the death. Van Beuningen found Arlington's assurance more credible because he observed a significant shift in English public opinion. No longer was the Dutch Republic the principal opponent they feared; it was now France, and people and Parliament alike saw the Triple Alliance as a Protestant league against a common Catholic threat. Dutch suspicions were further dispelled by the formal ratification of the Triple Alliance and settlement of the Anglo-Dutch dispute over Surinam.

If actions speak louder than words, then only those who had to believe in the friendship of Charles II could continue to do so. De Groot soon after his arrival in Paris was able to reinforce Rumpf's report that France and England were coming together against the Dutch. De Witt found such treachery on the part of the English monarch hard to believe, but he was deeply shaken when Temple was recalled in September. When the Englishman came to tell him that he was going home, the councilor pensionary replied with sadness and mild sarcasm. He did not think that Buckingham had gone to Paris "to see the country and learn the language," and he reminded Temple that it was Charles who had "engaged the States" in the Triple Alliance, whereas if they had accepted partition of the Spanish Netherlands (obviously in his mind still the best solution of the problem after cantonment), they would have retained the "ancient kindness and alliance" of France. To break the Triple Alliance, as Charles seemed to be doing, would be both to offend honor and violate the interests of the English nation.

Temple replied as he had before, confusing personal honesty and diplomatic veracity. He did not believe the king would act against his "honour and safety," but if this were true, he would have no part of it. If he came back to his post, De Witt would "know more," and if he did not, he would "guess more." In reply, De Witt merely smiled and said he would try to cure his suspicions.

His suspicions in fact did not go far enough. He now expected Charles II to leave the Dutch in the lurch when the French attacked them, keeping a balance between them to England's advantage. He told Boreel and Van Beuningen to warn the English ministers that if that was the English plan, the Dutch would respond by making the best settlement they could with France. He still did not grasp the full extent of Charles's treachery, nor that he no longer had any French card to play if need be. He was trapped in his illusions by his political needs as much as the Orangists were in theirs; worse, the prospect of war against France and England at the same time would seem to argue for advancement of the Prince as a last desperate stroke to win back the friendship of Charles II. But that was to De Witt a choice between alternative forms of enslavement for the Dutch Republic, in other words, no choice at all.

At least he did not share the naive belief of the Orangists that the Prince of Orange, who left for his long-delayed visit to England in November, would salvage the alliance. The meeting of Charles II and William III was hardly the embrace of like-minded men, however warm personally. William was shocked by his uncle's description of the Protestants in England as a subversive faction, and his protestation of his own unsullied faith made the king decide not to tell him the truth about the Dover Treaty. William, no more aware of Charles's ultimate intentions toward the Republic than was De Witt, therefore continued to rely upon Charles's support for his advancement. But he forthrightly told his uncle that he sought the downfall only of De Witt and his "cabal," not of the Dutch Republic itself, to which he was bound in honor and fidelity. Charles must "not be bound too closely" to France either. The king's reply was a brief admonition that William would not become the head of the Dutch state on his own.

Even before William had departed for London, Charles had given the strongest possible proof of his antipathy for the Dutch short of actual armed assault. This was a decision to keep Temple at home and to sent in his stead none other than Downing. As Wicquefort described it, this was putting one who frankly hated the Republic in the place of one who loved it. Arlington put it in even blunter words to the French ambassador: Downing was better "fitted to pick a quarrel." The decision was prompted by Emperor Leopold's embarrassing request to be admitted into the Triple Alliance, which Temple would support if allowed to. The return of Van Beuningen to Holland in December left the Dutch with Boreel alone in London either to repair the damaged friendship or to sniff out the English plans, tasks at which he had so far done poorly.

De Witt saw the refusal of Charles II to discuss the Emperor's request as an indication of a lukewarm attitude toward the Triple Alliance itself; but he continued to believe that this implied at worst neutrality, not belligerency, when war would come between France and the Republic. He began to explore another possible approach to relations with England, an appeal to the nation over the head of its king. Late in January 1671, he asked Boreel to find out what the "most intelligent and resolute" members of Parliament thought about the situation. This was too dangerous an approach to follow up for the time being, because there was probably nothing that would more certainly make Charles an implacable and open enemy of the Republic. That it would be giving tit for tat for the use he was making of the Orangist party in the United Provinces did not matter; the king of England was not interested in equity but in power. When the deputies of Leiden early in February put forward a proposal such as was merely hinted at in De Witt's request to Boreel, it was turned down.

Another proposal, to bribe the chief English ministers, did not win De Witt's favor. He had no confidence in bribes, revealing that an attempt to win over Clarendon and another minister of Charles II before the recent war had been useless. Only a commitment based upon self-interest was worth anything, and Dutch money would be better spent on ships and soldiers.

De Groot in Paris persevered in his tasks, but soon discovered that he could not argue the French out of their obvious intention to go to war, but also found out much about their plans. He wrote not only the usual dispatches to the States General and the States of Holland, which he had to assume would quickly come to be known to the French, but also to De Witt, who was both trustworthy and still the principal partisan of a pro-French policy. He went beyond even these letters, however, by confiding his deepest thoughts and bleakest fears to his friend Wicquefort, the historian and diplomatic intelligencer who served De Witt as a kind of French secretary after his expulsion from France in 1659. What Wicquefort learned from De Groot would become known to De Witt with little chance of going astray.

De Groot got wind of the decision to put off the declaration of war from 1671, as provided by the Treaty of Dover, until 1672, because of the muddled diplomatic situation in Germany, well before the new date was incorporated into the "simulated" treaty negotiated with Buckingham in December. But even he failed to learn that the English would be French allies, not just neutrals. He urged with all the vigor of phrase at his command that the Dutch turn rapidly and resolutely to arming themselves to meet the coming assault.

De Witt found this message helpful in spurring rearmament, noting that it was characteristic of the Dutch nation not to believe in a danger until it was right in front of them. De Groot's warnings grew more urgent in December when it was announced that Louis XIV would visit Dunkirk in the spring with an army of 30,000–40,000 men. Its public purpose was to construct new fortifications, but De Groot suspected it might be employed against the Dutch.

Meanwhile he did what he could to counter the heavy burdens that Colbert was putting upon Dutch trade and goods. On October 17, he submitted to Lionne a formal memorial presenting the arguments for free trade a century before they were given classic expression by Adam Smith. Lionne found the memorial persuasive, but told De Groot that in such matters it was Colbert who was listened to, and he added that he saw no reason why any favors should be shown to the Dutch unless they first changed the maxims responsible for the estrangement between their countries – a plain reference to the Dutch opposition to Louis XIV's ambitions in the Spanish Netherlands.

The Dutch responded with reprisals against French imports, but Colbert was not dismayed. The States General had violated their treaties with the king "on other, more important occasions," and he would reply as proper. Yet the "little war for trade," as Colbert called it, would be almost useless unless it reduced the ability of the Dutch to wage the big war that was coming. De Witt, from the opposite side, saw the issue in exactly the same way. The "true cause" for the onslaught would be the Peace of Aachen and the guarantee given afterwards by the Triple Alliance to Spain. No one, he wrote to De Groot, should be taken in by assertions that the tariff controversy was the course of the war. There can hardly be clearer statements of the primacy of the strategic conflict over the Spanish Netherlands as the origin of the war of 1672.

Yet the battle of tariffs and bans served to harden the French feeling that the Dutch were ungrateful and deserved what was planned for them. De Witt saw the reprisals as necessary, more to reaffirm Dutch courage and resoluteness than because he hoped they would bring much change in French policy. He was especially indignant that in Zeeland, which was late in approving the retaliatory measures, it was the Prince of Orange's town of Flushing that resisted the decision most strongly.

De Groot actually put the issue in terms which caught the psychological dimensions of Louis XIV's ambition. He wrote two letters to Fagel during December 1670 which De Witt advised the *griffier* not to read to the full States General, since they would then certainly come into the hands of Pomponne, the French ambassador, and would destroy whatever credit De Groot had at the French court. The dispatches were not read and Fagel probably destroyed them, because they are not in the archives; but we have a clue to what he wrote by remarks in a later dispatch in January. The people around Louis XIV were urging him on toward attainment of glory, which they said consisted of achieving everything within France and abroad "by plain force" (*de haute lutte*). If this was true – and anyone who reads the French monarch's writings cannot deny the power of this trait in his personality, although he would also add the king's equally strong desire to be sure and safe when he acted, as De Groot later recognized – then there was little hope for De Groot's mission. That was how De Groot felt, but he had to stay on till the bitter end, both for the information he acquired and the warnings he sent.

Unlike Boreel in London, De Groot had friends both personal and political who confided to him information and judgments which, if Louis XIV had known what they were doing, would probably have cost them their heads. Some were opponents of royal absolutism, although outright advocates of republicanism, like Marshal Frederick von Schomberg, were certainly very few. Others were Huguenots, who were beginning to feel the sting of royal persecution.

De Groot told De Witt late in February of an astounding visit he had just had from a Frenchman so highly placed that he was able to tell the Dutch ambassador everything about the treaty negotiated by Buckingham except that it was a duplication of the Treaty of Dover, without the promise of Charles II's conversion to Catholicism but setting back the date of the war a year. The aim of the allied monarchs was not just the defeat of the States General but the transformation of the United Provinces into a monarchy with the Prince of Orange as its sovereign. The attack would not come across the Spanish Netherlands but by a naval assault even before the declaration of war and a land invasion of the eastern Netherlands from Germany by troops bypassing Spanish territory.

De Groot was stunned, for this was even worse than he had anticipated, and he did not take it as literal truth (how accurate it was he would discover little more than a year later). De Witt shared his friend's astonishment and incredulity, but did not dare inform the States of Holland or the Delegated Councilors that he had received such a troubling letter. The news would get out and cause disturbances and trouble among the people.

Just who De Groot's informant was has never been discovered. French historians have paid virtually no attention to this revelation of disaffection at a very high level of the French government. This is all the more surprising because the disclosure of the French war plans was repeated a year later, presumably by someone else, and De Groot then said it was confirmed by indirect word from Condé, "who has always shown himself to be one of my best friends." Was

Condé the informant the first time? He fits the facts as few others would: someone not in the king's highest council, who were alone informed of the Treaty of Dover; yet who would know the most secret operational plans for the war. But whether Condé's reconciliation with the king after the Peace of the Pyrenees was feigned really mattered little to the Dutch, however significant it would be to historians of France; Condé, or whoever the informant was, did not dare to take his position publicly and could not shake the course of events. And Condé, whatever his private opinions may have been, commanded the army that invaded the United Provinces in 1672.

The rest of 1671 proved uneventful. De Groot accompanied Louis XIV to Dunkirk in May, and his fears that it would prove to be a cover for a sudden attack upon the United Provinces were not sustained. In November he learned that Pellisson, the king's historiographer, was working on a declaration of war against the Dutch Republic. He was therefore somewhat surprised that the French court gave itself so wholeheartedly to the enjoyment of theater and ballet, and he hoped even so late as December that the king might at the very last moment swing away from his course as too risky.

The only argument that De Witt thought might carry weight was the danger to France if William III came to power as a protégé of Charles II, but he saw that it would take a divine miracle to get Louis XIV to change his mind. Nonetheless it was the argument that De Groot was instructed by the States General to present to the king in December. The ambassador himself saw how little persuasive force it would carry: the king and his ministers no longer found any cause for worry in the Prince's promotion, thinking he would be easier to handle than the republican government had been. De Groot's hope shifted from forestalling war to the possibility that it would be brief if violent, a "straw fire."

Soon after the New Year, De Groot presented to Louis XIV a letter from the States General urging conciliation between France and the Republic, and he asked the king against whom France was arming. Louis replied with a transparent evasion: that would become known in the spring. He stated frankly that the reason for the estrangement between himself and the Dutch was the States had broken their alliance with him, and that he would do what his dignity required. De Groot now abandoned his own fierce opposition to the promotion of the Prince of Orange, although it was not any expectation that Charles would therefore change his plans that motivated him, only the possibility that the English king's subjects – fearing that with Louis's support he would try to impose absolutism and Catholicism upon them – would compel him to turn away from France.

Such hopes were not idle, but were based upon real political possibilities in England that would take time, and another defeat at sea, to lead to political action. In the meanwhile, Charles felt free to go his own way. He even found a pretext for war against the Dutch in a conflict over precedence at sea during the summer of 1671. The royal yacht *Merlin* was sent to bring Lady Dorothy Temple home, and on its return it sailed through the main Dutch fleet lying at anchor off Walcheren; the king's own flag flew from its masthead because Lady Dorothy, as the ambassador's wife, could be said to represent the sovereignty of the king in her person, as her husband undoubtedly did. The captain of the little yacht demanded that every Dutch warship, fifty-six of them in all, give him a salute in recognition, but De Ruyter merely dipped his own colors. Charles was simultaneously insulted and delighted: this was sufficient grounds for war. But the *Merlin's* captain was arrested and sent to the Tower because he had not responded by firing his guns at De Ruyter.

Downing came to The Hague in January and soon played tough, as the king wanted him to. He protested De Ruyter's failure to give the salute of his whole fleet to the *Merlin*, not as a courtesy but as owed to the king by right. He was rebuffed and his recall was announced only a month after his arrival. He left at once for home although he did not have specific orders to quit his post, and he was arrested too on reaching London for having alerted the Dutch by his unauthorized departure.

De Witt did in fact take the return of the detested ambassador as a harbinger of war. So too did Constantine Huygens, the Prince of Orange's secretary, who wrote a sarcastic query to Arlington asking whether the English had forgotten the maxims of Queen Elizabeth's day (support for the Dutch, obviously, although against Spain, not France). De Witt might have been pleased by such patriotic fervor, but he also knew that Orangists still thought the promotion of the Prince could avert war.

The helplessness of Boreel now meant that someone more able

was needed in London, and Meerman was sent there in March in a last desperate move to win Charles back to the Triple Alliance, which seemed the only ground for Louis XIV's projected attack upon the Republic. Meerman reached London on March 18, just as the duke of York was preparing to take the English fleet out to sea. Four days later Meerman wrote to De Witt that Charles II had boastfully told him the duke's fleet would attack the Dutch ships returning from Smyrna and suggested he return on the same vessel that had brought him from Holland. Meerman asked permission to leave for home because there were things to report which he dared not put on paper.

The Republic was as ready as De Witt could make it. He had not awaited the revelation of the full extent of the Anglo–French rapprochement to begin work on strengthening the Dutch diplomatically and militarily.

The quest for allies to take the place of the Triple Alliance defectors had begun by the summer of 1670, when it was only too obvious that England had turned its back upon the league of 1668. The importance of Sweden, its third member, became all the greater. The problem with Sweden continued to be that it had nothing very much to fear from French territorial aggrandizement and was held to the league only by its desire for subsidies. But when it came to giving out money, Louis XIV could more than match the States General.

Yet, once De Groot had quitted his brief Swedish embassy to take up the more burdensome post as ambassador in Paris, there was only another, inadequate, junior diplomat, Nicholas Heinsius, to represent the interests of the States General in Stockholm. The return of Pomponne from The Hague to Stockholm in 1671 was a clear sign that France was making every effort to draw Sweden out of the Triple Alliance, into neutrality or into armed hostility against the Dutch. De Witt could find no one better to follow Pomponne to the Swedish capital than William van Haren, a Friesland deputy to the States General who was the councilor pensionary's open political foe. By the time Van Haren arrived in Stockholm in October, Pomponne had already departed for France to become the new French foreign minister in the place of Lionne, who had died a month earlier. Pomponne had not yet accomplished his purpose, and Van Haren did what he could to hold the Swedes within the Triple Alliance (for the English had not formally pronounced its demise). Although De Witt had support for a closer alliance with the Swedes, the Dutch would not pay them as much as they wanted and they decided early in 1672 to sign a treaty of neutrality with Louis XIV.

Elector Frederick William of Brandenburg was no less hungry for subsidies than the Swedes, but it was not the only issue for him, as it was for them. He had many bones to pick with the government at The Hague, ranging from a decades-old squabble over a debt owed to Dutch bondholders to his antipathy for the régime of the "True Freedom" that barred his nephew William III from his forefathers' offices. On the other hand, he did not want to see the United Provinces, the strongest Protestant power on the mainland of Europe, utterly defeated and destroyed, for that would put both his faith and his own independence in the gravest peril. He was tempted by French offers to pay well for his alliance, but would go no further than to offer his mediation. His shilly-shallying led the Prince of Orange to wonder when his uncle in Berlin would join the French camp. This was a concern that might have reassured the councilor pensionary about William's loyalty to the Dutch cause, although it was the Prince's connection to Charles II that worried De Witt most.

By the autumn of 1671, Frederick William found himself being drawn to the Dutch side in the impending conflict by the compelling force of basic interests. He informed the Dutch of the French approach to him and his preference for an alliance with the States General. A capable minister was needed to negotiate with the elector. When Van Beverningk, back from a mission to Spain, refused to go as far as Berlin, De Witt turned to Adrian Godard Reede, lord of Amerongen, who if he paraded his support for the Orangist cause was nonetheless an experienced diplomat.

Amerongen's task was eased by a French decision in February 1672, taken after Pomponne's return from Stockholm, to seek the alliance of Sweden rather than Brandenburg and other German princes. The Dutch thereupon offered the elector both funds and the eventual return of the towns in his Rhineland territories, notably Orsoy, Wesel and Rheinberg, where they had had garrisons ever since they retook them from the Spaniards during the Thirty Years War. Fearful of committing himself too far, Frederick William was encouraged by Emperor Leopold to back the Dutch, and he signed an agreement to provide military assistance to the

Republic after the French declaration of war, although it did not include any promise to return the Rhenish towns.

Leopold I's attitude was another sign that the impending war was causing a fundamental shift in the European balance of forces. The outbreak of the War of Devolution had sharpened his sense of Habsburg rivalry with the Bourbon house of France and he permitted his wide-ranging diplomat Lisola, who had already a reputation as a fierce opponent of France, to build an alliance to defend the Spanish Netherlands. Although De Witt (like Lisola) was unaware of the secret treaty for partition of the Spanish monarchy in the event of the death of King Charles II of Spain made between Louis XIV and Leopold I on January 19, 1668, the councilor pensionary sought to improve relations with the emperor without granting him entry into the Triple Alliance, which Lisola so urgently requested. When De Witt persuaded the States General to name a resident at the Imperial court in 1669, however, it was with the goal of expanding the Triple Alliance in accordance with Lisola's wishes.

In Vienna the new resident, Gerard Hamel Bruynincx, an old schoolmate of De Witt's, began to build up good relations. But he was not able to prevent the cautious Leopold from agreeing with Louis XIV late in 1671 to remain neutral in the event of war between France and the members of the Triple Alliance, although the 1671 accord excluded French operations in Germany, thus leaving Leopold with his hands free to some extent, at least in Germany. As war came closer, the emperor began to swing toward the Dutch side, although without abandoning his neutral status. But he supported, as we have seen, the elector of Brandenburg's shift in favor of the Republic, and, with the Triple Alliance in shreds, even indirect assistance was of great value to the Dutch.

As for Spain, mistrust and historical antipathy continued to plague the relations with the ancient foe, though the common threat from France drove them toward collaboration. The Dutch ambassador in Madrid had died in 1669, but he was replaced a year later by the able Van Beverningk, who had been reluctant to take on new diplomatic duties but had been persuaded by De Witt, Van Beuningen and other leaders of Holland. He left in December 1670 with good prospects, for the new governor general in the Spanish Netherlands, the count of Monterey, had already proved to be an excellent administrator as well as a supple realist committed to improved relations with the Dutch. The situation Van Beverningk found in Spain was more difficult, for the queen regent continued her attempts to force the States General into open confrontation with Louis XIV. He did, however, to De Witt's relief, gain her consent to arbitration of Spain's disputes with France concerning the extent of the territories ceded by the Peace of Aachen; when he returned home in July 1671, he had persuaded her also to give instructions to Monterey to break with France as soon as the United Provinces were attacked. It did not matter greatly that the assistance promised would consist of auxiliary forces only: the step forward was significant. De Witt had already promised the Spanish ambassador at The Hague, Gamarra, that the States General would aid the Spanish Netherlands in case of direct French attack upon them, and would undertake to conclude neither truce nor peace with Louis XIV without Spain. This promise had not yet been turned into a formal treaty when Gamarra died in August; but it moved forward even before Manuel de Lira arrived as the new ambassador in November. The treaty was successfully concluded in December 1671.

The importance attached to this Dutch–Spanish treaty was such that measures to make it effective began even before the formal ratifications were completed in February 1672. A deputation of three headed by Cornelius de Witt was sent to Brussels to work with Monterey on military preparations. Cornelius found Monterey a man after his own heart, full of grim determination and ready to strike hard and quickly. Although Cornelius had been named a deputy in the field, assigned to accompany the Dutch army on the outbreak of war, his brother urged him to remain at Brussels until formally recalled. John even went further, suggesting to Cornelius that the time had come to take the initiative against Louis XIV, although a first strike against the French military storehouses in the Rhineland would have to have Spain's prior approval. But he soon abandoned the idea as too risky, and he was reluctant to meet Monterey's demand for Dutch troops to be stationed in the southern Netherlands under his command. Finally, in March 1672, six regiments were sent, but subject to recall if the French attacked the United Provinces first. The war began, however, with an English attack upon the Smyrna fleet, and Cornelius was recalled to serve as deputy aboard the fleet with De Ruyter, as he had done in 1667, and he was replaced at Brussels by Van Beuningen.

**:

.**

: ** concerned

As the situation worsened, De Witt began to consider the possibility of recruiting Bishop Galen of Münster as an ally of the Republic but that warrior prelate was too embittered against the Dutch not to respond to the offer of Louis XIV to join in the attack upon the United Provinces in 1672. De Witt made no effort to gain the elector of Cologne, whose close ties to France were well known; and it was from his territory that the major French assault upon the Republic was eventually launched.

All in all, De Witt's diplomatic successes in these two years were few and small, yet they played an essential part in the war once it came. Whether the councilor pensionary would remain at the helm of the state depended, however, on his ability to prepare the country for the immense challenge and whether he himself could accept the inevitable ascent of the Prince of Orange, certainly as commander of the army and in all probability with a share in the political leadership.

The intertwining of the military and political roles of the Prince was demonstrated soon after his election to the Council of State in 1670. A deputy sent by the States General to pay an official visit to Louis XIV in the part of Flanders recently conquered from Spain reported to Their High Mightinesses on his return. The presiding deputy, a Frieslander, proposed that William be invited to attend the session and be seated at the table in an armchair, as had been usual with the Princes of Orange in the past. De Witt thought the proposal a trick to pay special honor to William beyond what Holland had accorded him, and the resistance of Holland wore down the other provinces. It was a triumph that brought only symbolic advantage to the States party, while confirming the Prince in his conviction that De Witt would not easily assent to his further advancement. Van Gendt recognized that the situation had changed by resigning as the Prince's governor; while the States of Holland, by disbanding the education committee, acknowledged that the Prince of Orange, who would be twenty years of age in less than four months, now stood on his own feet.

For the next year the most difficult of De Witt's problems were not concerned directly with the Prince, but with worsening relations with important towns in Holland and with the other provinces, principally Zeeland. Valckenier, holding Amsterdam in a firm grip of his own, abandoned the policy of friendliness toward the councilor pensionary that he had adopted after the episode of the "Eternal Edict." He now felt safe to give vent to his jealousy of De Witt, and also wished to mend his fences with the Orangist party. His immediate motive, however, was to meet the desire of Amsterdam to have the load of taxation upon its trade and shipping lightened. De Witt, alarmed lest the revenues of the admiralties be reduced at a time when they had to pay the costs of enormously expanding the navy, sought help from Van Beuningen, who was in England, and from Fagel. This enabled him to win a majority in the States of Holland for a compromise that provided immediate revenues enabling the admiralties to cope with the preparations for a war visible on the horizon.

The dispute between De Witt and Valckenier had become bitter and personal, but the Amsterdammer fell victim to his own arrogance. A coalition formed against him in the town council, defeating him for reelection as burgomaster in February 1671. Van Beuningen, who had also broken with De Witt, likewise failed in his candidacy for another of the city's four burgomasterships. Yet, although the new victors were led by De Witt's brother-in-law, Peter de Graeff, and their general relations with him were friendly, they persisted in Amsterdam's characteristic reluctance to put broad provincial and national interests ahead of their city's particular rights and needs. It was all to the good for De Witt's broad political control that Valckenier, preferring to cast his lot on the side of the Prince of Orange, was not even a candidate in the municipal elections a year later.

De Witt took a different tack with Fagel, Valckenier's friend who had also returned to the Orangist side. When the *griffier* of the States General, Nicholas Ruysch, fell ill during the autumn of 1670, De Witt first thought that his cousin Nicholas Vivien might replace him. The opposition to the candidacy of Vivien, as both a Dordrechter like Ruysch and politically and personally De Witt's man, was so strong that the councilor pensionary turned instead to Fagel, who was duly elected after Ruysch's death in November. Some at the time believed that De Witt had gained the election of another friend; but the well-informed Wicquefort later thought he had tried to get Fagel out of the way by giving him work without power. If so, it was a trick that failed. Fagel soon began to build up his office and his influence, apart from and potentially in rivalry with the councilor pensionary. Most important was the privilege Fagel possessed ex officio to be present at all meetings of the States

General and to present relevant materials and his own ideas – a privilege parallel to De Witt's own role in the States of Holland, the one the councilor pensionary had employed so effectively.

De Witt's relations with Zeeland illustrate the complexities that the Prince of Orange introduced into Dutch politics. The councilor pensionary of Zeeland, Peter de Huybert, although in recent years on good personal terms with De Witt, was an outspoken advocate of the Prince's cause. This did not make him, however, a friend of England. He realized that Charles II would be at best neutral, at worst an open enemy, when France and Münster eventually attacked the Dutch Republic, and he wanted measures to ensure that unwanted guests would receive a fitting reception. Yet he did not dare oppose the resistance offered by Odijk, William's deputy as First Noble, to this policy until the Prince himself ordered that the measures be supported.

The Prince played his hand with skill and patience. He attended the Council of State regularly, and the courtesies accorded him showed that he was more than just another member. He treated De Witt with personal respect, giving a magnificent banquet in his honor in November 1670, before he crossed over to England for the visit he had put off while the issue of his election to the Council of State was still in deliberation. In England, as we have seen, he surprised King Charles by the vehemence of his Protestant feelings, and he was not made privy to the Treaty of Dover. Just how intense William's feelings as a Dutchman were the English king did not yet suspect, and he expected his nephew to fall into line when the Republic was defeated. The young Prince kept silent about his attitude not only before his royal uncle when in England, but also before his own entourage in Holland and before the leaders of the States party. Had he confided his feelings to De Witt, the councilor pensionary might have been reassured and have accepted more readily William's election as captain general, made inevitable with the approach of war.

By December 1671, the decision was taken by the States of Holland to support the Prince's election to the captaincy general, the highest military office in the Republic. De Witt clung desperately to his hope that somehow the army command could be given to someone else. His argument that William was too young and lacked experience fell on deaf ears, as did his assertion that membership in the Council of State, a political office, was incompatible with a military post under the terms of the "Eternal Edict." He continued to fear that William would some day be able to institute "slavery," by which he clearly meant the combined captaincy general and stadholdership that his forefathers had possessed and William II had used with such dire effect in 1650. These fears were not shared by all Dutchmen; indeed, many members of the States party now accepted the old Orangist conviction that the English king's friendship could be won by putting his nephew into high office. One of Amsterdam's burgomasters put the argument for William most cogently: his person was worth an army of 20,000 men.

De Witt finally gave way on the election, but was able to keep intact the principle that the captain general could not at the same time be a stadholder of any province. William could in any case be under the control of deputies of the States General who would accompany him on a campaign. Even at this late stage, in January 1672, Holland held out for William's election for the campaigning season of 1672 only, not for life. A compromise was then worked out. The States of Holland accepted immediate election of the Prince as captain general for 1672, but with an assurance that he would receive the office for life when he reached his twenty-third birthday. The States General on February 24 proceeded with his election on these terms. Wicquefort, like his friend De Groot in Paris, thought De Witt had acted too slowly and too reluctantly, sacrificing whatever chance he had had to repair his reputation among the people and to gain William's confidence.

There was general jubilation at the Prince's election, but many Orangists still feared and distrusted the influence of the councilor pensionary. They did not share William's continuing respect for De Witt, which remained intact despite their political antagonism. They even suspected that De Witt sought the Prince's death: the councilor pensionary shied away from having him assassinated, some said, only because the threat of William's advancement ensured his own leadership of the States party, and others held that God had interposed his protection to spare the Prince's life. Their suspicions were utterly false, but they probably reveal their own desire for murder of De Witt by the thrust of a dagger or the shot from a pistol.

The task that William had sought so eagerly and De Witt had been so reluctant to see him gain was one that would have daunted an older, wiser, more experienced general. Yet, in the inner exile that had been his fate until so recently, the Prince of Orange had found the self-assurance to take on the responsibility. The army of the United Provinces was not much readier for a great war than it had been for the little war against Münster seven years earlier. The councilor pensionary had never learned to know or trust the land forces of the Republic as he had the navy. During the first English war he had had the advice of Field Marshal Brederode, whom he had made into a friend; but the army had not been called into action in that war. Thereafter he had had no military men at his right hand. During the Münster episode John Maurice had already been visibly weak and worn-out. De Witt had procured the appointment of the foreigner Wirtz, hoping to find in him a politically subservient commander for the land forces, but Wirtz, discovering that the soldiery would not tolerate him in the supreme post, shifted his allegiance in 1671 to the ascendant William III. De Witt found himself relying more and more upon the advice of Colonel Joseph Bampfield, a former English officer in the royal army who had fled to the United Provinces under suspicion of treason and espionage. Utterly beholden to De Witt for his resumed career and livelihood, he spied upon English royalists in the Netherlands for the councilor pensionary and also gave him counsel on military affairs. A report he submitted to De Witt in 1669 depicted an army unreformed since the debacle of the Münster war, which would have to face in the French the best army in Europe. The first need was to recruit a new top commander, and Bampfield suggested Marshal Schomberg, a Protestant in the service of Louis XIV, but Schomberg demanded conditions that the Dutch found unacceptable and he did not join the States army until after the Revocation of the Edict of Nantes in 1685 and the intensified persecution of Protestants that followed.

French troop movements in September 1671 – which turned out to be directed toward invasion of Lorraine – frightened the Republic into beginning the expansion and improvement of the army. Dutch anxieties were increased when De Groot wrote from Paris that the French disdained the Dutch army as a badly led opponent which sheltered behind fortifications in a state of collapse. De Witt used the letter to shake the States of Holland into greater activity, and work on improving the fortifications, especially the great fortress of Maastricht in the southeast, was begun. De Witt continued to be confident that Dutch cash would bring in enough recruits, both common soldiers and officers to command them, when the need arose; but he failed to understand that time and skill were required to turn them into an effective fighting force. The election of William III as captain general gave the army the commander-in-chief it wanted, but he could not work magic overnight, and he too needed training and experience in the field. Van Beverningk, the most important of the deputies in the field, became a close collaborator with the Prince, and he also worked well with De Witt as the fated day of the outbreak of war approached.

By that time De Witt had proved himself as vigorous in the task of bringing the Dutch army up to strength as he had earlier in his efforts for the navy. With De Ruyter in command of a strengthened fleet, there was no need for the councilor pensionary to worry about its fate, beyond the normal uncertainties of storms and battles.

11

Collapse of the "True Freedom" March–August 1672

The long-expected hostilities began at sea as a repetition of the beginning of fighting between England and the United Provinces in 1664. Once again the Smyrna fleet was attacked by an English naval force before a formal declaration of war, though the place of battle changed from off Cadiz in southwest Spain to the English Channel off the Isle of Wight. Luckily, the outnumbered Dutch convoyers were able to beat off the assailants during a two-day battle on March 23 and 24, and bring home their flock of merchantmen with small losses. De Witt was proud of the achievement, scornful about the double perfidy of Charles II – toward the Dutch Republic and toward his own people – and hopeful that in time it would receive its deserved punishment. The States General did not await a tardy English declaration of war but picked up the challenge and issued their own manifesto first on April 7.

The French declaration of war had been issued the previous day, with full formality, the manifesto being handed to Rumpf, the chargé d'affaires who had remained in France after De Groot's departure three weeks earlier. The French court was revengeful but not perfidious. In mid-February, Pomponne, the new foreign minister, had given an audience to De Groot in which he made no secret of his king's intentions and suggested that De Groot leave for home before the manifesto was made public.

The only motivation for the war given in the manifesto, which was extraordinarily brief and terse, was that the States General had offended the king of France and any delay in retribution would diminish his glory. De Witt accepted the French declaration without the contemptuous wrath that he had poured upon the English, taking it at face value. It provided "clear proof," he said, that Louis XIV was going to war against the United Provinces because they had thwarted his plans to absorb the Spanish Netherlands into his own realm. If there had been any other reasons, he added, they would have been made explicit. Historians from the eighteenth century down to our own have thought the French manifesto more devious, preferring an explanation that gave the tariff conflict initiated by Colbert as the origin of the war. Louis XIV and De Witt alike would have been puzzled by such refusal to see the obvious; but in their age such things as glory and dynastic right had not yet gone out of fashion.

De Witt did not waste time on elaborate debate over the responsibility for the war, but turned at once to meet the immensely multiplied burdens that were placed upon him. He toiled almost around the clock, at meetings of the States of Holland, the States General, and their committees, and at his desk, reading and writing dispatches. His first, almost his only, task became to prepare the country and its armed forces for the challenge to national independence, probably the most dangerous since the first years of the Republic. In one respect, however, and only for a while, the outbreak of hostilities simplified his tasks. Politics ceased and war took over. Not until the course of battles had run decisively one way or another would politics resume its normal place as the primary work of the statesman. In the meantime the councilor pensionary of Holland and the captain general worked together, putting aside all that had divided them in the past. The mature man of forty-six, with two decades of experience in leading the state, and the young man of twenty-one, a novice still but a quick learner, between them shouldered the enormous responsibility of saving their country. It was a collaboration in spite of contrary ideologies and ambitions for a common cause, and neither was deterred by the overwhelming odds against success.

Although the onslaught by land was the more threatening, it would not come until the French army had reached the Dutch frontiers, and its march would take a month or two. The naval conflict with England that was opened by the attack upon the Smyrna fleet was the first priority, and De Witt gave it his full attention. He retained his unstinted admiration for De Ruyter, but continued to believe that the admiral performed best with plenipotentiary commissioners of the States General at his side. He again chose his brother to be one of the three, and urged the States of Zeeland to name Van Vrijbergen, who had been with Cornelius at Brussels, as the other. Both were elected by the States General on April 16; but Van Vrijbergen, to Cornelius's deep regret, declined to serve. The Brussels post was given to Van Beuningen; once largely neglected, it was now the most important diplomatic post and he was clearly the best available man.

However great De Witt's confidence in De Ruyter and his brother, the councilor pensionary knew that the naval war might prove fatal for the Dutch if the English managed to link up with French naval forces before the Dutch fleet put to sea from its roadsteads at Texel and Zeeland. The admiralties, as usual, did not move quickly enough to suit De Witt's impatient temper, and he hurried to Den Helder to help De Ruyter bring out the main fleet from Texel. He was not impressed by the pilots' assertion that there was insufficient draft in the Slenk, the favored passage, and went out himself in a dinghy, as he had done before, to test the Spaniards' Gate, although this time the admiral came along as well; the plumb line showed twenty-one to twenty-two feet, more than enough water, but contrary winds delayed the exit until May 9.

The States of Zeeland, in defiance of direct orders from the States General, delayed the sailing of the ships in their waters until the Texel fleet was at sea. This doomed the bold plan De Witt had conceived to bring the war to the enemy in one of their home ports, either the French at La Rochelle or Brest or the English in the Thames estuary, before the enemy forces had combined. De Ruyter now would have to meet the foe in the Channel or off the English, Flemish or Dutch coasts, and decisions as to the broad strategy would have to be taken aboard. De Witt trusted the judgment of his brother and De Ruyter, but nonetheless he urged them to attempt a repetition of the great raid of 1667 into the Thames and the Medway, destroying the shipyards and half-built ships and creating panic in London. Success might well take the English out of the war and enable the United Provinces to face the approaching French army on land with undivided attention. When the fleet changed the expected course for the Thames, De Witt became impatient. His brother scolded him for interference and told him that the raid had to be abandoned: the English were not to be caught off guard a second time and were ready with a strong fleet. If the government at The Hague – and this of course meant the councilor pensionary of Holland himself as well as the States – insisted, he and De Ruyter would obey, but they would have to receive specific orders, so that the responsibility did not rest on them.

In the great crisis of his country, De Witt was reluctant to rely on others. In this attitude there may have been some vanity of which he was unaware, but there was probably even more present that identification of the self with the state that we are more accustomed to find in a Louis XIV, and which De Witt certainly would have denied with vehemence. Two decades of guiding the ship of state had given him a self-confidence that was matched only by that of the Prince of Orange, who was born to be a leader. Cornelius de Witt, for all his hard manner, lacked his brother's supreme presumption. He shared the caution of the admirals, especially after the junction of the enemy fleets was confirmed. The councilor pensionary, mastering his own impatience, became concerned to guard Cornelius against retribution if things should go wrong: he had learned from bitter experience that regents and people alike would support a well-argued decision before it was acted upon, but after a battle is lost, "everyone says he would have been wiser." Cornelius, he advised, should therefore take the precaution of informing the government beforehand, especially if the decision was a bold one. De Witt would take care to obtain prior approval, and Cornelius would thus be protected in case of defeat. For all of De Witt's experience of the passions and irrationality of politics, he remained something of a lawyer who puts his trust in the text of laws.

On June 7, battle was engaged off the English coast at Sole Bay. When the English, although holding the advantage of the wind, withdrew from the fight the next day, Cornelius knew that a vital victory had been won. It came in the nick of time. The French were already breaking through the Dutch defenses in the Rhineland, and De Witt breathed a little more easily at not having to face two simultaneous disasters.

Two weeks later Cornelius, incapacitated by a severe respiratory infection, came ashore. It was a sign of the rising passions in the country that rumors at once spread that he had been compelled to quit the fleet because of a fistfight with De Ruyter, who had wanted to resume battle on June 8, and had been prevented by Cornelius, who wished to spare the French squadron. De Ruyter was appalled at the tale, which was totally untrue: he and Cornelius had worked together in "all brotherly and candid friendship."

When De Witt was able to call upon him for this testimony early in August, however, events had already taken a course that made this accusation the least of problems.

The Dutch victory off Sole Bay ensured that the outcome of the war would be on land, not at sea. The lesser foe, England, had been warded off; the greater enemy, France, still had to be thwarted of its triumph. At sea, the Dutch had faced the hostile fleets pretty much as an equal in numbers of ships and guns and certainly in quality of command. The situation on land was not so satisfactory. The United Provinces were inferior to France in numbers of troops and in generalship. No one could sensibly compare the military novice William III with superb commanders such as Turenne and Condé. Yet, although the Dutch position was more imperiled than it had been since the siege of Leiden a century before, it was not utterly hopeless. When Louis XIV's declaration of war was issued, it was thought unlikely that the assault would come across the Spanish Netherlands, where the French impetus might be stalled for months, giving the Dutch time to improve their state of readiness. More probable was a drive round the southern Netherlands and down the Rhine valley from Germany, as De Groot had been repeatedly forewarned by French friends.

It was only days before this anticipation was confirmed. The crucial Dutch defenses became those in the easternmost provinces of Gelderland and Overijssel. The great river line of Rhine–Waal would not serve as a barrier, as it could be crossed far upstream, but it would at least divide the invading armies. Lesser rivers, of which the IJssel was the most important, might slow down the French, especially if the water was high enough and the crossings were well defended. The sturdiest barrier would be the polderland beginning just west of Utrecht and extending from the wide Zuider Zee to the Waal near Gorinchem, for – once flooded – the polders could be crossed only by narrow and easily defensible dike roads. But all would depend upon the ability of the army to withstand the blows of the French while the army was recruiting troops, strengthening fortifications and screwing up its nerve under its already adored commander, the Prince of Orange. Two vital elements remained essential for an effective defense. The first was the military leadership of William, who had not yet experienced battle. The second was the stability of the civil order, since – with almost all the troops drawn off to the fighting zone – the governments of the towns and provinces would be at the mercy of the burgher guards and, if they failed, of the rabble mob.

William III left for his command post at Doesburg, near the German frontier, on April 19, with the assurance of the full collaboration of the councilor pensionary of Holland. He was accompanied by Van Beverningk and two other deputies from the States General. Like William, Van Beverningk put aside the political and personal issues that had estranged him from De Witt in recent years. He became both the Prince's enormously helpful right arm in administrative work and the principal channel of communication between the army headquarters and the government at The Hague, where De Witt remained the effective political leader of the nation. The councilor pensionary looked to the Prince of Orange to supply warnings and appeals that could reinforce his own forthright efforts to rouse the country to the most intense effort. It was he and the Prince, as well as Van Beverningk, who saw the course of the impending battle as a whole, not just meeting the needs of individual towns and provinces.

By the middle of May, the situation was becoming clearer and more dangerous. The French armies, instead of halting to reduce the key Dutch fortress of Maastricht in the southeast, marched past, leaving only a force to screen off its defenders, and entered the lands of the elector of Cologne, the principal ally of Louis XIV in Germany. There great stocks of military supplies had been accumulated, and the troops were able to cross the Rhine easily by bridge. At The Hague, the military affairs committee, at the suggestion of De Witt who had returned from Texel, began to work out plans for the contingency of a French breakthrough across the IJssel, which was so low it could be waded. One emergency measure was to put a flotilla of ships at or near Kampen to take the troops in the pay of Holland over the Zuider Zee to strengthen the resistance in the polder country; another was to authorize the deputies in the field to act on their own with the authority of the States General.

The situation was so serious that William wrote to De Witt to commit himself again to serve the country to the best of his ability and to seek his further assistance, even by sending armed peasantry from Holland to the army. De Witt did what he could. He did not permit troops to be drawn from the Prince's main forces along the IJssel line for defensive posting elsewhere, especially in Zeeland

and States Flanders, and the peasant reinforcements were sent quickly, although they were reluctant to serve. Nonetheless, the Dutch force that would have to meet the main French blow remained pitifully small, less than 10,000 infantry and 5,000 cavalry plus about 1,000 in garrisons in the IJssel towns. De Witt responded also by pressing the States for rapid recruitment of additional troops, enough to more than double the Dutch army, and by persuading Monterey, the Spanish governor general at Brussels, to lend the Dutch 2,000 Spanish cavalrymen.

On June 3, the French were already besieging the Dutch-held towns in the German Rhineland. Van Beverningk reported to Fagel and De Witt that a council of high officers called by the Prince had divided between those who favored resistance where the army stood and those who wanted the army to take refuge in fortified towns. The fainter spirits, in defiance of tradition, were the military men, except for William, who wanted to try to hold at least some of the places in Germany; the bolder voices were those of the deputies in the field. Van Beverningk, refusing to take the final decision upon himself, urged that the military committee meet at once at the Prince's camp at Zutphen.

Van Beverningk's letter reached The Hague the next morning. De Witt first worked out plans for immediate reinforcements to bring the army up to a strength of 30,000, including armed peasants and *waardgelders* (troops hired by the towns), and then brought these proposals to the States of Holland for approval. He held up William's conduct as a model to be followed and scorned the pessimism of Wirtz. Political rivalry was obviously the last thing on his mind when he quoted to Their Noble Great Mightinesses William's declaration that if the enemy crossed the IJssel, they could assume that he himself was dead.

The measures proposed by the councilor pensionary were accepted, and he wrote at once – it was now evening – to Van Beverningk to lift his faltering spirit. He was confident, or at least hopeful, that with determination and steadfastness and with the help of the God of Hosts, the Dutch would prevail. Both the States of Holland and the States General, he assured Van Beverningk, favored meeting the enemy head-on and flinging him back in battle. A new deputation from the States of Holland was on its way. He had wanted to go himself, but was held in The Hague by the prospect of a naval battle (this was only a very few days before the battle of Sole Bay).

Two days later came news that tested the steadfastness on which De Witt counted so much. Three of the Rhenish towns besieged by the French had fallen to them, two by capitulation. The fate of another, Rheinberg, was uncertain. A mood of gloom fell over The Hague. It may have encompassed the councilor pensionary himself. According to one report, he told some members of the government that if Rheinberg were lost, the country was half lost. What can be done to save it? they asked him. He shrugged his shoulders and replied that they must treat with the enemy, a possibility he had never before been willing to consider. The contemporary historian Petrus Valkenier, who tells us this story, was an Orangist, to be sure, and wrote some years later; but he was also a well-informed and relatively dispassionate commentator. His report therefore cannot be dismissed out of hand, but even if true it would only prove that De Witt's dogged heroic attitude was achieved by an act of will, not by sober evaluation of the facts.

Whether the councilor pensionary's nerve snapped for a moment on the sixth of June, we do not know. What is certain is that by the seventh he obtained the States General's consent to giving the deputies in the field full powers of decision after consultation with the captain general, a method of political–military collaboration he had used to good effect at sea and which had been employed during the Eighty Years War. The next day he reported that the gravest peril – a French breakthrough toward Holland itself – was at hand, and urged the most vigorous measures for the defense of the province to the very end. Amsterdam should be made ready to hold out if need be, as Copenhagen had successfully done against the Swedes in 1659. The funds in the hands of the receiver general should be transferred there, as well as the artillery and other weapons in the armory at Delft. The States of Holland and the States General should prepare to move to Amsterdam as well. The following day, with still direr predictions received from Van Beverningk, De Witt continued to insist upon defense to the last man and urged that the dikes be opened. "The Lord God has a hundred ways to save us," he wrote to Van Beverningk.

No decision was taken on moving the seat of government, and De Witt envisaged the possible disintegration of the Republic of the United Provinces. The province of Holland had done its best for the Union; only its victory could liberate the other provinces from French conquest. But he still hoped to stop the French, particularly after the naval triumph at Sole Bay.

Out in the field William displayed similar courage, and he became implacable toward cowardice and incompetence. His first important victim was Colonel Montbas, a French cavalry commander in the Dutch service who was a brother-in-law of De Groot. On June 11, in accordance with orders to pull back if the French approached, he had withdrawn from his post at the frontier east of Nijmegen. Refused entry into Nijmegen, which kept its gates closed, he continued to the Prince's headquarters. There, to his surprise, he was arrested and held for trial by court martial for disobedience to orders. There had been some vagueness and misunderstanding in his instructions, but the Prince was intent on stiffening the backbone of the army by exemplary punishment of a high-ranking offender. The fact that he was a favorite of De Witt's may not have been the specific reason for his being singled out, but it explains why his arrest was taken as a sign of treason within the States party by a populace increasingly frightened and panicky.

On June 12, the French army, with Louis XIV watching, at last crossed the Dutch frontier, fording the Rhine at the tollhouse near Lobith. The military significance of the passage of the Rhine did not lie in its inherent difficulty – militarily it wasn't much, as Napoleon was to remark more than a century later – but the French propaganda machine in the service of a vainglorious monarch puffed it up into an astounding achievement. It would have been such, indeed, if it had been the main stream of the Rhine or Waal that had been crossed by calvary on horseback. But the Rhine here was not the mighty "Rhein" of Germany or the equally wide and swift "Waal" of the Dutch, the continuation of the main stream of the river with a change of name. The "Rijn," which in Roman days had indeed been the principal stream, was now little more than a wide creek that turned northwestward just inside the frontier. Its crossing was a simple operation that was almost botched by the headstrong assault of the French calvary, during which Condé was wounded. The defenders fled, however, after a few volleys. The operation was strategically significant for it opened up the Betuwe, with the IJssel river beckoning to the enemy not many miles to the west.

Again we come to the possibility that De Witt's nerve snapped. Again we have a single source that can be neither accepted nor rejected outright, for it is Wicquefort, the historian–intelligencer in De Witt's service. According to Wicquefort, De Witt got the news of the crossing of the Rhine deep in the night of June 12. He ran to Fagel's home and awakened the *griffier*, telling him that the only way to save the country was to surrender upon the best conditions obtainable. Fagel replied that four times before in its history the country had been in worse difficulties and God had saved it; the Dutch should trust Him to do so now. Did this really happen? The difficulty with the two reported episodes of June 6 and 13 lies not just in the absence of confirmation but also arises precisely from the conflict with everything else we know that De Witt said and did at this time.

In any case, De Witt's conduct the next day when the States of Holland assembled and he was asked what he thought should be done was not that of a man in a funk. He faced squarely the stark fact that possible military disaster was near and that the Dutch might have to seek peace from Louis XIV. He proposed therefore that the States General send a notable person to the king to learn his specific demands and then return so that the French terms could be discussed. But at the same time the measures for defense to the utmost – the move of the government to Amsterdam, the flooding of the polders, and the construction of fortifications – should be adopted at once.

The members split as to what to do, but the division did not follow party lines. Most of the towns in the States party camp followed De Witt's lead, but not all Orangists followed the Prince of Orange's policy of sturdy resistance. Haarlem and Leiden in particular, which had been the fiercest supporters of the Prince's cause, now argued with equal vehemence for accepting almost any conditions that Louis XIV should offer. Amsterdam, on the other hand, which had come around to favoring William's promotion, wanted resistance to the bitter end. The delegation to Louis XIV was decided upon, and it was named that same evening by the States General. Fagel, who as *griffier* should have signed the resolution of Their High Mightinesses, refused to do so; De Witt declined to do so as outside his powers, and others had to put their signature to it. The deputation named consisted of three persons, spanning the political spectrum: De Groot, the ablest of De Witt's friends; Odijk, the agent of the Prince of Orange in Zeeland; and Van Gendt, the nobleman from Gelderland who had worked so closely with De Witt during the past decade. Although De Witt

John de Witt

had proposed the deputation, he had little hope for its success, and he continued to advocate the toughest measures of resistance.

The greatest immediate peril, in his eyes, was the turbulence, rioting and widespread disobedience that spread over the country. A bitter witticism that went the rounds summed up the situation: the government was *radeloos* (at its wit's end), the people *redeloos* (void of reason), and the country *reddeloos* (beyond saving). An English equivalent, accurate in spirit if not the letter, would be "hapless, helpless and hopeless." The principal fault, De Witt told the States of Holland on June 20, lay with the regents – the members of the governing class – who themselves failed to act with courage. He was a stoic and a rationalist who had no understanding of the moods and thoughts of common men; they needed, he thought, to be commanded to do what was necessary for their own good as for that of the state. He had no gift of phrase to touch their hearts, and to them he seemed the cold, hard embodiment of the devil.

The desperateness of the situation was made the greater by the first reports from the deputation sent to Louis XIV. The deputies had traveled to the headquarters of the French king far to the east, at Keppel castle, in a single day, June 14, the long journey lasting from early morning to midnight. The French commissioners refused to state what their king wanted; it was up to the Dutch to make offers, which Louis would then take under consideration. De Groot, who took upon himself the main burden of negotiations, traveled the next night to the headquarters of the Prince of Orange, to consult with him. De Groot was in The Hague to report on the morning of June 17. After a long debate, he was ordered to return to continue the negotiations with the French monarch. Though he was given full powers, De Groot asked both the States General and the States of Holland to make their intentions and commands explicit. Can we conclude peace if Louis XIV demands only the Generality Lands and will respect the territorial integrity and full sovereignty of the seven United Provinces? He received no clear answer, and had to leave without detailed orders. Their High Mightinesses had given him a gift of powers that could destroy him, for whatever concessions might be made would be blamed upon him... and his friend De Witt.

He found understanding for his perilous situation at the headquarters of the Prince of Orange, where he once more halted on

194

the way to Rhenen, Louis XIV's new headquarters. Van Beveringk confessed he would not want the hard task De Groot had been given, and William III concurred. De Groot said in response (as he later recalled) that the country was not so unfortunate that it could no longer find men who would risk their lives to save it. Willingness to consider capitulation is a different kind of bravery from confronting death in battle: ordinary men do not distinguish it from cowardice – and would not in the weeks to come.

De Groot went on to Rhenen, where Odijk refused to present De Groot's suggestion that the Generality Lands might be sacrificed. The Dutch delegation met the two chief commissioners of Louis XIV, the war minister Louvois and the foreign minister Pomponne, however, and put forward De Groot's proposals, with Odijk openly dissenting. Louis XIV's reply was shattering: he would keep what he had already taken and what he should take before peace was made, or equivalent territory; moreover, the States General would have to pay a war indemnity of 24,000,000 guilders to himself and his allies. The Dutch delegates did not know that the French king had rejected Pomponne's opinion that De Groot's proposals be accepted, in favor of Louvois's argument that De Witt would now accept anything that Louis XIV cared to demand. The king admitted that Pomponne was right in principle, but felt that he would gain greater glory if he followed Louvois's advice. On June 23, De Groot returned to The Hague to present the French king's demands. At the very least he was gaining time.

What De Groot also did not know as he set out was that the political situation in The Hague had been transformed by an act of violence. Two days before, De Witt had been attacked and wounded while returning home from the Binnenhof. The assault was the culmination of a campaign of vilification that focused the general panic of the populace against the man whom they most hated, the councilor pensionary of Holland. The pamphlets that seemed to rain from the sky, as one contemporary historian put it, found a hundred different ways to place the blame for the impending catastrophe upon De Witt. In such a time, betrayal is an easier, more satisfying explanation of dire events than such prosaic facts as the relative size of populations, or the maze-like complexity of international politics, in which even the best of minds can get lost. The councilor pensionary's very ability to persuade the States of Holland and the States General to adopt his policies became a crime. He was painted as secretly plotting with Colonel Montbas to turn the country over to Louis XIV so that he could continue to rule it on the French king's behalf. It was believed that he had sent great sums from his private fortune for safekeeping to the Bank of Venice and other far-off depositories at a time when his country needed all the money it could lay hands on.

We do not know who most of the authors of these pamphlets were, although it is clear that they were literate men with a feeling for the pulse of the people. There is no indication of a concerted campaign behind them, and we should not commit the logical fallacy of which at least a few of them were guilty, holding that the very absence of evidence is proof of a conspiracy. But there had been plotters on the Orangist side before, such as the man in the shadows behind Buat, and it is not at all unlikely that they were already at work to bring down the man whom they hated more than any other in the world. Some of the pamphleteers, prompted or not, went beyond mere denunciation to calls for action – the councilor pensionary and his brother should be burned alive or beheaded!

Such hot words, when catastrophe lies encamped and ready to move no more than a day's journey away, can take flame in the minds of young men, ready for bold deeds but doing none. Such were four young men of good family in The Hague on June 21. Two were sons of a member of the Court of Holland, Jacob van der Graeff, who had been left to guard their home while their parents sought refuge in Delft; the other two were friends. All shared the Orangist commitment of the elder Van der Graeff. Idling away the time on the Vijverberg, across the moat they saw the lights on in the assembly hall of the States of Holland and knew that the councilor pensionary had not yet gone home. That he was toiling to save the country was beyond their imagining; they thought of him only as a traitor to be removed. They decided that the time to act had come, and they would be the actors. They drew lots and one brother, Peter, went with a friend, named De Bruyn, to confront De Witt as he came out through the Gevangenpoort gate on the Square. The other brother, named Jacob like his father, remained to one side. Two servants were with the councilor pensionary, one in front with a torch and the other behind carrying a bag with letters.

The assailants knocked the torch out of the servant's hand, then the friend tried to kill De Witt with his rapier. De Witt grappled with them, and he and Peter van der Graeff fell to the ground, with De Witt on top. Peter's brother Jacob ran up, thinking De Witt had a sword in his hand, and he attacked De Witt with his knife. De Witt fell wounded while his servant fought off the attackers. Then he got to his feet and walked the few hundred feet to his home on the Kneuterdijk. Two doctors were called, and they found him suffering from contusion and minor wounds. A fever kept him to his bed, so that he had to report his condition and his inability to work to the States of Holland the next day.

The assailants escaped, although the Van der Graeff brothers were recognized. Jacob did not flee with the others to the Prince of Orange's camp but went home. He was arrested there. He was the only attacker who was brought to trial. Although the Prince was informed by the States of Holland that they had taken refuge in his camp, they were not sent back to face the court. This is the only hint that they might have been prompted to their deed rather than acting solely on their own; but such implacable enemies of De Witt as Zuilestein and the Prince's equerry would have thrown a cloak of protection about them in any case.

On the orders of the States of Holland, Jacob was tried not by the local court in The Hague which usually had jurisdiction over such offenses, but by the Court of Holland, because the victim was an official in the service of Their Noble Great Mightinesses and the crime was therefore one of *lèse-majesté*. Jacob did not deny his guilt and even repented his action; he had believed he was acting in defense of the church against the enemy. The only question was the severity of the verdict. Although De Witt was accused of demanding that no mercy be shown, his first biographer, a contemporary, tells a different story. He regretted that young men of good family had been "entrapped" in such foul work, and he forgave him. He could hardly have spent much time discussing the case, for his fever worsened and the few persons allowed to visit him stayed only briefly. The decision to condemn Jacob to death by beheading was taken on June 27, despite efforts to obtain a delay of four to six days in anticipation of a change of government in that time. The executioner swung his great sword two days later; it took two blows to end the young culprit's life. He was exalted at once as a martyr, like Buat before him.

Although De Witt lived, the attackers' essential objective – to remove him from the leadership of the country – had been achieved. His recovery lasted until July 12, for a high fever hung on intermittently although the wounds were quick to heal. Vivien, whom he had called to The Hague to assist him early on the day of the attack, as pensionary of Dordrecht assumed the duties of the councilor pensionary's office.

What he could not become, certainly not on a moment's notice, was the leader that De Witt had been, both of the country and of the States party. Intelligent and diligent though he was, he lacked not only the experience but also the hard-driving, most extravagantly self-confident quality of his cousin. The leadership of the state fell open. The guidance of affairs in The Hague was taken over by the *griffier*, Fagel, whom De Witt had helped place in his office, but Fagel did not aspire to the national leadership, which he wished to see in the hands of the Prince of Orange. As for the leadership of the States party, it remained empty while the country continued in convulsions of disorder and near revolt.

The news that the councilor pensionary had been wounded became a signal for demands throughout the province of Holland that the Prince of Orange be proclaimed stadholder. The Eternal Edict of 1667 would have to be torn up, figuratively and literally. The demands were backed by violence against reluctant regents.

The movement began in De Witt's own Dordrecht, where his friends were still in power, and was led by a burgher and a regent named Adrian van Blyenburch who had long been battling with the dominant party. It fed upon the hatred among the guildsmen in particular against the De Witts, once Jacob and now Cornelius, as hard-hearted opponents of their interests and their influence. Rioting crowds encircled the town hall and threatened to do violence to burgomaster Halling, an old friend of the De Witts, unless a delegation was sent to bring the Prince of Orange to Dordrecht. The delegation was named, went to William's camp on July 25, and found him not at all eager to do what was wanted. He remembered how embittered the towns of Holland had been by his father's interference in their affairs in 1650, but gave in to their pleas that they might be killed by the mob if they returned without him.

His appearance in the city on June 28 calmed the rioters,

although they halted his coach and demanded that he be made stadholder at once. They compelled the town secretary to draw up a proclamation abolishing the Eternal Edict, an action that was legally beyond the powers of the municipal government but was nonetheless politically potent. William declined to accept the stadholderate unless the States of Holland, which had adopted the edict, released him from his oath to abide by it, and he rode back to camp. The town magistrates all fearfully signed the revocation, even bed-ridden Cornelius de Witt, but only after his wife and children pleaded for their own safety. In a final act of scorn, he put the initials "v.c." (*vi coactus*, "Under duress") beside his signature, although he had to blot them out when they were noticed and interpreted.

The success of the Dordrechters was immediately imitated almost everywhere in Holland and Zeeland. The town governments had no force with which to suppress the rioters. Apart from four guards companies, the entire army had been sent to the zone of battle, which had moved westward while these events were taking place, with Louis XIV taking Utrecht on July 27. What armed force was available was in the hands of the burgher guards, and most of these were vehemently Orangist. The political bastions of the "True Freedom" crumbled in quick succession. Not until the States of Holland renounced the Eternal Edict on July 3 and elected William III as the province's stadholder did the disorders cease.

De Witt had been spared the ordeal of attendance by his wounds and fever. We know little of what he thought or felt in these days, for he wrote no letters. Wicquefort, again our only source, depicts a man aware that his time in power had passed but unwilling to depart from the letter of his sworn duties and his oath to the edict. Warned that he was in danger in The Hague, he refused to go to a safer place to recuperate unless the States of Holland told him to; he would not ask them, however. But his friends were no longer in control of Their Noble Great Mightinesses, and nothing was done.

With William stadholder of Holland, and Zeeland too, of course, the void of leadership in the United Provinces was filled. The wish of the great majority of the nation had been met, and those who continued to believe in the trampled principles of the "True Freedom" had for the moment at least to hold their tongues. Indeed, over the next few months the municipal governments were systematically purged of States party adherents in a series of *wetsverzettingen*, the "changing of the government" not by normal elections but by the quasi-constitutional authority conferred on the stadholder in a crisis.

In these days of clamor, violence and change, the debate over De Groot's mission to Louis XIV continued with mounting fury. Strong-minded even when working with De Witt, De Groot now lacked his friend's judgment to steady his own in the face of the stupendous responsibility put upon him. Asked by the States of Holland what reply he suggested to Louis XIV's conditions, he urged continued resistance if at all possible, but otherwise to go on with negotiations in order to save the United Provinces as a free, sovereign state. He did not tell them that he had little hope that there could be a successful military defense, but his preference for a negotiated peace was transparent. According to some contemporary chroniclers, De Witt was consulted and replied, with a shrug of the shoulders, that although he would not give advice, what De Groot suggested might be best. It is doubtful that he was well enough on June 25, while gripped by fever, to have done so, but no contrary evidence exists.

The next day, over the protests of Zeeland, the States of Holland called upon the States General to send De Groot back to the French king's camp with full powers to the three deputies to conclude peace. Their High Mightinesses split, with Holland joined only by Gelderland, Overijssel and Groningen – the former two occupied and the latter fighting off an invasion by Münster. Fagel again refused to sign the resolution, and this time he virtually called De Groot a traitor. The States of Holland now reassembled for renewed and bitter debate without De Groot. The advocates of resistance gained the upper hand, until finally it was only Leiden, once the stronghold of Orangism, that still proposed capitulation to Louis XIV.

When De Groot reached Rhenen once more, the deputies offered terms that would have given France Maastricht, a war indemnity of 10,000,000 guilders and the Generality Lands, provided that the United Provinces remained free, sovereign and Calvinist. The debate in Louis XIV's council was resumed, with Pomponne again urging acceptance and Louvois opposing, and once more the king chose the harsher course. The deputies were informed that he would accept terms that ceded most of the eastern and all of the southern Republic to him, while the independence of the remaining United Provinces would be whittled down to a mere pretence. In spite of their full powers, the deputies would not take such a responsibility of capitulation upon themselves; and De Groot, accompanied by Van Gendt, returned to The Hague. He was met by vitriolic vilification as a puppet of France, a traitor as Fagel had hinted. Amalia and William, however, did not join in these denunciations; she told De Groot to his face that he had acted honorably, and the Prince sent a similar message in writing.

The States of Holland and the States General first met to hear the reports of the deputies on July 1, but the next few days were fully taken up with the reestablishment of the stadholderate. When they returned to the question on July 7, the situation had been transformed. The French élan had weakened, their supplies were depleted and the Dutch "water line" of flooded polders west of Utrecht was holding.

Two leading English ministers, Arlington and Buckingham, arrived in the Republic on July 3, on their way to Louis XIV's headquarters, which were now at Zeist, east of Utrecht. They were seen by the deluded populace as bearers of peace, and even De Groot hoped that talks with them before they reached Zeist might yield an armistice with England and therefore ensure better terms with France. To William, whom they called upon in his camp at Bodegraven, west of Utrecht, they offered establishment as sovereign ruler over what would be left of the Dutch Republic, under the protectorate of the king of Great Britain. He rebuffed them sharply; he was, he told them to their surprise, a loyal servant of the States and preferred to be a stadholder by their grant; he would face death before accepting a peace imposed by conquest.

How much this passionate patriotism was the result of De Witt's tutoring when he was "Child of State," and how much the expression of his own commitment of his fate and fortune to the country of which he saw himself the natural leader, cannot be determined. Nor can we say how much De Witt would have eased William's path to power if he had known earlier of such attitudes. In any event, the Prince's distrust of his uncle was justified, for the two English ministers, once at Zeist, backed the French terms completely. The Franco-Dutch negotiations thereupon collapsed, and the Dutch deputies returned to The Hague.

The campaign against De Witt and his friends rose to new

heights of vilification. Every argument against the councilor pensionary that had been developed over more than two decades was repeated now, and new ones added. But they amounted basically to a few points: he was a traitor in the service of France, because he had striven to maintain the French alliance; he was an "atheist," because he had not had the States of Holland do the bidding of the orthodox Calvinist preachers; he was guilty of corruption, exceeding his powers and using his influence for the private benefit of his friends; and, most of all, he was a usurper, depriving the Prince of Orange of his rightful place at the head of the state. The tone of the pamphlets was more hateful and violent than ever, with one demand ringing throughout: "If he'd be killed, we'd all be safe!"

Some pamphlets appeared in defense of De Witt and the "True Freedom," but they were few in number. De Witt himself disdained to reply to most of the accusations; he had always held broad public opinion in scorn as ignorant and bigoted. Only one pamphlet, called *Warning to All Right-Minded and Loyal Inhabitants of the Netherlands*, broke through this shield of contempt by charging him not only with broad, legally empty offenses but with malfeasance in office. Two accusations in particular aroused his ire: that he had diverted to his own pocket funds entrusted to the Delegated Councilors of Holland to pay for espionage reports ("secret correspondence"); and that he had failed to give full support to the army in the field.

He turned to the States of Holland and to the Prince of Orange to seek official rebuttals of the "foul calumnies." Their Noble Great Mightinesses obtained from the Delegated Councilors a declaration that De Witt had never received any secret funds from them; but William was less forthright in a statement about the councilor pensionary's positive efforts for the army. His secretary, Constantine Huygens, wanted the Prince to send no reply at all, lest he gave offense to the people, to whom he was under obligation (a clear reference to the role of the riots in making him stadholder). The Prince's supporters were unhappy, Huygens warned, because William had written to the towns calling for strict enforcement of public order. The Prince did write the letter De Witt requested, but deftly, affirming that the councilor pensionary had worked to strengthen the army and navy, but declining to give details, as he had other things to do. In the popular mind, this was taken to mean that De Witt had really been at fault.

Another allegation in the pamphlet, that De Witt had used his position to borrow money at low interest in order to buy government bonds that paid a higher rate, he did not refute publicly. He explained his conduct to Vivien, first orally and then in a letter which was published after his death. He had been lent money by individuals who preferred to entrust it to him personally; it was a perfectly legitimate transaction "in a land of business." Everything he owned, land or bonds or other personal property, lay within the United Provinces, so that, with regard to his wealth, he "must stand and fall with Holland." This confession of willingness to benefit by his public office offended the ethical sensibilities of the great Dutch historian Robert Fruin, who failed to catch the assumption, which De Witt made explicit, that men serve their country best when it is to their private advantage to do so as well as their public duty.

Although his wounds were healed and the fever gone by the middle of July, De Witt did not go back to his work as councilor pensionary. In part he was simply regaining his strength, of course, but under other circumstances he would not have been restrained by such a consideration. He knew that his time in politics was past. He did not flee, like De Groot, who escaped with his family to the Spanish Netherlands on July 22, a day after the Prince refused to discuss his negotiations with Arlington and Buckingham in his presence. De Groot had gone too far in his final meetings with the French, William said, beyond what his mandate from the States General permitted. It was a virtual accusation of selling out his country, such as Fagel had made a month before. Whether De Witt's judgment that his friend's flight was overhasty rather than prudent was right may therefore be doubted, especially since De Groot had been barely saved from a knife attack in Rotterdam a few days earlier.

De Witt visited the Prince on August 1, both to pay his respects to him and to discuss his own situation. According to quite reliable reports, William asked him to stay on as councilor pensionary, with the same influence and credit that he had enjoyed before he was injured. It was a gracious offer, but probably no more than a formal courtesy, although we should not underestimate the Prince's respect for De Witt's abilities. There was no longer need to fear him, for his political power had been broken. De Witt declined. He would be of no use, he said, and Fagel, who was both able and on good terms with the Prince, would be his best successor as councilor pensionary.

Three days later De Witt went to the States of Holland to resign his office. He defended his conduct over the years but made it plain that it was also Their Noble Great Mightinesses whom he was defending, because they had been his masters and had taken all decisions. The true responsibility for the disaster which had befallen the country lay not upon them, but upon Zeeland and Friesland, which had so often failed to respond to the country's needs. (He did not need to remind the assembly that these were the most strongly Orangist of the seven provinces.) He asked that he be allowed to take a seat on the High Council, as provided at his election. While he waited outside the chamber, the assembly debated; they granted his request, but with reluctance. His career was at an end. He gave thanks to God for being able at last to put down "a very heavy burden, with many troubles in these difficult times."

The States of Holland drew up a list of three candidates, Fagel, Van Beverningk and Van Beuningen, to replace De Witt as councilor pensionary, and it was presented to the Prince of Orange for his choice on July 18. William selected Fagel, but had to overcome the Haarlemmer's reluctance to take on a post which presented such dangers to its holder. He finally agreed, however, and was elected on August 20.

12

The worst of days
July–August 1672

De Witt's public life was concluded, apart from his seat in the High Council, which was a refuge from politics rather than its continuation. The Prince of Orange seems to have been satisfied with the completeness of his triumph over the States party and the leader who had guided it so effectively over two decades. Not only was the erstwhile councilor pensionary of Holland no longer able to do him harm; he gave every sign that he no longer wished to. Without him the States party was beheaded; it could be dealt with at leisure, by *wetsverzettingen* or by elections in regular course where the Prince's influence would assure victory to his friends. Had it been up to William alone, De Witt would probably have slipped quietly into obscurity. What this would have meant when the States party eventually recovered from its fright and challenged the Prince is merest speculation; De Witt might have seized the chance to reassert his political leadership, or he might equally well have counseled against any effort to restore the "True Freedom."

William, his attention fixed on the waging of the war, did not have time for revenge; he left politics to Fagel and other loyal followers as much as possible. His attitude was not shared by those who had been his guides and friends during the hard years of internal exile. Some were old soldiers who felt undiminished bitterness against De Witt, whom they considered Buat's murderer; others were half-English or married to English wives, like Zuilestein. All lacked the respect that William felt for the Dutch constitutional system, with himself at its core as stadholder, of course; they lived in a mental world filled with ideas of dynastic kings and condottiere soldiers, of power held by right or seized by force.

They loathed De Witt. Less attuned to political reality than William, they also feared a quick resuscitation of the States party under De Witt's leadership. They had always suspected him of trying to poison or otherwise get rid of the Prince, putting in his mind thoughts that prowled eternally in their own. They believed in a world where politics was practiced with the dagger, and were ready to use the fury of the populace to gain their way if they had to; they had none of the distaste for King Mob that William inherited from his mother and grandmother, and none of his respect for the law. Buat's failure did not dissuade them from conspiracy and violence.

There is little direct evidence for the work of these plotters, among whom Zuilestein must be put first. There is much for the plot itself, directed at the removal of De Witt. After all, they had muttered among themselves for years about the need to slay the councilor pensionary: are we to believe that they would make no attempt when the chance was there? Zuilestein had been William's beloved governor for a few years; but the young man had moved beyond him in the qualities of human understanding and political principle. Zuilestein and his friends grew impatient as they watched William's mildness toward De Witt and his willingness to work with him. They mistrusted the stadholder's friendship and collaboration with Van Beverningk and Van Beuningen. They realized they would have to act apart from the Prince and without his knowledge or participation.

The question arises whether the attack upon De Witt by the Van der Graeff brothers and their friends on June 21 was the first blow struck in the conspiracy of which we get glimpses during the next two months. The one strongest argument against this hypothesis is not that Jacob van der Graeff told a tale of a spur-of-the-moment decision by youthful idlers, but that he confessed so easily and repented so fully. A historian not prone to paranoiac theories would accept this account at full value, were it not for one disturbing fact. The same June 21, at about the same time that De Witt was being assailed in The Hague, four armed men came to Cornelius's home in Dordrecht and tried to enter by force; only the arrival of the watch, summoned by servants, led to their flight. They were not recognized and were probably not Dordrechters. Were the two simultaneous episodes merely coincidental, or where they an attempt to decapitate the States party twice over? It is impossible to say either way with any assurance, but, in view of what followed some two weeks later, the coincidence remains troubling.

The riotous events that swept Holland after the attack upon the councilor pensionary and led to the elevation of William III to the stadholderate came so swiftly and rested upon such broad popular feeling that there is no need to postulate any conspiratorial origins. They were more an expression of panic fears and of what may be called "Orange democracy" – the belief of the common man that the Prince of Orange was their protector and savior against the foreign enemy and the regents at home – than of any artificial agitation. Cornelius de Witt may have been threatened with death when he balked at signing the revocation of the Eternal Edict on June 28, but the crowd had gone off peacefully when he removed the insulting initials "v.c." Assassins would not have been so easily satisfied.

The taint of conspiracy clings much more tightly to the events that began on July 7 with the appearance of a ne'er-do-well named William Tichelaer at Cornelius de Witt's home in Dordrecht and finished on August 20, the "worst of days" that ends our story. For the next pages the tale of John de Witt's life must recount what happened to Cornelius, for it was through his brother that John would be reached.

Tichelaer was by trade a barber-surgeon in the village of Piershil on Putten Island, where Cornelius was steward, the head of local government. He had a mixed reputation: both a sedulous churchgoer and a troublemaker who consorted with a woman of dubious morality. With her and another couple he had gone to the main army camp after the outbreak of war, and when he returned he had so many coins jingling in his purse that he did not bother to reopen his barber shop as once. That he had taken his lady a-whoring is pretty certain; but whether her earnings explain the size of his new-found fortune is not. He may, nay must, have been given another job to do when he returned home. Who his taskmasters were may be guessed, but cannot be proved.

However that may be, Tichelaer on that seventh day of July came to Cornelius de Witt to ask that he revoke a sentence pending against him from two years before, when he had been convicted of attempted rape of a young woman of the village who had fled to Dordrecht to escape his importunities. He had been fined 1,000 guilders, a huge amount for a man of his occupation, and had been perpetually banished from Piershil. He wanted to see Cornelius alone and went away when told he had visitors, and did the same the next morning. Only an hour later did he enter, finding Cornelius in his bedroom, resting. There are two accounts of what then happened, one from Cornelius and members of his household, and other from his visitor.

According to Tichelaer, when he asked Cornelius to have the fine against him annulled, the steward told him he would first have to perform a service for him. He would have to assassinate the Prince of Orange, who was contemplating marriage with a daughter of the duke of York. Then he would not only have his fine forgiven, but he would be paid 30,000 guilders and receive the office of bailiff of Beyerland, his birthplace. Cornelius heard a noise at the door and asked Tichelaer to see if his wife was there, but when he looked there was no one.

According to Cornelius, it was Tichelaer who had raised the question of doing something about the Prince of Orange. He wanted, he said, to prevent the Prince from bringing the Dutch Republic into eternal slavery through an alliance with England. When Tichelaer mentioned William's possible marriage to a daughter of the duke of York that would put the future of the country into peril, Cornelius replied that on the contrary it would help the Dutch if he made such a marriage. He would listen only if Tichelaer had something good to say; if he had evil deeds on his mind, he should hold his tongue, for otherwise the steward would inform the government. There were other discrepancies between Tichelaer's account and the testimony of Cornelius, his wife, son and a servant: whether the visit lasted between a half and a full hour, as Tichelaer averred, or only a quarter of an hour, as the others asserted; whether Cornelius almost whispered, as the visitor declared, or spoke in his usual loud voice, as the rest said; whether the door was closed tight or was slightly ajar, so that the servant could hear what was said.

As soon as Tichelaer left, Cornelius's wife Maria, told by the servant that the visitor was the notorious barber of Piershil, sent for Muys van Holy, the town secretary, and at Cornelius's request he in turn informed the burgomaster. With this Cornelius let the affair drop as beneath contempt.

This was a fatal error, for he did not look behind the strange episode at what dangers might be lurking there for him. He assumed that everyone would take his word as against that of a Tichelaer, forgetting that there were those quite willing to make use even of infamous rascals. We assume that Tichelaer had said nothing specific about an attack on the life of William III, for then Cornelius would certainly have had him held and charged and would himself have informed the Prince (we must remember that by this time his brother John had put aside all thought of opposing William's leadership). Indeed, we may go further in our assessment. The words that Tichelaer attributed to Cornelius were characteristic not of Cornelius but of Tichelaer's own wild way of thought. We may even wonder whether the figure of 30,000 guilders was the one his prompters promised him if he succeeded in trapping the steward.

As for the tale about marriage between William III and a daughter of the duke of York (this was five years before his marriage to Princess Mary), Tichelaer turned out under examination to know nothing about the duke's children, their number, sex or age. It was just the kind of idea that would have been on the minds of members of the Prince's entourage, and they attributed to Cornelius what they would have done to prevent it if they had been in his place. In any event, Cornelius in the whole episode was guilty of guileless underestimation of those who hated him and his brother.

Tichelaer went back to the Prince's camp at Bodegraven but waited three days before he presented himself to Jan de Bye, lord of Albrantswaart, the Prince's equerry, and then to Zuilestein. His public reason for going to them was to report the villainous offer made to him, which he had delayed doing out of fear of the mighty steward. Yet, considering his earlier visit to the camp on a less nefarious mission and his return with money of unexplained origin, the probability cannot be dismissed that it was they who were the prompters of the attempt. The evidence may be only circumstantial, but there are seldom "smoking guns" in a conspiracy. The whole affair has the smell of a trumped-up business to destroy Cornelius de Witt, and through him his brother.

Whether because the bait was not snapped up by the intended victim, or because Albrantswaart and Zuilestein were truly not behind the affair, the equerry went to inform William. The stadholder thereupon turned the accusations over to the Court of Holland for investigation and trial, since either Cornelius de Witt or Tichelaer was guilty of a crime, the one of planned assassination, the other of the vilest perjury.

The judges faced a devilishly ticklish task. The evidence in other circumstances would have led to the throwing out of the case against Cornelius and the arrest and conviction of Tichelaer. On the one side was Tichelaer, a man whom even Zuilestein called a knave, whose past was disreputable and whose story rested on no one's testimony but his own. On the other was Cornelius de Witt, who for all the political hatreds he had borne had never been accused of this kind of crime. His testimony was substantiated by that of his household, which by its nature could be suspected of bias, but displayed precisely the kind of minor inconsistencies that a concocted tale would not have. There was no reason whatever for Cornelius, if he had really been planning the assassination of William III, to have attempted to recruit so unreliable a character as Tichelaer, particularly since he was well known as a supporter of the Prince's cause. Indeed, it was Tichelaer who came to him unsolicited. Would any sane man have trusted so foul a proposal to someone he did not know? Finally, although in our own day considerations of class are supposed to play no role in court, they were considered proper and normal in seventeenth-century Holland. In ordinary times the word of a Tichelaer, a man of no rank, would never have been taken against that of a Cornelius de Witt, a regent, without overwhelming independent evidence. (I state here the situation as it appeared at the time; Tichelaer's repudiation of himself when an old man may be left for later.)

Yet, if the judges brought Tichelaer to trial, their investigations would have to go behind him to possible instigators, and this meant getting very close to the Prince of Orange himself. The Court was not famed for its independence of political authority, and it knew full well which way the wind was blowing since the beginning of July. Jacob van der Graeff, who could be expected to be embittered at a De Witt beyond any chance of impartiality, was not sitting, but the others, particularly the president of the Court, Adrian Pauw van Bennebroek, were notoriously weak men.

The Court therefore decided on July 23, after taking testimony from Tichelaer, to put Cornelius under arrest while continuing their investigations. (The trial, it should be noted, did not follow the English or modern American pattern, with prosecutor and defense counsel presenting cases before impartial judges who pronounce sentence once an independent jury has decided guilt. As was the usual form of trial on the continent, the court sat as both investigators and judges.) Cornelius was taken from Dordrecht two days later and brought to The Hague, where he was placed in the Kastelnij, the civil jail. He could not comprehend the reason for his arrest and was confident that his testimony would bring his release. John, fully recovered from his illness by this time, set to work with vigor to prove his brother's innocence. He did not rely on his own legal knowledge, presumably somewhat rusty after several decades out of practice, but consulted leading lawyers. He began to worry that all might not go well when he saw that Tichelaer was still free.

Under examination, Cornelius retold what had happened during Tichelaer's visit to him. His story was confirmed by Muys van Holy as well as by the servant who had been told by Cornelius's wife to eavesdrop. Tichelaer's appeal to the sheriff of Piershil for an attestation of his good character boomeranged, for the Court was told of his trip to Bodegraven with a clear indication that he had been a pimp, and of his return with money in unaccustomed quantity. Nonetheless the judges' enquiries shifted from the case at hand to the irrelevant, but politically significant, question of Cornelius's refusal to sign the act of revocation of the Eternal Edict on June 29. The only connection it could have was to support a claim that he continued his opposition to the Prince of Orange in the form of planning an assassination.

Not until the deputies of Dordrecht protested to the States of Holland, not only against the arrest and transfer of Cornelius de Witt as a violation of their city's jurisdiction in criminal cases, but also against Tichelaer's continued freedom, was the accuser arrested. Even then, when he was put in the Gevangenpoort, the little criminal prison between the Buitenhof and the Square, Cornelius too was transferred there from the Kastelnij. John was indignant at such perfect equality between the accuser, who had proved nothing, and the accused, whose innocence was evident. He feared what this might forebode. He kept busy doing what he could on behalf of his brother, but he found himself powerless. His influence was destroyed, men dared not listen to his arguments, and he may well have realized, although he did not put the thought into words, that it was he whom unseen forces were seeking to destroy through his brother. A man of reason, he was also a man of action, and he was doomed to inaction while the judges were busy in the dim little rooms of the Gevangenpoort.

The judges did their work under duress. The law ran one way, the political needs another. By itself, Tichelaer's testimony was inadequate to convict. Yet they did not dare find Cornelius de Witt not guilty and set him free. A bare majority decided that they would have him subjected to torture so as to demonstrate that they were doing their best to extract a confession from him that he had done what Tichelaer claimed. This decision ran against the grain of Dutch criminal law, for it provided for torture only when there was "half proof" from several witnesses or independent evidence. According to a later report, a person of importance close to the Prince told the judges that they would have to convict the prisoner.

During the evening of August 15, rumors spread that Cornelius had escaped and a crowd assembled around the Gevangenpoort and remained there all night. The next morning one of the judges and the prosecutor had Cornelius stand in the window of his room on the second floor of the little prison, but the crowd still refused to go away. The Court sent a request to William, who was then at Alphen, to send troops to protect Cornelius's person, but he replied that he trusted that they would do their duty. However, a small force of cavalry and some burgher guards were put on watch the next day at the Gevangenpoort. But the mob had done its work. The Court, feeling a menace not only to Cornelius but also to themselves, had decided to go ahead with torture of the accused prisoner; for without a confession, there would not be adequate evidence for a conviction.

Another day was spent in ordinary examination of Cornelius, again directed to his conduct on June 29 when the Eternal Edict was revoked in Dordrecht rather than to Tichelaer's visit. Nothing more came out than that he had spoken harshly and scornfully of the crowd. A lawyer who lived on the Square next door to the Gevangenpoort and kept track of what was going on heard that Prince William and a close friend had come secretly to The Hague and met with others in his confidence at Odijk's house for three hours before returning to camp. The same observer also learned that a number of burgher guardsmen were told by their captains to keep their weapons at hand in case they were needed. All of this, if true, might hint at William's participation in the plotting going on behind the scene, but there is no confirmation. Whatever the truth of the matter, he certainly knew of the danger to Cornelius. At the very least, the question remains what he did, if anything, to ward it off.

On the 19th, Cornelius was tortured twice, first without the judges present and then with them in the bleak basement room. The instruments of pain were the "boot," which compressed the foot, and a barrel over which he was tied with knotted ropes while a weight of fifty pounds hung from his toes. Refusing to confess during the three and a half hours that the "sharp examination" lasted, he endured, endlessly repeating a passage from Horace's *Odes* that speaks of men holding out against terror and being raised to immortality. At the end, he quoted Horace to reaffirm his innocence. Spiritually, it was the executioner who was broken by the experience, but he was warned not to reveal how severe the torture had been. A few months later, as he was dying, he confirmed what had happened, and in a letter asked Cornelius's widow to forgive him.

The judges were still caught in a cleft stick. The law required that for a valid conviction they must have either a confession or the testimony of two witnesses (one of "irreproachable reputation" might do, but that could hardly apply to Tichelaer). What went on as they debated remains obscure, because the "secret book" in which the records of the trial were kept has vanished. They did not know how to determine a verdict for a crime they could not prove, yet they did not dare find for innocence. Apparently they divided, three to three, and the decision was left in the hands of the Prince, who concurred in a sentence of exile. John who had spent the day with the deputies of the States of Holland from various towns, did not learn of the decision until the following morning.

It was a proceeding without parallel that took place in the main room of the Gevangenpoort that morning. The verdict itself was a legal monstrosity: Cornelius de Witt, the accused, was not found guilty of the charges against him, but Tichelaer, who had brought them, was released unconditionally, although the failure to find Cornelius guilty meant that his accusations were false and he himself was guilty of perjury. The sentence was forfeiture of all of Cornelius's offices, perpetual banishment from the province of Holland and payment of all legal costs of the trial. No ground was given other than that "relevant matters" had been taken into consideration. This was justice as practiced in Alice's Wonderland, or, rather, it was judicial injustice at the command of political terror.

To make the scene still stranger, one of the judges was overheard talking to Tichelaer, who was watching from a corner of the room. Exile was the best that could be achieved, he explained. It was strange but real, for what it demonstrates was that at least one of the judges and Tichelaer were engaged in a diabolic operation to destroy the De Witt brothers. No wonder Cornelius de Witt, astounded, asked the judges in wrath what kind of men they were. Two at least did not dare reply to him, but they gave vent to their own distraught consciences elsewhere. One told his wife the night before that there was "nothing" in the verdict. Another admitted to a friend that the sentence was like that which Pilate passed on Jesus, but he was afraid to say any more about what had happened. What made them so frightened – the mob outside, or the men behind it?

An hour later, at about nine-thirty in the morning, Tichelaer walked out of the door and spoke to the assembled mob. At his side were known Orangists who had been instigating the crowd. He repeated, as he had been told to, that the verdict proved his innocence and Cornelius's guilt, and they responded with threats to the life and homes of the judges for not condemning Cornelius to death, but were deterred by the civic guards standing by on the Square.

Just afterward John came to the Gevangenpoort from his home a few hundred yards away to take his brother to a relative's house at Loosduinen, a village to the south of The Hague. The call to him was brought by the jailer's servant girl, but it remains unclear precisely who sent her. One account tells of the jailer pleading with Cornelius to leave at once; he replied that he was unable to walk to his brother's house and asked that a message be sent to him. The servant girl took it to John, who received it while being shaved. Wicquefort says that the message actually came from a person "on station" (*apostée*) to lure him into the hands of the mob. The lawyer who was keeping a diary on the events heard that Odijk, Zuilestein and Tromp had met that morning in an inn on the Square, where they had the jailer's servant girl brought to them and then sent her to De Witt's house. A family friend who was in the house on the Kneuterdijk expressed surprise that the message was not brought by someone more official than a servant and urged John to await confirmation. His daughter Anna, sensing what was afoot, pleaded with him to stay at home, to think of his own safety and that of his children. He would not listen: his brother had called for him, and that was all that mattered. He had never feared the mob, and he would not now.

John went with his coach as close to the Gevangenpoort as he could manage and walked through the gate to the entrance. The crowd was sullen and did not reply to his question as to what was happening. Once John was in his brother's room, their first concern was for each other. Cornelius thought John should not have come, but should have withdrawn to safety and helped his brother's family. (This report, given in a number of sources, would confirm that it was someone other than Cornelius who sent the servant girl to John.) They agreed that if they had an opportunity to examine Tichelaer, they could make him come out with the truth. They talked of an appeal to the High Council, which the prosecuting attorney came to tell them he had already lodged.

At about eleven o'clock, after John had paid the legal costs imposed in the sentence, they were ready to leave. No sooner had the door been opened, however, than there was a shout that the "traitors" were coming, and the guards ordered them to return into the jail or be shot. John attempted to argue with them, telling them what he had done for the citizenry. In reply they cocked their guns, and one man fired but missed. They went back in and asked the jailer if there was another door by which they could leave. Although in fact there was one the jailer replied that there was none. He lied, obviously, out of fear for his own safety: the De Witts were trapped, and must not escape.

The mob, increasingly restless, repeatedly sent burghers upstairs to make sure that the brothers were still there. Once in the room with them, and away from the scalding passions of the crowd, they began to show deference to the once so mighty men who were now in their power. The last of three inspection teams found Cornelius on his bed, dressed in his underclothing and a Japanese dressing gown, while John sat in a chair. John urged his brother's innocence and his own upon them with quiet eloquence, and they accepted his invitation to lunch with them. When the inspectors – two officers of the civic guard and four ordinary burghers – were slow in coming back, the crowd began to shout and throw stones. Armed men clambered to the rooftops to make sure the De Witts did not escape. At about one o'clock, the whole civic guard was called out and stationed outside the Gevangenpoort, but the captain found his force too small to hold off the mob if it should begin to stir, and at his request the Delegated Councilors sent three cavalry companies to take up positions in the Buitenhof. They were prevented by the crowd from going through the gate and remained in formation on the Square, so that the door to the Gevangenpoort was not under their protection.

The States of Holland, which was meanwhile meeting nearby in the Binnenhof to consider the election of a new councilor pensionary, upon being informed of developments by the Delegated Councilors, instructed them to take every measure necessary to protect the De Witt brothers. If need be, the troops should fire, and more reliable civic guard companies should be put on duty. An express courier was sent to Alphen, about fifteen miles away, with an urgent request to William to send more troops and to come in person, for his very presence would restore calm. He declined, although troops could have been spared because the French had started to withdraw from their most advanced positions.

The cavalry already on station in the Square proved adequate to intimidate the mob. Their commander, Count Claude de Tilly, warned the officers of the civic guards that there would be a bloodbath if their men shot first, but this was more than they wanted. As long as the cavalry remained where they were, the De Witts were safe. What followed can again be either mere coincidence or part of a plan deftly and steadily managed by invisible but not inactive men. (How many coincidences add up to evidence of a conspiracy?) In mid-afternoon rumors were spread that thousands of peasants intent upon looting were moving upon The Hague, and orders were sent by the Delegated Councilors to Tilly to post his troops at the bridges by which the town could be entered. The orders were oral and he would not accept them until they were confirmed in writing. These soon arrived, written by the secretary of the States of Holland, who was a cousin of the De Witts, and signed by the chairman who had earlier had the troops sent to the Gevangenpoort; it may therefore be assumed that they were responding to a perceived danger and were not part of any scheme to strip the brothers of protection. Tilly took his orders, commenting acidly, "I shall obey, but now the De Witts are dead men," and marched off his troops. Four o'clock had not yet struck.

The final scene of the last act of the tragedy began. It was time for the brothers' foes to act, now or perhaps never. According to Kopmoijer, the lawyer-diarist who is probably the best source for these events, the trio of Odijk, Zuilestein and Tromp met again at the inn on the Square. They called in key members of the Blue Banner Company of civic guards, which was passionately Orangist, and told them they must get the crowd to do its work before evening. Two members of The Hague government who were in difficulties – an alderman, John van Banchem, who blamed his troubles on John de Witt, and the town treasurer, who was being investigated as an embezzler – made their way to the Square by back alleys and whipped up the mob, most of whom were hungry and some drunk as well.

Just after Tilly and his cavalrymen left, the rumor that The Hague was about to be invaded by looters was heard again. It set off a cry for slaying the De Witts at once and then going to stop the intruders. When the jailer refused to open the door of the Gevangenpoort, the hinges were shot off and two smiths smashed the lock with sledgehammers. One of the civic guard companies attempted to prevent the break-in, but desisted when the men realized they would have to fight with another company as well as the crowd. Officers and burghers ran up the narrow stairway and found Cornelius in bed and John at its foot. They were calmly reading, Cornelius a book of plays by contemporary French dramatists and John the Bible, at the passage where the death of Jezebel at the teeth of dogs is forecast.

The burgher officers and the prosecutor, who had been on watch all afternoon, stood aside lest they meet the brothers' fate. Blows were struck at Cornelius, but only his cheek was touched. John, as if he had anticipated nothing all day, asked why the violence. The reply came that he had to go downstairs. Why? To be killed. Do it here. No, you must die where all can see. Cornelius was dragged from his bed, and his brother led him, half dressed, down the stairs. Behind, their captors pushed and cursed. Halfway down, John put his arm upon his brother's shoulder and said, "Adieu, brother." John was wounded in the neck, but they were driven on.

At the door, John saw the mob and turned to go back, but was pushed forward. He attempted to speak but he and Cornelius were shoved toward the scaffold that stood outside the gate near the Vijverberg, where it was planned to tie them to the stake and kill them by musket fire. They did not reach the scaffold alive. Cornelius died first, under the thrusts of muskets, swords and pikes. John was knocked to his knees, looked up as in prayer, and cried out, "Men! citizens! what are you doing?" Pulling his cloak over his face, he did not see the pistol shot that killed him. The burghers continued to shoot into the dead men, cheered on by a crowd of about a thousand, including preachers who intoned their approval of what they called the Lord's work. Those who looked on with horror kept still, as did the magistrates of The Hague who came up and watched from a house next to the prison.

The corpses were next dragged to the scaffold and hung by the feet. Someone observed an "eminent person" gazing on, nodding approval, and asked whether they were hanging high enough; instead of replying, he pulled down his hat over his eyes and walked away. He was identified, although not certainly, as Tromp. Except for the violence against the two victims, there had been no injuries to anyone. An Orangist pamphleteer was struck by the order that was maintained amidst disorder. Did he realize that he was describing the look of a massacre that had been planned?

What was not planned was what followed. In the crowd had been not only burghers – the members of the respectable citizenry – but also the rabble, the ever-turbulent, ever-dangerous bottom segment of the population. For them the mere killing was not enough. They ran to the scaffold as soon as the civic guards formed up and marched off, beginning the desecration and violation of the dangling corpses. They stripped the bodies bare, cut off parts including the genitals, slit the bodies open and pulled out the hearts and entrails – as if they were slaughtered cattle, wrote a pamphleteer afterwards. The parts were speared on quills and hawked about for stivers. A few participants in the gory tableau even roasted parts of the cadavers and ate them. There is no parallel to this cannibalism in all Dutch history, yet it is confirmed by many sources. The political meaning of the killing was stated plainly but eloquently in the signs that were hung from the corpses, "Land Prince" for John and "Water Prince" for Cornelius. Their crime had been to be rivals of the Prince of Orange.

As night fell, the crowd dribbled away, but it was not until one o'clock in the morning that servants and friends of the De Witt family could risk removing the bodies. So badly mangled were they that John could be distinguished only by the recently healed scars on his body. They were brought by coach back to the house on the Kneuterdijk. The next night they were buried quietly in the Nieuwe Kerk next to the grave where Wendela, whom death had spared this worst of horrors, lay. Although there was talk of digging up the corpses so as to burn them and scattering the ashes to the wind, violence was now limited to tearing down the arms of the De Witt family which, according to custom, had been hung outside the church during the funeral.

So died John de Witt and his brother, who gave their lives for each other.

Epilogue: afterwards and afterthoughts

Life went on, as it must. Johanna van Beveren, the eldest of Jacob de Witt's daughters, who had come to help before the tragedy on the Square, took charge. Early in the day she had sent Jacob, now the patriarch of eighty-three, with the children to a refuge six blocks away, at the home of two Anabaptist sisters who were seamstresses for the De Witt family. The morning afterwards she sent them to stay with their guardian and uncle, Peter de Graeff, at his country house at Ilpendam, beyond the IJ River well to the north, and then went herself with her father to her own home in Dordrecht. Cornelius's widow Maria returned to Dordrecht the same day. On the canalboat to Rotterdam, she sat in silent despair until a passenger exultantly held up one of her late husbands' fingers, and then she cried out in protest. Even those whose sympathy went out to her bit their lips and kept silent.

There would have been another victim of the mob on the evening of the massacre had not a kind landlord thwarted the outrage of a philosopher shaken out of his contemplative calm. Spinoza, who was then living in The Hague, sought to go out to put up a sign in the Square with the words *ultimi barbarorum* (you are the worst of barbarians); but his landlord locked the door and assuredly saved his life. The great admiral De Ruyter, who did not hear the news till six days later, responded in a way that does honor to the warrior: he broke into tears for the friend he had lost. A committee was named to examine the papers of the former councilor pensionary, which were confiscated by the States of Holland, in order to determine whether there was any evidence in them that De Witt had been a traitor in the service of France. One of the members, no friend of De Witt in the past, when asked what had been found, answered simply, "Nothing but honor and virtue." It would have been better for the fatherland, he added, had others served it equally well.

Amalia van Solms spoke with quiet dignity of her pain that "so noble a mind" should have died so cruelly. Constantine Huygens's son, Christian, living in Paris as a member of the French Academy of Sciences, was first horrified and then meditative. Wise men do not take part in politics, was his Stoic conclusion. Fagel, who had been elected on the very day of the massacre to the office De Witt had laid down, accepted three days later in a speech that praised his predecessor. De Witt's qualities, he said, were greater than his own, but it was the very importance of the office as he had built it up by his service that had made him the target of criticism beyond measure and brought him to disaster.

What of the man who mattered most, the man whom De Witt had barred from office for two decades and yet taught, when a Child of State, how to exercise it well? William III heard the news of the murders at about seven o'clock that evening. He turned pale and was visibly distraught and unhappy. Many years later Hans William Bentinck, his closest friend, still remembered that he had never seen the Prince so shaken as when he learned of the massacre. William himself told a friend some time later that if De Witt had lived, he would have preferred him as a collaborator before anyone else. And after William became king of England, he called De Witt one of the greatest men of the century and one who had served his country loyally. Yet, at the moment, he could not say such things, probably even to himself. He was the prisoner of the movement that had brought him to power and office, and not yet its master.

He went to The Hague the next day, not in order to guide an investigation into the responsibility for the murders but in order to muffle any such perilous enquiry and to give rewards to the doers of the foul work. He put his cloak of protection around the assassins and paid them off with jobs and pensions. Tichelaer got 800 guilders a year until 1702, when William III died; three years later he was also named a deputy to Cornelius's successor as steward of Putten. But the Prince knew him for what he was and spoke of him with foul words of contempt. Tichelaer too knew himself for what he was, and in old age, facing eternal judgment, he confessed that his accusations against Cornelius de Witt had been false. He did not name instigators, however, and our decision as to whether he acted alone or was prompted and commanded – and if the latter, by whom – must continue to rest upon the whole mesh of events rather than upon documentary evidence. Van Banchem was made a bailiff of The Hague by William, but his rascality came to the surface again four years later when he was arrested for embezzlement; while on trial, he died before conviction. Adrian van Walen, who had fired the shot that killed John de Witt, continued a life of crime and died on the gallows.

There were others who benefited by the restoration of the Prince in the following days and weeks who were not involved in the massacre on the Square. Kievit, the alderman in Rotterdam who had been implicated in the Buat affair, returned from his exile in England and was pardoned and restored to office. The municipal government of Amsterdam resigned on August 22, without waiting to be dismissed. Valckenier became for a while the Prince's man in the great city, although in the *wetsverzetting* in September it was Van Beuningen who was elected burgomaster, and Valckenier did not become one of the city's four chief magistrates until the following February. In the other towns of the province of Holland, De Witt's relatives and friends withdrew from office, as did Vivien in Dordrecht, or were dismissed in *wetsverzettingen*. The "ins" were out, the "outs" in.

Yet, when the urgencies of consolidating his power had passed, William displayed towards members of the De Witt clan a generosity that hinted at the feelings Bentinck had glimpsed when the Prince first heard the news of the massacre. Some who were willing to work with him he retained in office, like De Witt's cousin Ascanius van Sypesteyn, the army's wagonmaster general, and Hamel Bruyncinx, who served the Republic with skill and devotion as its minister to Vienna. William did not interfere when the States of Holland acted to protect Cornelius de Witt's widow against blackmail, or when Jacob de Witt died in 1674 and the family was permitted to hold a public funeral with full ceremony. It was Bentinck himself who arranged in 1687 for De Witt's son John to be presented to William, with assurances that the Prince, although acknowledging the father's faults, would not hold them against his children.

In all of this extraordinary combination of harsh political realism and lack of personal vindictiveness, William most resembled De

Witt himself. This may give a clue to his contradictory conduct. It is extremely unlikely that he was involved in the conspiracy against the De Witts. Indeed it is almost certain that the plotters, aware of the Prince's feelings, did not let him know what they were doing. Yet it is equally obvious that William suspected that something was brewing and did not act to prevent it. In August 1672, William III did not display moral greatness. Like De Witt, he could not bring himself to make the healing gesture of forgiveness and reconciliation when it might still have worked. As with De Witt, his commitment to his friends was so strong that it could overpower other feelings. Like De Witt, he did not mind using evil men for his own purposes and thus – as did De Witt – besmudged the purity of his own reputation.

In political character too, he was remarkably like De Witt. He was no reformer, but made use of the political system he found to achieve his own purposes without attempting any structural or constitutional changes (his flirtation with the dukedom of Gelderland in 1675 was quickly abandoned when it met wide opposition). He won the war against Louis XIV – it was Spain that would be the territorial loser in the Peace of Nijmegen in 1678 – following a diplomatic policy already sketched by De Witt before the war began; indeed, this writer at the tercentenary celebration of the peace in 1978 called it "De Witt's revenge" gained by William III. Of course they differed in social status, in doctrine and in their fortunes. But William's successes in the service of their common fatherland may to some significant degree be called the achievement of the councilor pensionary of Holland. It was another of history's ironies, a victory that John de Witt did not live to see.

John de Witt became a potent historic memory. Only within the last decade or two has he ceased to be a name familiar to every Dutch schoolchild (my evidence for this is a single incident a few years ago, when Jan de Tex and I, strolling across the Leusden heath, met rollicking youngsters of twelve or so, not one of whom had ever heard the name of De Witt – sadly, we were sure that this was not untypical). De Witt remained the symbol of the persistent anti-stadholderian force in Dutch political life down to the end of the Republic of the United Provinces; along with Oldenbarnevelt he was its greatest martyr. Indeed, a debate waged in the year 1757 over the stadholderate took the form of a controversy regarding the

significance of De Witt in Dutch history, and it was therefore called
the "War over the De Witts."

For more than a century De Witt's name was used in a
frightening political phrase: to treat someone *op zijn De Witts* – "as
if he were De Witt" – meant threatening a political personality
with the murderous violence of the mob. De Witt and his brother
became enshrined together in literature when their death became
the opening event in Alexandre Dumas's novel, *The Black Tulip*;
although Dumas distorted history almost beyond recognition, his
evocation of their massacre is unforgettable. Less widely known,
but even more powerfully gripping as well as accurate, are the
etchings that Romeyn de Hooghe made of the slaying and the
desecration of the brothers.

Dutch historians in the nineteenth and twentieth centuries have
continued to discuss the figure of De Witt. (Only foreign historians
characteristically doubled the name, treating Cornelius as almost
as important as John. The councilor pensionary would probably
have been both amused and pleased to see the steward of Putten
raised so high.) The kingdom of the Netherlands that rose up in
1813–15 reconciled in practice the two ruling forces in Dutch
history, the regent aristocracy and the House of Orange. This made
the theoretical evaluation of De Witt and the "True Freedom"
particularly difficult. On the one hand the great councilor pensionary embodied the principles of personal freedom and parliamentary
power so dear to the liberals who in the course of the nineteenth
century transformed the kingdom into a constitutional monarchy.
On the other hand, he had not been a friend of the House of Orange,
to which they remained devoted. As for the democrats and the
socialists who became increasingly important as the nineteenth
century grew into the twentieth, they also found De Witt an
ambiguous figure. They liked his republicanism, which they
equated with their own principles, but were put off by his
aristocratic attitude and policy. Furthermore, they did not know
what to make of the "Orange democracy" which hated and slew
him. The socialists in particular shared its hatred of the regents,
whom they viewed as identical with the capitalist bourgeois of their
own time, but not its belief that salvation and emancipation would
come from the House of Orange. In general, the historical debaters
could not fight their way free of anachronism, treating a past epoch
as in fundamental aspects identical to the present.

This may be the explanation why Robert Fruin, the greatest of historians of the Netherlands, never wrote the life of De Witt for which he assembled materials over many years. To some extent he was a writer of essays and articles rather than of books, but the two books he did publish are masterpieces of story telling and telling interpretation. It is not at all unlikely that the more he grappled with the figure of De Witt, the more a satisfactory picture eluded him. There is a paradox, therefore, in the fact that the one competent biography of De Witt by a Dutch historian came from the pen of the royal House Archivist in the twentieth century, Nicholas Japikse. He displayed for De Witt an admiration and a respect that a later biographer can only honor. Japikse's own intellectual life has not been studied as Fruin's was, and we can only speculate how he achieved such praiseworthly fairness.

The author of this book, as well as of the large biography of De Witt on which it is based, has drawn freely and fully from the work of his two great predecessors. Still he has an obligation to present his own vision of the councilor pensionary. The man De Witt, as I see him, was admirable for his intelligence, vitality and courage. Yet he was flawed, as are all human beings. He lacked the imaginative power and the human sympathy to feel his way into the emotional and intellectual world of other people. Warm within the circle of close family and good friends, he was almost icy to those outside that charmed perimeter who did not respond to his persuasiveness. He had no sense for the power of the friendly gesture given unreluctantly and in time. Extraordinarily intelligent, he was not a thinker as such, one who takes apart and puts together the great principles that govern our lives.

Yet it is not as a private man but as a statesman that we are interested in De Witt, and it is as such that we must judge him. In the arena of domestic politics, it is probably impossible to avoid some anachronism, some introduction of the values which we each hold dear in our own time. For someone who sees personal and political liberty as the be-all of good and just government, De Witt stands out heroically, as admirable as any statesman of the entire early modern epoch. Nonetheless he could not cure, and did not try to, the social plagues of his age, and he did not try to perfect the mechanism of the Dutch state. He was satisfied to use it to the best of his abilities, to serve the interests of the province of Holland and the Dutch Republic as he understood them. He never established himself in the affections of the "lower classes" and scorned their love for the Prince of Orange; he was a "regent" to the core. After William II's coup of 1650, it was virtually inevitable that his death would lead to the experiment – for it was an innovation, whatever the councilor pensionary thought – of stadholderless government. De Witt made it work for twenty years, and it is impossible to say whether it would have endured and become permanent if disaster in war had not for a while utterly changed the political situation in the Republic.

But war did come, and it came despite his most desperate efforts to find an escape. He should not have relied so long on France, it has been said, or failed to gain the friendship of England. This is a judgment that misses the point. So long as Charles II of England and Louis XIV of France stuck to their purposes and thought they could achieve them in alliance with each other, there was virtually nothing that De Witt could do but wait for the great blow and do what he could to prevent it from being fatal. The extent to which his rival and successor as leader of the Dutch state, William III, in performing the near miracle of defeating the conquerors, built upon the councilor pensionary's work, has not been sufficiently emphasized. Ultimately, therefore, his career did not end in utter failure, although it ended in the worst of horrors.

A bibliographical essay

The sources on which this book is based are indicated in full detail in my large biography of John de Witt (*John de Witt, Grand Pensionary of Holland, 1625–1672* (1978)), of which this is a much briefer and wholly new version. The following remarks for readers who wish to go further are comments on useful studies which bear on the subject.

During the nineteenth century the outstanding Dutch historian of the time, Robert Fruin, undertook the writing of a major scholarly biography of De Witt. He never actually began the writing of the book itself, so that we are deprived of what almost certainly would have been a masterpiece, for no historian has ever had a more impressive command of the sources or possessed a deeper familiarity with the relevant events and personalities. Fortunately, we have Fruin's research notes and running commentary, assembled and amplified by W. G. Kernkamp and N. Japikse in their edition of De Witt's correspondence for the Historisch Genootschap (*Brieven van Johan de Witt*, 4 vols., 1906–13; *Brieven aan Johan de Witt*, 2 vols., 1919–22). Much of De Witt's diplomatic correspondence was published in the eighteenth century (*Brieven geschreven ende gewisselt tusschen den Heer Johan de Witt . . . ende de Gevolmaghtigden van den Staedt der Vereenighde Nederlanden . . .*, 7 vols., 1723–7). We also have the numerous articles Fruin wrote on this period, republished both in his *Verspreide Geschriften* (11 vols., 1900–5) and in the separate reprint of volumes IV and V under the title *De Tijd van De Witt en Willem III: Historische Opstellen* (2 vols., 1929).

The only full-length scholarly biography published in the nineteenth century came from the pen of the French historian G. A. Lefèvre-Pontalis (*Une république parlementaire au dix-septième siècle: Jean de Witt, Grand Pensionnaire de Hollande*, 2 vols., 1884; English translation, *John De Witt, Grand Pensionary of Holland*, 2 vols., 1885). It is a work based on extensive study in the archives, but is shallow and distorted in its understanding and unbalanced in its presentation; it makes our regret that Fruin did not write his biography all the greater. The first biography that met the requirements of scholarship was written by N. Japikse (*Johan de Witt*, 1913; 2nd rev. edn, 1927). It is based on superb knowledge of the sources. What makes it particularly remarkable is that the author, who was the royal House Archivist, displayed deep sympathy for his protagonist despite his own strong Orangist connections. From a quite different ideological point of view, the essay on De Witt in J. Romein and A. Romein-Verschoor, *Erflaters van Onze Beschaving* (4 vols., 1938–40) is notably perceptive and sensitive.

Among works that bear strongly on De Witt and his era, none excels *Oranje en Stuart*, by P. Geyl (1939; English translation, 1969). It is unusual among studies of the Dutch seventeenth century in that it sides strongly with De Witt in his struggle with the House of Orange, and with the regent aristocracy against its rivals above and below. Based overwhelmingly on published sources, this work is most valuable for its fresh vision and historical subtlety. Biographies of William III by N. Japikse (*Willem III: De Stadhouder-Koning*, 2 vols., 1930–3) and S. Baxter (*William III and the Defense of European Liberty*, 1966) complement each other, for each brings a different mastery to his work, Japikse of the Dutch side and Baxter of the English. For both William is the hero, but Japikse does not go anywhere near as far as Baxter in making De Witt into a villain. Both provide a balance for a vision too focused on De Witt himself, or too much caught up by De Witt's attractive qualities (*mea culpa?*).

One other work should be added for the light it throws upon the rivalry between the Dutch Republic and England that played so powerful a part in De Witt's career. This is Charles Wilson, *Profit and Power* (1958), which puts emphasis upon economic forces. The work of S. Elzinga, *Het Voorspel van den Oorlog van 1672* (1926), unfortunately lacks Wilson's breadth and balance; it is more useful for its information than for its explanation of events. My own study, H. H. Rowen, *The Ambassador Prepares for War: The Dutch Embassy of Arnauld de Pomponne, 1669–1671* (1957) is a picture of Dutch (as well as French) politics from the Triple Alliance to the outbreak of war. The famed *Observations upon the United Provinces of the Netherlands* by Sir William Temple (1672, and many subsequent editions) remains a masterpiece of knowledge and insight to this day.

Index

Index

Index

Index

Keyser, Nanning, 34
Kievit, John, 130, 134, 137, 165, 222

Leiden, 9, 55–6, 71, 111, 168, 188, 193, 200; University of, 9, 58–60
Lenin, Vladimir I., 52
Leopold I, Holy Roman Emperor, 102, 136, 144–5, 168, 175–6
Lionne, Hughes de, 99–100, 130, 149, 152, 169, 174
Lira, Manuel de, 177
Lisola, Franz Paul, baron von, 143–4, 176
Lobith, 192
Loevestein, 1–3, 14, 27, 34
London, 11, 25, 27, 42–4, 47, 88, 96, 98, 124, 129, 133, 135, 146–7, 150, 152, 160, 164, 168, 171, 173–5, 186
Loosduinen, 214
Lorraine, 182
Louis XIV, king of France, 11, 35, 79, 82–3, 91, 98–106, 120–2, 128, 131, 134–7, 143–7, 150, 156–7, 160, 164–6, 169–78, 184–5, 187–8, 192–6, 199–201, 223, 226
Louvois, Michel le Tellier, marquis de, 195, 200
Lowestoft, 115
Luxemburg, 145

Maastricht, 102, 182, 189, 200
Madrid, 5, 150, 176
Maria Ana, queen-regent of Spain, 145–6, 150, 158, 177
Marie Thérèse, queen of France, 83, 102, 104–5, 145–7
Marlborough, 11
Mary Stuart, Princess of Orange, 3, 32, 45, 67, 73–4, 76, 108–12, 127–8, 206
Mary II, Princess of Orange and later queen of England, 209
Maurice, Prince of Orange, 6, 7, 36, 54, 65, 91, 119
Mazarin, Jules Cardinal, 11, 35, 79, 82–3, 90, 99, 101
Medemblik, 27, 32
Meerman, John, 146, 151, 155–6, 174
Mennonites, 59
Middelburg, 30, 110, 115, 162
Monck, George, 80
Montagu, Sir Edward, 88
Montbas, Jean Barton, marquis de, 192, 195–6

Münster, 119, 121, 131, 182, 200; Peace of, 1, 101, 135
Musch, Cornelius, 16
Muys van Holy, family, 7
Muys van Holy, Arend, 208, 211

Napoleon I, emporer of the French, 118
Nassau, House of, 65
Navigation Acts, English, 23, 41–2, 93, 137
Nes, Aert van, 124
Netherlands, Spanish, 5, 50, 81–3, 98–106, 124, 128, 130–1, 135–7, 143–7, 149–50, 156–9, 167, 170–1, 176–7, 185, 188, 203
Netherlands, United, see United Provinces
Netherlands, New, 137
Newton, Sir Isaac, 52, 60
Nieupoort, William, 24–5, 27, 44–5, 79–80, 111
Nieuwpoort, 147
Nijmegen, 192; Peace of (1678), 223; quarter, 109
Nobility (Ridderschap) of Holland, 17, 36–7, 48, 66, 72, 110, 154, 161
Norway, 84, 87, 117

Obdam, Jacob van Wassenaar, lord of, 40, 72, 87–8, 115–16
Odijk, William Adrian of Nassau, lord of, 162, 180, 193, 195, 212, 214, 217
Oirschot, 151–2
Oldenbarnevelt, John van, 6–7, 23, 33, 36, 53–4, 59, 65, 223
Oliva, Peace of, 89
Orange, House of, 8, 19–20, 28, 30, 41, 45, 57, 65–6, 68, 72–3, 82, 91–2, 111–12, 120, 141, 224–5
Orangist party, 2–3, 19–20, 23–5, 27–31, 33, 42, 46, 54, 69, 72–3, 75, 103, 107–9, 111–12, 128, 130, 138, 141, 154, 167–8, 173, 179, 181, 193, 196, 207, 214, 224
"Ordre de l'Union de la Joye," 47
Orsoy, 175
Ostend, 103, 147
Oudart, Nicholas, 110, 129
Overijssel, 65, 74–6, 119–20, 129, 188, 200

Paris, 11–12, 98–9, 129, 135, 155, 158, 167, 169, 181–2, 221